FISCAL YEAR 2016
BUDGET
OF THE U.S. GOVERNMENT

OFFICE OF MANAGEMENT AND BUDGET
BUDGET.GOV

Scan here to go to
our website.

Table of Contents

Page

THE BUDGET MESSAGE OF THE PRESIDENT

To the Congress of the United States:

After a breakthrough year for America, our economy is growing and creating jobs at the fastest pace since 1999, and in 58 months we have created over 11 million jobs. Our unemployment rate is now lower than it was before the financial crisis. More of our kids are graduating than ever before. More of our people are insured than ever before. We are as free from the grip of foreign oil as we've been in almost 30 years. Thanks to the hard work, resilience, and determination of the American people over the last six years, the shadow of crisis has passed.

With a growing economy, shrinking deficits, bustling industry, and booming energy production, we have risen from recession freer to write our own future than any other Nation on Earth. It's now up to us to choose what kind of country we want to be over the next 15 years, and for decades to come. Will we accept an economy where prosperity belongs to a few and opportunity remains out of reach for too many? Or will we commit ourselves to an economy that generates rising incomes and chances for everyone who makes the effort?

Over the last six years, we've seen that middle-class economic works. We've reaffirmed one of our most fundamental values as Americans: that this country does best when everyone gets their fair shot, does their fair share, and plays by the same set of rules.

The ideas I offer in this Budget are designed to bring middle-class economics into the 21st Century. These proposals are practical, not partisan. They'll help working families feel more secure with paychecks that go further, help American workers upgrade their skills, so they can compete for higher-paying jobs, and help create the conditions for our businesses to keep generating good new jobs for our workers to fill. The Budget will do these things while fulfilling our most basic responsibility to keep Americans safe. We will make these investments and end the harmful spending cuts known as sequestration, by cutting inefficient spending, and closing tax loopholes. We will also put our Nation on a more sustainable fiscal path by achieving $1.8 trillion in deficit reduction, primarily from reforms in health programs, our tax code, and immigration.

First, middle-class economics means helping working families afford the cornerstones of economic security: child care, college, health care, a home, and retirement. We will help working families tackle the high costs of child care and make ends meet by tripling the maximum child care credit for middle-class families with young children, increasing it to up to $3,000 per child, expanding child care assistance to all eligible low-income families with children under four by the end of 10 years, and making preschool available to all four-year-olds.

The Budget also provides middle-class families more flexibility at work by encouraging States to develop paid family leave programs. Today, we're the only advanced country on Earth that doesn't guarantee paid sick leave or paid maternity leave to our workers. Forty-three million workers have no paid sick leave, which forces too many parents to make the gut-wrenching choice between a paycheck and a sick kid at home. It's time to change that. For many families in today's economy, having both parents in the workforce isn't a luxury, it's an economic necessity.

Second, middle-class economics means making sure more Americans have the chance to earn the skills and education they need to keep earning higher wages down the road. The Budget calls for new investments and innovation that will expand preschool and invest in high-quality early education for America's youngest learners, provide more help to disadvantaged students and the schools that serve them, better prepare and support teachers, and transform our high schools so they help all students graduate prepared for college and career.

In a 21st Century economy that rewards knowledge more than ever, our efforts must reach higher than high school. By the end of this decade, two-thirds of job openings will require some higher education, and no American should be priced out of the education they need. Over the course of my Administration, we have increased Pell Grants, and the Budget continues to ensure that they will keep pace with inflation over time. The Budget also includes a bold new plan to bring down the cost of community college tuition for responsible students, to zero. Forty percent of college students attend community college; some to learn a particular skill, others as a path to a four-year degree. It is time for two years of college to become as free and universal in America as high school is today.

Even as we help give our students the chance to succeed, we also must work together to give our workers the chance to retool. Last year, the Congress came together and passed important improvements to the Nation's job training system with the bipartisan Workforce Innovation and Opportunity Act. To build on this progress, the proposals in this Budget support more in-person career counseling for unemployed workers and double the number of workers receiving training through the workforce development system. My plan would also expand the successful "learn-as-you-earn" approaches that our European counterparts use successfully by investing in the expansion of registered apprenticeships that allow workers to learn new skills while they are earning a paycheck. The Budget would also ensure that training leads to high-quality jobs by investing in projects that feature strong employer partnerships, include work-based learning, and develop new employer-validated credentials.

As we welcome home a new generation of returning heroes, the Budget makes sure they have the chance to live the American Dream they helped defend. It invests in the five pillars I have outlined to support our Nation's veterans: providing the resources and funding they deserve; ensuring high-quality and timely health care; getting veterans their earned benefits quickly and efficiently; ending veteran homelessness; and helping veterans and their families get good jobs, education, and access to affordable housing.

Third, middle-class economics means creating the kind of environment that helps businesses start here, stay here, and hire here. We want to build on the growth we have seen in the manufacturing sector, where more than 750,000 new jobs have been created over the last 58 months. To create jobs, continue growth in the industry, and strengthen America's leadership in advanced manufacturing technology, the Budget funds a national network of 45 manufacturing institutes, building on the nine already funded through 2015. As part of the manufacturing initiative, the Budget also launches a Scale-Up Fund, funded through a public-private partnership to help ensure that if a technology is invented in the United States, it can be made in the United States. The Budget proposes an investment fund to help startup companies produce the goods they have developed. Taken together, these investments will help ensure that America keeps making things the rest of the world wants to buy and will also help create manufacturing jobs for the future.

Our Nation thrives when we are leading the world with cutting-edge technology in manufacturing, infrastructure, clean energy, and other growing fields. That is why the Budget includes investments in cutting-edge advanced manufacturing research—to make sure we are leading the way in creating technology that supports our manufacturing sector; biomedical research—like our BRAIN initiative, which studies the brain to offer new insight into diseases like Alzheimer's, and Precision Medicine, which can improve health outcomes and better treat diseases; or, agricultural research—looking at climate resilience and sustainability. These investments have the potential to create high-wage jobs, improve lives, and open the door to new industries, resulting in sustainable economic growth.

As our economy continues to grow, our Nation's businesses and workers also need a stronger infrastructure that works in the new economy—modern ports, stronger bridges, better roads, faster trains, and better broadband. The Budget proposes to build a 21st Century infrastructure that creates jobs for thousands of construction workers and engineers, connects hardworking Americans to their jobs, and makes it easier for businesses to transport goods. The Budget would do more to repair and modernize our existing roads and bridges, while expanding transit systems to link communities and support workers.

These proposals will put more money in middle-class pockets, raise wages, and bring more high-paying jobs to America. To pay for them, the Budget will cut inefficient spending and close tax loopholes to make sure that everyone pays their fair share. The Budget closes loopholes that punish businesses investing domestically and reward companies that keep profits abroad, and uses some of the savings created to rebuild our aging infrastructure. The Budget closes loopholes that perpetuate inequality by allowing the top one percent of Americans to avoid paying any taxes on their accumulated wealth and uses that money to help more young people go to college. The Budget simplifies the system so that a small business owner can file based on her actual bank statement, instead of the number of accountants she can afford. It is time for tax reform that at its core is about helping working families afford child care and college, and plan for retirement, and above all, get a leg up in the new economy.

Of course, we cannot separate our work here at home from challenges beyond our shores. By winding down the wars overseas and lowering war spending, we've strengthened our economy and shrunk our deficits. But we still face threats to our security that we must address.

The Budget supports our efforts to degrade and ultimately destroy ISIL. We are leading over 60 partners in a global effort that will take time and steady resolve. As I made clear in my State of the Union address, I am calling on the Congress to show the world that we are united in this mission by passing a bill to authorize the use of force against ISIL.

The Budget supports our efforts to counter Russian pressure and aggressive actions in concert with our European allies, by funding support for Ukraine's democracy and efforts to reassure our NATO allies.

We also must look beyond the issues that have consumed us in the past to shape the coming century. This Budget provides the resources we need to defend the Nation against cyber-attacks. No foreign nation, no hacker, should be able to shut down our networks, steal our trade secrets, or invade the privacy of American families. In addition to increasing funding to protect our Nation against cyber-attacks, I continue to urge the Congress to finally pass the legislation we need to meet this evolving threat.

The Budget invests in our efforts to confront the threat posed by infectious diseases like Ebola—here at home, and internationally. It provides resources to support the Global Health Security Agenda, increases funding to eradicate polio and other global health challenges, and creates a new Impact Fund for targeted global HIV/AIDS efforts. In addition, the Budget increases funding for domestic preparedness efforts to more effectively and efficiently respond to potential, future outbreaks here at home and dedicates funding for States to develop HIV Plans to help them reach the goals of the National HIV/AIDS Strategy.

The Budget also capitalizes on historic opportunities in Asia and the Pacific—where we are modernizing alliances, opening new markets, and making sure that other nations play by the rules—in how they trade, resolve disputes, and do their part to confront the biggest challenges we face.

No challenge poses a greater threat to future generations than climate change. Fourteen of our planet's 15 warmest years on record have all fallen in the first 15 years of this century. The world's best scientists are telling us that our activities are changing the climate, and if we do not act forcefully, we'll continue to see rising oceans, longer, hotter heat waves, dangerous droughts and floods, and massive disruptions that can trigger greater migration, conflict, and hunger around the globe. The Pentagon says that climate change poses immediate risks to our national security. And as discussed in the Budget, the significant costs to inaction on climate change hit the Federal Government's bottom-line directly, as worsening climate impacts create Government liabilities. That's why this Budget takes action on climate by supporting the Climate Action Plan that I released in 2013 with investments to accelerate carbon pollution reductions, to build on-the-ground partnerships with local communities and help them put in place strategies for greater resilience to climate change impacts, and to support America's leadership abroad on this important moral and fiscal issue.

Beyond these critical investments, the Budget also supports my Management Agenda, which seeks to create a Government for the future that is more efficient, effective, and supportive of economic growth. The Budget includes initiatives to improve the service we provide to the American public; to leverage the Federal Government's buying power to bring more value and efficiency to how we use taxpayer dollars; to open Government data and research to the private sector to drive innovation and economic growth; to promote smarter information technology; and, to attract and retain the best talent in the Federal workforce. The Budget includes proposals to consolidate and reorganize Government agencies to make them leaner and more efficient, and it increases the use of evidence and evaluation to ensure that taxpayer dollars are spent wisely on programs that work.

The Congress can also help grow the economy, reduce deficits, and strengthen Social Security by passing comprehensive immigration reform. Last year, I took a series of executive actions to crack down on illegal immigration at the border; prioritize deporting felons, not families; and allow certain undocumented immigrants who register and pass criminal and national security background checks to start paying their fair share of taxes and stay in the United States without fear of deportation. I also took action to streamline the legal immigration system for talented STEM students, entrepreneurs, and business. These actions will raise average wages for all American workers and reduce the deficit. But this is only a first step toward real reform, and as I have said before, the Congress should act on the more comprehensive reform that only changes in the law can provide. Independent economists say immigration reform will grow our economy and shrink our deficits by almost $1 trillion over 20 years. It is time to fix our broken system and help grow our economy by passing comprehensive immigration reform.

The Budget also builds on the progress we have made ensuring that every American has the peace of mind that comes with quality, affordable health insurance. The Affordable Care Act has helped to provide millions more Americans get covered. It has forced insurance companies to play by the rules by prohibiting discrimination for pre-existing conditions and eliminating lifetime insurance caps. It has also helped to put our Nation on a more sustainable fiscal path by slowing the growth of health care costs. The Budget includes additional reforms and cost saving proposals to continue encouraging high-quality and efficient health care.

This Budget shows what we can do if we invest in America's future and commit ourselves to an economy that rewards hard work, generates rising incomes, and allows everyone to share in the prosperity of a growing America. It lays out a strategy to strengthen our middle class, and help America's hard-working families get ahead in a time of relentless economic and technological change.

Fifteen years into this new century, and six years after the darkest days of the financial crisis, we have picked ourselves up, dusted ourselves off, and begun again the work of remaking America. We've laid a new foundation. A brighter future is ours to write. This Budget will help us begin this new chapter together.

BARACK OBAMA

THE WHITE HOUSE,
    FEBRUARY 2, 2015.

BUILDING ON A RECORD OF ECONOMIC GROWTH AND PROGRESS

> "It is indisputable that our economy is stronger today than when I took office. By every economic measure, we are better off now than we were when I took office."
>
> —President Barack Obama, Northwestern University, October 2, 2014

When the President took office in 2009, the economy was shrinking at its fastest rate in 50 years and shedding over 800,000 private sector jobs per month. The unemployment rate reached 10 percent that year, a level not seen in over 25 years. The housing market was in a free fall and the American manufacturing industry was thought to be in irreversible decline, with the auto industry nearing collapse. The deficit hit a post-World War II high, and health care costs had been rising rapidly for decades.

Today, the U.S. economy is recovering and, in 2014, achieved a number of important milestones. American businesses set a new record for the most consecutive months of job growth: 58 straight months and a total of 11.2 million new jobs, and counting. In 2014, the economy added more jobs than in any year since the 1990s. Significantly, nearly all of the employment gains have been in full-time positions. At the same time, the annual unemployment rate in 2014 fell 1.2 percentage points from the previous year, the largest annual decline in the last 30 years.

11.2 Million Jobs Added Over the Past 58 Months

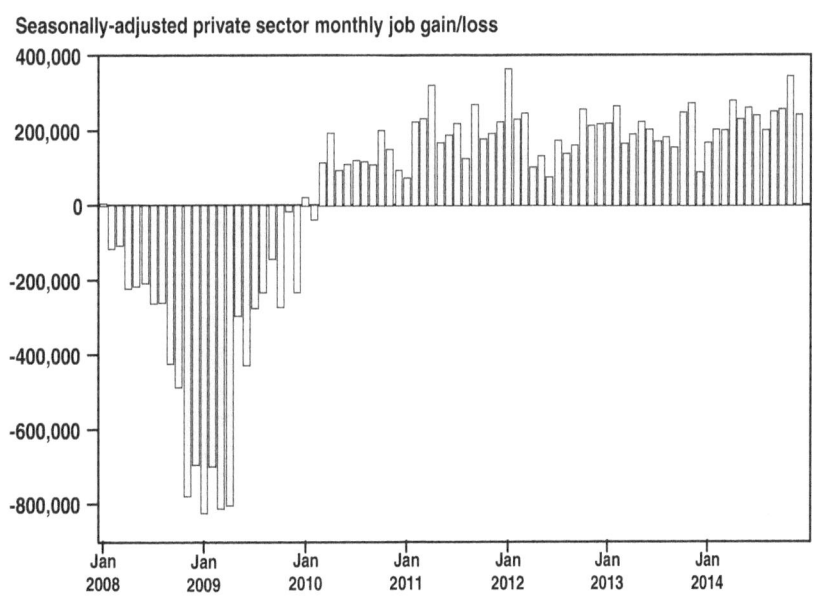

Seasonally-adjusted private sector monthly job gain/loss

Source: Bureau of Labor Statistics.

Over the last four years, the United States has put more people back to work than Europe, Japan, and every other advanced economy combined. As the economy strengthened, the unemployment rate fell from a high of 10 percent in 2009 to 5.6 percent at the end of 2014. Long-term unemployment declined from 6.8 million in April 2010 to 2.8 million in December 2014 and fell even faster than overall unemployment over the past year.

For the first time in two decades, the United States has started producing more oil than it imports. Domestic natural gas production set a new record high in 2014. The manufacturing sector continues to experience its strongest period of job growth since the late 1990s. Rising home prices are bringing millions of homeowners back above water, restoring nearly $5 trillion in home equity.

The progress in the economy since the President took office has been steady and it has been real. The President's decisive actions during the financial crisis brought the economy back from the brink, to the increasingly strong growth seen today. The Administration pushed the Recovery Act to jumpstart the economy and create jobs; rescued the auto industry from near collapse; fought for passage of the Affordable Care Act to provide insurance coverage to millions of Americans and help slow the growth of health care costs; and secured the Dodd-Frank Wall Street reform legislation to help prevent future crises. The American people's determination and resilience, coupled with the Administration's work, are driving the economy full steam ahead.

Helping, Not Hurting the Economy: The End of Austerity and the Move Away from Manufactured Crises

During the first years of the Administration, the President and the Congress worked together to enact measures that jumpstarted and strengthened the economy, and made it more resilient for the future. In addition to the Recovery Act, the Affordable Care Act, and Dodd-Frank Wall Street reform legislation, the Congress took bipartisan action in 2010 to temporarily reduce payroll taxes and continue emergency unemployment benefits.

Unfortunately, policies adopted in subsequent years hurt, rather than helped, the economy.

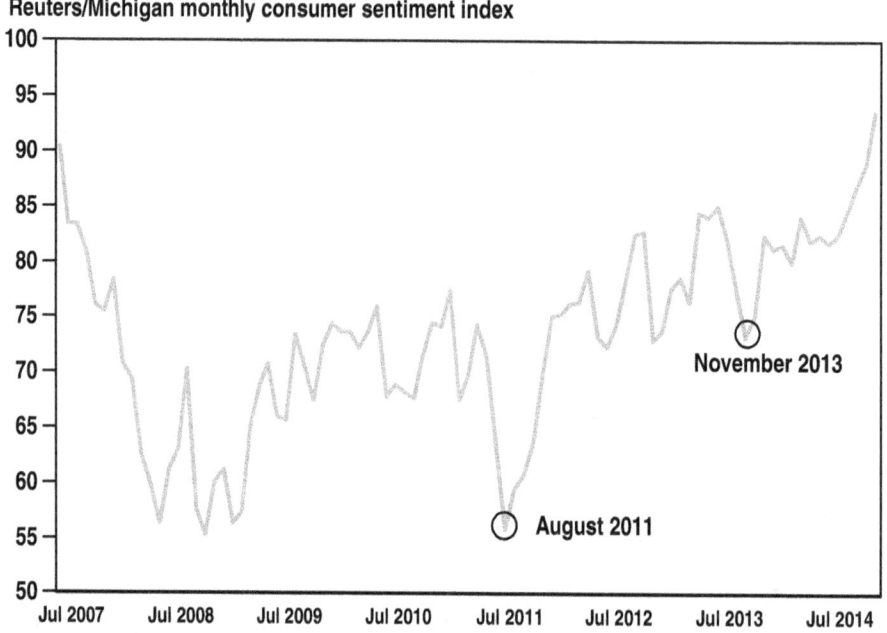

Consumer Confidence has Returned to Pre-Crisis Levels

Reuters/Michigan monthly consumer sentiment index

Source: University of Michigan: Consumer Sentiment (NSA, Q1-66=100).

A Retrospective on 2013 Sequestration

When the Congress failed to enact the balanced long-term deficit reduction required by the Budget Control Act of 2011, a series of automatic cuts known as sequestration went into effect, cancelling more than $80 billion in budgetary resources across the Federal Government in 2013. Beyond the economic impacts, these cuts also had severe programmatic impacts, shortchanging investments that contribute to future growth, reducing economic opportunity, and harming vulnerable populations. For example:

- *Hundreds of important scientific projects went unfunded.* The National Institutes of Health funded the lowest number of competitive research project grants in over a decade, providing roughly 750 fewer competitive grants in 2013 compared to the previous year. These unfunded grants included more than a hundred competitive renewal applications that were considered highly meritorious for additional funding in peer review, limiting research into brain disorders, infectious disease, and cancer. Also as a result of sequestration, the National Science Foundation awarded 690 fewer competitive awards than the previous year, resulting in the lowest total number of competitive grants provided since 2006, limiting scientists and students' ability to pursue cutting-edge, potentially revolutionary discoveries.

- *Tens of thousands of low-income children lost access to Head Start.* Over 57,000 children lost access to Head Start and Early Head Start in school years 2012-2013 and 2013-2014, forgoing critical early learning experiences and health and nutrition services intended to help improve their cognitive, physical, and emotional development. As a result, Head Start enrollment dipped to its lowest level since 2001. In addition, Head Start centers were forced to reduce the number of school days by more than 1.3 million.[1]

- *Fewer low-income families received housing vouchers.* A total of 67,000 Housing Choice Vouchers were lost, resulting in reduced access to affordable, safe, and stable housing for low-income families. Although the Department of Housing and Urban Development and Public Housing Authorities took extraordinary steps to prevent families from losing assistance, many vouchers were withdrawn from families that were in the process of looking for housing or not reissued when families left the program, while many of the families remaining in the program faced higher rents.

While the Bipartisan Budget Act of 2013 replaced a portion of the damaging and short-sighted sequestration cuts in 2014 and 2015 with long-term reforms, they did not go far enough. Without further congressional action, sequestration will return in full in 2016, bringing discretionary funding—or, spending that is approved through the appropriations process—to its lowest level in a decade, adjusted for inflation. In fact, assuming roughly the current allocation of resources across programs, a return to sequestration levels in 2016 would mean the lowest real funding level for research since 2002—other than when sequestration was in full effect in 2013—and the lowest real per-pupil funding levels for education since 2000, a major disinvestment in exactly the areas where investment is needed to support growth.

---

[1] Head Start programs reported the number of days of service reduced because a shortened school year was required to implement the unprecedented reductions in their funding. The total number of days grantees reported eliminated from their school year is multiplied by the number of children affected by those cuts to produce the estimate that 1.3 million days of service were eliminated.

Sequestration cuts that took effect in March 2013 reduced the gross domestic product (GDP) by 0.6 percentage points and cost 750,000 jobs, according to the Congressional Budget Office (CBO). In 2011, and again in 2013, congressional Republicans sought to use the Nation's full faith and credit as a bargaining chip, driving down consumer confidence and driving up economic policy uncertainty measures. The Federal Government shutdown in October 2013 created further uncertainty and reduced growth in the fourth quarter of 2013 by at least 0.3 percentage points.

Beginning in 2014, however, policymakers moved away from manufactured crises and austerity budgeting, helping to lay the groundwork for job market gains and stronger growth. The President worked with congressional leaders from both parties to secure a two-year budget agreement (the Bipartisan Budget Act of 2013) and enact full-year appropriations bills that replaced a portion of the harmful sequestration cuts and allowed for higher investment levels in 2014 and 2015.

The Council of Economic Advisers estimated that the 2013 budget deal will create about 350,000 jobs over the course of 2014 and 2015, meaning that it has likely contributed to the marked improvement in the labor market this past year. Moreover, thanks in part to the budget deal, 2014 will likely have been the first year since 2010 that Federal fiscal policy did not significantly reduce economic growth.

Increased certainty and a break from the threat of shutdown and other fiscal crises also added to growth, according to several independent analyses. For example, an analysis by Macroeconomic Advisers found that fiscal uncertainty cost 900,000 jobs from 2009 through mid-2013. The crises also negatively impacted consumer confidence, which fell markedly around the time of the 2011 and 2013 manufactured crises, and, along with small business optimism, has only returned to pre-recession levels in the past year (see previous chart). Business leaders, economists, and the Federal Reserve Chair have all attributed stronger growth in part to reduced fiscal headwinds and uncertainty, and business leaders have urged policymakers to avoid a return to manufactured crises and needless austerity.

Fiscal Progress

Since 2010, Federal deficits have shrunk at an historic pace—the most rapid sustained deficit reduction since the period just after World War II. The turn away from austerity in 2014 was accompanied by another steep drop in the deficit, bringing it to 2.8 percent of GDP—the lowest level since 2007, about one-third the size of the deficit the President inherited, and below the 40-year average. Over the past five years, actual and projected deficits have fallen due to three main factors.

First, economic growth has helped accelerate the pace of deficit reduction. Growth in recent years has increased revenues and reduced spending on "automatic stabilizers" programs, such as

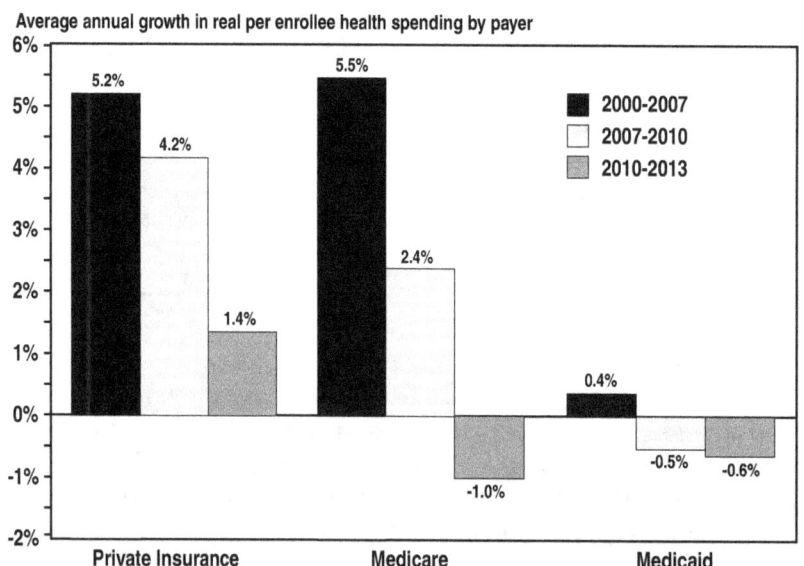

Recent Growth in Health Spending has been Slow in Both the Private and Public Sectors

Average annual growth in real per enrollee health spending by payer

Source: Centers for Medicare & Medicaid Services; U.S. Bureau of Economic Analysis; Council of Economic Advisers calculation.

unemployment insurance, that automatically increase during economic downturns.

Second, since 2010, policymakers have put in place more than $4 trillion in deficit reduction measures through 2025, not counting additional savings achieved by winding down wars in Iraq and Afghanistan. These measures include restoring Clinton-era tax rates on the wealthiest Americans and discretionary spending restraint. Sequestration cuts account for a minority of the discretionary savings achieved since 2010, and have had a negative impact on critical services and public investments in future growth (see above, A Retrospective on 2013 Sequestration).

Finally, deficits are falling due to historically slow health care cost growth. The years since 2010 have seen exceptionally slow growth in per-beneficiary health care spending in both private insurance and public programs (see previous chart). As a result, 2011-2013 saw the three slowest years of growth in real inflation-adjusted per-capita national health expenditures since record-keeping began in 1960. While some of the slowdown can be attributed to the Great Recession and its aftermath, there is increasing evidence that much of it is the result of structural changes. These include reforms enacted in the

Affordable Care Act that are reducing excessive payments to private insurers and health care providers in Medicare, creating strong incentives for hospitals to reduce readmission rates, and starting to change health care payment structures from volume to value.

The health care cost slowdown is already yielding substantial fiscal dividends. Compared with the 2011 Mid-Session Review, aggregate projected Federal health care spending for 2020 has decreased by $216 billion based on current budget estimates, savings above and beyond the deficit reduction directly attributable to the Affordable Care Act.

The chart below shows how slower health care cost growth and policy changes are contributing to improving the medium-term budget outlook. In the 2011 Mid-Session Review, published in July, 2010, the Administration projected a 2020 deficit of 5.1 percent of GDP if current policies were to continue. The Budget projects a baseline deficit of 3.3 percent of GDP in 2020, a reduction of 1.9 percentage points, or $491 billion. One major contributor to the improvement is lower-than-expected Federal health spending. Revisions to health spending forecasts based on the historically slow growth of the past several years (and

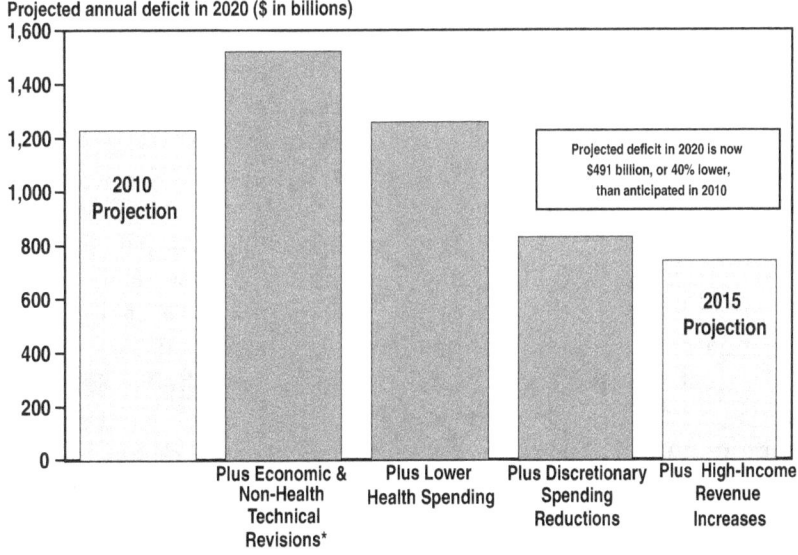

Health Savings and Policy Choices have Significantly Reduced Projected Deficits

* Also includes minor policy changes (e.g., mandatory sequestration).

based on the assumption that only a portion of the slowdown will continue) account for about half of the net improvement in the projected deficits. Another important factor is the high-income revenue increases enacted in the American Taxpayer Relief Act of 2012, which contributed about a fifth of the new improvement. Discretionary spending restraint has also played a large role, although the impact of sequestration is much less than the impact of the pre-sequestration Budget Control Act caps and prior appropriations action and less than the savings from winding down wars.

An under-appreciated aspect of the Nation's recent fiscal progress has been the way these same factors, discussed above, have led to a significant improvement in the long-term outlook (as discussed in more detail in the Long Term Budget Outlook chapter of the *Analytical Perspectives* volume). Moreover, as discussed below, a number of the President's Budget policies, and particularly the proposed reforms to health and immigration, will not only substantially reduce deficits over the next 10 years, but will have a growing impact in reducing deficits beyond the next decade.

The Budget: A Roadmap for Continued Economic and Fiscal Progress

The progress that has been made to date is significant, but not sufficient to address either the Nation's economic or fiscal challenges. The Budget increases investments that will accelerate growth and expand opportunity, while also finishing the task of putting the Nation on a sustainable fiscal path.

Investing in Growth and Opportunity. The Bipartisan Budget Act of 2013 reversed a portion of sequestration and allowed for higher investment levels in 2014 and 2015, but it did nothing to alleviate sequestration in 2016. In the absence of congressional action, non-defense discretionary funding in 2016 will be at its lowest level since 2006, adjusted for inflation, even though the need for pro-growth investments in infrastructure, education, and innovation has only increased due to the Great Recession and its aftermath. Inflation-

adjusted defense funding will also be at its lowest level since 2006.

The Budget finishes the job of reversing mindless austerity budgeting and makes needed investments in key priorities, even while setting the Nation on a fiscally responsible course. The proposed increases in the discretionary budget caps make room for a range of domestic and security investments that will help move the Nation forward. These include investments to strengthen the economy by improving the education and skills of the U.S. workforce, accelerating scientific discovery, and continuing to bolster manufacturing. They also include program integrity initiatives that will reduce the deficit by many times their cost. As described in the Investing in America's Future chapter, the Budget proposes to further accelerate growth and opportunity and create jobs through pro-work, pro-family tax reforms and through mandatory investments—or, direct spending that is determined outside the appropriations process—in surface transportation infrastructure, universal pre-kindergarten, child care assistance for middle-class and working families, and other initiatives.

Putting the Nation on a Sustainable Fiscal Path. The Budget achieves $1.8 trillion of deficit reduction over 10 years, primarily from health, tax, and immigration reform. As described further in the Investing in America's Future chapter, the Budget includes about $400 billion of health savings that grow over time, extending the life of the Medicare Trust Fund by approximately five years, and building on the Affordable Care Act with further incentives to improve quality and control health care cost growth. It also reflects the President's support for commonsense, comprehensive immigration reform along the lines of the 2013 bipartisan Senate-passed bill. The CBO estimated that the Senate-passed bill would reduce the deficit by about $160 billion over 10 years and by almost $1 trillion over two decades, while the Social Security Actuary estimated that it would reduce Social Security's 75-year shortfall by eight percent. In addition, the Budget obtains about $640 billion in deficit reduction from reducing tax benefits for high-income households.

Under the Budget, deficits decline to about 2.5 percent of GDP. Starting in 2016, debt declines as well, reaching 73.3 percent of GDP in 2025, a reduction of 1.9 percentage points from its peak. The key test of fiscal sustainability is whether debt is stable or declining as a share of the economy, resulting in interest payments that consume a stable or falling share of the Nation's resources over time. The Budget meets that test, showing that investments in growth and opportunity are compatible with also putting the Nation's finances on a strong and sustainable path.

The economic growth and progress the Nation has seen in the President's first six years in office prove that America's resurgence is real. As the President said it would be, 2014 was a year of action and a breakthrough year for America; a year that saw accelerated job growth, sharp declines in unemployment, uninsured rates at near-record lows, and a continuation of historically slow health care price growth. Now it is time to invest in America's future to drive economic growth and opportunity, secure the Nation's safety, and put the Nation's finances on the road to a more sustainable fiscal outlook. The Budget does just that.

INVESTING IN AMERICA'S FUTURE

> *"We have to make our economy work for every working American. And every policy I pursue as President is aimed at answering that challenge."*
>
> —President Barack Obama, Northwestern University, October 2, 2014

Today in America, we are seeing real, tangible evidence of economic recovery from the crisis the President inherited. In a 58-month streak, the longest on record, American businesses have created more than 11 million new jobs, and almost all of the employment gains since 2010 have been in full-time positions. All in all, the economy added more jobs in 2014 than in any year since the 1990s.

The Administration's investments in American manufacturing have helped fuel its best stretch of job growth since the 1990s. America is now the number-one producer of oil and the number-one producer of natural gas; this has meant decreasing dependence on imported oil and increasing competitiveness for American industry. The rescue of the auto industry officially ended in December 2014, and the American auto industry is on track for its strongest year of new vehicle production since 2005; about half a million new jobs have been created in auto production and sales since mid-2009, when Chrysler and General Motors emerged from bankruptcy.

Since the President took office, the deficit has been cut by about two thirds. The Nation has seen the slowest health care cost growth in 50 years, with the largest reduction in the number of uninsured Americans in decades. The high school graduation rate is above 80 percent for the first time in history. Both the crime rate and the incarceration rate are falling.

We now have the chance to make sure that all Americans are able to benefit from the economic recovery. America's promise has always been that if we work hard, we can change our circumstances for the better. The economy cannot truly succeed until we live up to that promise. The Budget lays out a strategy to reach that promise, by investing in the drivers of growth and opportunity for all Americans.

To ensure America remains a magnet for jobs, the Budget builds on investments in manufacturing and innovation—including through clean energy technology programs and tax policies that position America as a global clean energy leader with a strong and modern energy infrastructure. To fix the Nation's roads and bridges and create more middle class jobs, it continues the progress toward building a 21st Century infrastructure. The Budget invests in education and job training to give American workers the skills they need to compete in the global economy. It also provides resources to programs that help create opportunity and economic mobility for all, and it reforms the tax system to better support and reward work.

To further the progress made to prevent another crisis such as the one we saw in 2008, the

Budget supports the financial stability efforts launched through the Dodd-Frank Wall Street Reform and Consumer Protection Act. The Budget also invests in climate preparedness and resilience—providing necessary tools, technical assistance, and on-the-ground partnership to communities that are dealing with the effects of climate change today. In addition to directly helping these communities, preparing for the impacts of climate change is also part of strengthening the Nation's long-term fiscal outlook (see below, Federal Budget Exposure to Climate Risk).

The Budget recognizes that while America is a world leader in domestic economic growth, it must also continue to promote U.S. national security interests while mobilizing the international community to address global challenges to the Nation's safety and security. That is why the Budget further advances national security priorities by proposing the funding increases above current law needed to execute the President's defense strategy. The Budget supports America's continued fight to degrade and ultimately defeat the Islamic State of Iraq and the Levant (ISIL). The Budget continues the transition in Afghanistan, while also supporting European reassurance efforts to counter Russia's aggressive actions. It advances security, prosperity, and economic growth in the Central America Region to address the root causes of migration. The

Budget also confronts threats such as Ebola by strengthening U.S. global health security and continues to invest in the Nation's cybersecurity, while supporting efforts to maintain technological superiority. It continues the progress made to reassert American leadership in the Asia-Pacific region. The Budget also upholds the Nation's duty to care for its veterans who have risked their lives to serve America.

The Budget also shows that we can end sequestration, make the investments necessary to support economic growth, economic mobility, and national security, and continue to make progress in meeting the Nation's fiscal goals. To further strengthen America's long-term fiscal outlook and the economy, the Budget sets the Nation on a sustainable fiscal path, achieving $1.8 trillion of deficit reduction over 10 years, primarily from health, tax, and immigration reforms described in this chapter. The Budget proposes to maintain the Affordable Care Act's progress in constraining the growth of health care costs and spurring additional health care reforms to make the system work better for all Americans. It supports comprehensive immigration reform, which would not only grow the U.S. economy, but also strengthen the Nation's fiscal future, reducing deficits by almost $1 trillion over 20 years. The Budget also reforms the tax system to raise the revenue needed to keep our commitments to seniors,

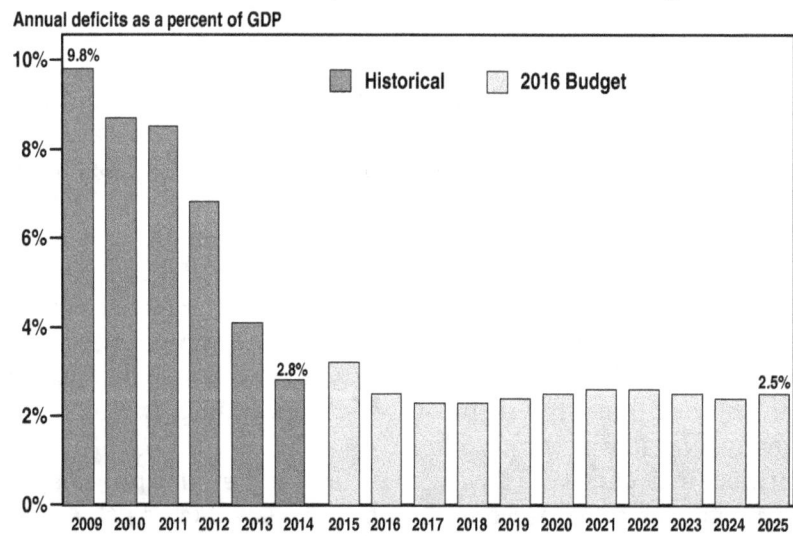

Deficits Remain Low Under President's Budget

without shortchanging investments in the next generation. All told, the Budget puts the Nation's economy on a more sustainable fiscal path, with deficits around 2.5 percent of the Gross Domestic Product (GDP) and debt as a share of the economy on a downward path after 2015.

In order to make these critical investments to create more jobs, grow the economy, and ensure the Nation's safety and security, while also putting the Federal budget on a more sound fiscal footing, the Federal Government must continue to move away from the mindless austerity and manufactured crises that have hurt the economy in recent years. As discussed in the previous chapter, Building on a Record of Economic Growth

and Progress, the Bipartisan Budget Act in late 2013 represented real progress—partially replacing sequestration cuts in 2014 and 2015, fully offset by long-term savings, in order to provide certainty and increase discretionary investments. The Budget builds on this progress by proposing additional investments in vital areas such as education, research, and national security, offset by a balanced package of spending cuts, proposals to close tax loopholes, and program integrity measures. These investments are crucial to the Nation's economic growth and national security. Failing to make them—and returning to the mindless austerity of sequestration in 2016— would weaken America's economy at a time of accelerating growth.

INVESTING IN JOBS AND ECONOMIC GROWTH

Accelerating Manufacturing Industry Growth

America is building again. The manufacturing sector has been a critical driver of economic growth and job creation since the President took office, adding more than 750,000 new jobs over the last 58 months. The Recovery Act and subsequent Administration efforts have helped reignite America's manufacturing industry, which many thought was in irreversible decline at the height of the Great Recession. These efforts helped create new clean energy manufacturing markets and rescued the auto industry, which is now on track for its strongest year of new vehicle production since 2005. The President is committed to continuing the manufacturing sector's growth in order to attract the kind of well-paying jobs that will help drive middle class economic security. The Budget reflects that commitment by investing in efforts to promote advanced manufacturing technology and efforts to ensure that manufacturing technology made in America can be used in America, to help create more jobs, and grow the economy.

Manufacturing Institutes. To support investment and accelerate innovation in U.S. manufacturing, the President has called for the creation of a National Network for Manufacturing

Innovation across the Nation. The Congress supported this initiative in a bipartisan fashion by passing the Revitalize American Manufacturing and Innovation Act in December 2014, which authorizes manufacturing innovation institutes to come together into a shared network and codifies authority for the Department of Commerce to coordinate this multi-agency initiative.

Leveraging the strengths of a particular region, each institute will bring together companies, universities, community colleges, and Government to co-invest in the development of world-leading manufacturing technologies and capabilities that U.S.-based manufacturers can apply in production. For example, the first manufacturing innovation institute, America Makes in Youngstown, Ohio, is focused on reducing the cost of 3D printing, connecting small businesses with new opportunities, and training American workers to master these sophisticated technologies. Although only in its third year of operation, the institute has research underway that will help accelerate the speed of 3D printing in metals by a factor of 10, is partnering to provide over 1,000 schools with access to 3D printers, and has launched new workforce training programs that have trained over 7,000 workers in the fundamentals of 3D printing. In addition to launching new products and filing new patents from the research already underway, the institute is serving as a magnet for investment in the region.

The Budget funds a national network of 45 manufacturing institutes that will position the United States as a global leader in advanced manufacturing technology. Specifically, the Budget builds on the nine institutes already funded through 2015 with more than $350 million in additional discretionary funds to support seven new manufacturing institutes in the Departments of Commerce, Agriculture, Defense, and Energy. The Budget also includes a mandatory spending proposal of $1.9 billion to fund the remaining 29 institutes in the network.

Scale-Up Manufacturing Investment Funds. The Budget also calls on the Congress to work together with the President to launch a public-private investment in a Scale-Up Fund as part of the Administration's innovative manufacturing initiative. This will help emerging advanced manufacturing technologies reach commercial viability, ensuring that if a technology is invented in the United States, it can be made in the United States. To address the gap in financing for these new manufacturing firms, the Budget proposes a $5 billion investment fund, administered by the Small Business Administration, which will be matched with non-Federal funds to increase investment in the first commercial production facilities for technology intensive manufacturing start-ups. These funds will help entrepreneurial firms secure capital to scale from idea to prototype, and into full commercial production. Once fully deployed, this fund could eventually leverage up to $10 billion in total public-private investment to build first-of-its-kind manufacturing production capabilities here in the United States.

Investing in Research and Development

America's long-term economic competitiveness and growth—including efforts to grow domestic manufacturing—depend on robust investments in research and development (R&D), which provide the foundation needed to further grow the economy. Federal funding for R&D has helped lead to new products, new capabilities, and new industries, resulting in sustainable economic growth and highly-skilled, high-wage jobs, as well as the creation of an astounding array of products and services that benefit every American. Today, we look to engineering and science to address the Nation's biggest challenges: creating jobs; improving the health of all Americans; enhancing access to clean energy, water, and food; addressing global climate change; managing competing demands on environmental resources; and ensuring the security of the Nation.

The Budget provides $146 billion for R&D overall, a 5.5 percent increase from 2015, targeting resources to areas most likely to directly contribute to the creation of transformational knowledge and technologies that can benefit society and create the businesses and jobs of the future. In addition to making permanent and expanding the Research and Experimentation Tax Credit (discussed later in this chapter), the Budget includes increases for several priorities.

- *Basic Research at the Department of Energy (DOE) and the National Science Foundation (NSF).* To continue the cutting-edge R&D that is essential to U.S. innovation and economic competitiveness, the Budget provides DOE's Office of Science with over $5.3 billion and NSF with over $7.7 billion. These investments support ground-breaking research and world-leading facilities across fields of science and engineering, including advanced manufacturing, clean energy, climate science, information technology, and life sciences.

- *Biomedical Research at the National Institutes of Health (NIH).* The Budget provides $31.3 billion to support biomedical research at NIH, providing about 10,000 new NIH grants that will help to better understand the fundamental causes and mechanisms of disease. The Budget provides increased resources for Alzheimer's, cancer and other diseases that affect millions of Americans, and enhanced support for the BRAIN initiative that is helping to revolutionize understanding of the human brain.

- *Precision Medicine Initiative.* The Budget includes $215 million to launch a Precision Medicine initiative that will accelerate the ability to improve health outcomes and better treat diseases. The Budget will help to begin the establishment of a voluntary national research group of a million or more Americans, expand research to define cancer subtypes and identify new therapeutic targets, modernize the regulatory framework for DNA-sequence-based diagnostic tests, and enhance interfaces for electronic health records and patient-generated data in assessment of individual health and population-level trends.

- *Agriculture R&D.* The Budget recognizes the importance of science and technology to meet challenges in agriculture, and provides significant investment increases in three major areas of agricultural R&D: 1) Competitive grants are funded at $550 million to support extramural research grants through the Department of Agriculture's (USDA) flagship Agriculture and Food Research Initiative, for advanced manufacturing public-private institutes, and for a new program to provide competitive support to land grant institutions; 2) USDA's in-house research programs are funded at $1.19 billion, which includes increases for current and new programs for climate change resilience and vulnerability, agricultural sustainability (e.g., vertical agriculture), translational genetics, antimicrobial resistance and pollinator health, as well as major investments in the repair and maintenance of USDA laboratories to increase their lifespan and respond to health and safety issues; and 3) $206 million in key infrastructure investments fully funds USDA's five highest laboratory construction and renovation needs, including the poultry biosafety and laboratory consolidation in Athens, Georgia.

- *Stewardship of Natural Resources and the Environment.* Sustainable stewardship of natural resources requires strong R&D investments in the natural sciences to strengthen the scientific basis for decision-making. The Budget provides robust R&D funding to support resource decision-making and environmental stewardship at the Department of the Interior (DOI), Environmental Protection Agency (EPA), National Oceanic and Atmospheric Administration (NOAA), and USDA. The Budget provides strong support for R&D related to the management of public lands, ecosystems, energy permitting, and Earth observations (such as earth observing satellites and monitoring of water, wildlife, and invasive species). The Budget also provides strong support for science to inform ocean and coastal stewardship, with investments in ocean observations and exploration, coastal mapping and assessment, coastal ecosystem research, and coastal habitat restoration. The Budget strengthens investments in the safety and security of the Nation through R&D related to hazards such as earthquakes, floods, and extreme weather.

Cutting Carbon Pollution and Investing in Climate Preparedness and Resilience

Deep, persistent drought. Longer, fiercer wildfire seasons. High tides flooding downtowns. Severe storms wreaking havoc. This is the picture from the front lines of climate change in communities across America. As they face these immediate climate crises, cities, towns, counties and Tribes of every size and in every region of the United States have stepped up to be part of the solution: identifying their vulnerabilities; cutting carbon pollution; creating jobs by investing in clean energy and energy efficiency; and finding innovative solutions to make their communities and infrastructure more resilient to climate extremes. Whether it is investing in clean energy technology, or in necessary tools, technical assistance, and on-the-ground efforts, the Federal Government has a key role to play as a strong and ready partner with communities and the State, local, and tribal leaders who are taking action on climate today.

The Administration's robust energy and climate efforts over the last six years provide a strong foundation for this necessary partnership. When the President took office, U.S. greenhouse gas emissions were projected to continue increasing indefinitely, but the President set a new course with an ambitious goal to cut emissions in the range of 17 percent below 2005 levels in 2020. Throughout the first term, the Administration took strong actions to cut carbon pollution, including investing more than $80 billion in clean energy technologies through the Recovery Act, establishing historic fuel economy standards, supporting policies that contributed to a doubling of renewable energy generation, and implementing ambitious energy efficiency measures.

In 2013, the President launched an ambitious Climate Action Plan that built on the progress during the first term and doubled-down on cutting carbon pollution, preparing the Nation for climate impacts, and leading internationally. The Plan puts the Nation on track to meet the President's 2020 goal and establishes a strong foundation to reach the new 2025 goal by cutting carbon pollution through new measures, including a Clean Power Plan, historic standards for heavy-duty engines and vehicles, new energy efficiency standards, and economy-wide measures to reduce other greenhouse gases.

Cutting Carbon Pollution. Cutting carbon pollution is essential to reducing the threat of climate change and represents one of the greatest economic opportunities of the 21st Century. Investments in pollution-cutting technologies and proven energy efficiency and clean energy solutions are investments in American jobs, American industries, and Americans' health.

That is why in June 2014, the EPA proposed the Clean Power Plan, a flexible, commonsense approach that builds on the actions States, cities, and businesses across the United States are already taking to address the risks of climate change by reducing carbon pollution from existing power plants.

The Budget includes $239 million to support EPA efforts to address climate change through commonsense standards, guidelines, and voluntary programs, including $25 million to help States develop their Clean Power Plan strategies.

The Budget also includes an incentive fund for States choosing to go beyond the Clean Power Plan, which will be finalized this summer. The Clean Power State Incentive Fund will provide $4 billion to support States exceeding the minimum requirements established in the Clean Power Plan for timing of State plans and the pace and extent of carbon pollution reductions from the power sector. This funding will enable States to invest in a range of activities that complement and advance the Clean Power Plan, including efforts to address disproportionate impacts from environmental pollution in low-income communities and support for businesses to expand efforts in energy efficiency, renewable energy, and combined heat and power through, for example, grants and investments in much-needed infrastructure.

To support the development of pollution-cutting technologies, the Budget invests approximately $7.4 billion in clean energy technology programs, advancing American clean energy leadership, supporting job creation, and increasing energy security. These programs conduct research, development, and deployment efforts that stimulate the evolution and use of clean energy sources such as solar, wind, and low-carbon fossil fuels, as well as energy-efficient technologies, products, and process improvements. The largest investors are DOE, the Department of Defense (DOD), NSF, and USDA. DOE provides about 75 percent of the clean energy technology funding and supports a wide array of efforts across the clean energy spectrum that will further reduce costs and increase the use of clean energy technologies. For example, these efforts include increasing the affordability and convenience of advanced vehicles and domestic renewable fuels. They will advance technologies to improve the efficiency of the residential and commercial buildings of today and tomorrow, making energy systems more easily integrated into the electric grid. DOE is also developing technologies that reduce the costs of carbon capture from fossil fuels, undertaking research to ensure the safe, permanent storage of carbon dioxide in underground geologic formations, and conducting R&D to measure and mitigate fugitive methane emissions from natural gas infrastructure. DOE is also supporting

R&D in advanced nuclear reactor technologies, life extension for existing power plants, and innovative fuel-cycle concepts.

To support the adoption and scale-up of proven energy-efficiency and clean-energy solutions, the Budget includes additional key investments. For example, the Budget invests roughly $100 million in core DOI renewable energy development programs to review and permit new renewable energy projects on Federal lands and waters. These funds will allow DOI to continue progress toward its goal of permitting 20 gigawatts of renewable energy capacity and related transmission infrastructure by 2020, as part of the President's Climate Action Plan. The Budget also includes proposals to reform and renew tax credits that incentivize the deployment of wind, solar, and carbon capture sequestration technologies. In addition, the Budget invests in communities that are experiencing an economic transition as a result of the Nation's energy transformation toward cleaner power sources. This includes targeted investments in economic development for areas such as Appalachia, where declines in coal production over several decades have created economic challenges for communities and families.

Investing in Climate Resilience and Preparedness. As a Nation, we need to better understand and prepare for the impacts of a changing climate, which has widespread implications for the well-being of communities, health of our natural resources, and national security. The failure to invest in climate solutions and climate preparedness does not just fly in the face of the overwhelming judgment of science—it is fiscally unwise. While it cannot be said with certainty that any individual weather event is caused by climate change, it is clearly increasing the frequency and intensity of extreme weather events, from floods to drought to the most powerful storms. The costs of climate change add up, and ignoring the problem only makes it worse.

That is why the Budget makes investments to increase the resilience of the Nation's communities and ecosystems, improve understanding of projected climate-change impacts, and assist communities in planning and preparing for climate change. The goal is simple: to proactively reduce the risks communities and ecosystems face, rather than waiting until after disaster strikes. These forward-thinking investments will not only save lives, but will save communities and taxpayers the costs associated with recovering from the next weather-related emergency for which they were not prepared.

- *Flood Resilience.* The Budget includes $400 million for National Flood Insurance Program Risk Mapping efforts, an increase of $184 million over current funding levels. This increase will further support efforts to help communities and businesses understand what areas pose flood risks. The Budget also includes robust investments that will supplement ongoing work across USDA in science and tool development and projects to improve ecosystem and community resilience. Specifically, the Budget includes $200 million for USDA to emphasize watershed-scale planning and land treatment efforts and aid communities in planning and implementing mitigation and adaptation projects for extreme weather events, including mitigating the risks associated with coastal flooding.

- *Coastal Resilience.* The Budget includes funding for two new coastal resilience programs—one at NOAA and one at DOI—that will help reduce the risks that a changing climate poses to ecosystems and communities. Funding at NOAA will help coastal regions plan for and implement activities related to extreme weather, changing ocean conditions and uses, and climate hazards, while DOI funding will focus on increasing the return on investment from Federal land protection and restoration, through projects on adjacent non-Federal lands that restore ecosystems and boost resilience in coordination with non-Federal partners. The NOAA Regional Coastal Resilience Grants, funded at $50 million, will provide competitive grants to State, local, tribal, private, and non-governmental organization partners to support activities such as vulnerability assessments, regional ocean partnerships, and development and implementation of adaptation strategies. The new program at DOI, also funded at $50 million, will be modeled after the agency's Hurricane Sandy Competitive Grant Program and will expand the footprint of healthy ecosystems to deliver valuable ecosystem services, including flood attenuation and storm risk reduction, to nearby communities.

- *Drought Resilience.* The Budget strongly supports USDA in its efforts to integrate climate considerations into existing programs and to use programs to drive resilience. For example, through its regional Climate Hubs, the Department will provide information and guidance to farmers, ranchers, and forest landowners on the latest technologies and risk management strategies to help them implement climate-smart tactics. This effort is complemented by $89 million for DOI's WaterSMART program, which promotes water conservation initiatives and technological breakthroughs.

- *Wildland Fire Resilience.* The Administration is committed to ensuring that adequate funds are available to fight wildland fires, protect communities and human lives, and implement appropriate land management activities to improve the resiliency of the Nation's forests and rangelands. To accomplish this, the Budget proposes to establish a new budget framework for wildland fire suppression, similar to how other natural disasters are funded. The Budget proposes a base funding level of 70 percent of the 10-year average for suppression costs within the discretionary budget cap. A cap adjustment would then be used for only the most severe fire activity, which comprises one percent of the fires, but 30 percent of the costs. This framework minimizes the adverse impacts from transferring funds from other programs, reduces fire risk, and allows landscapes to be managed more comprehensively.

- *Federal Emergency Management Agency (FEMA) Pre-Disaster Mitigation Grant Program.* The Budget provides $200 million for FEMA's Pre-disaster Mitigation Grant Program, an increase of $175 million over current funding levels. This funding will predominately support mitigation planning, facilities hardening, and nonstructural risk reduction measures, such as buyouts and elevation of structures. Studies on mitigation activities conclude that Americans save $3-$4 for every dollar invested in pre-disaster mitigation.

- *Climate Resilience Toolkit.* The President's Budget provides $20 million to continue expanding and improving the recently-released online Climate Resilience Toolkit, which provides scientific tools and information to help Tribes, communities, citizens, businesses, planners, and others manage their climate-related risks and opportunities, and improve their resilience to extreme events. Through this online Toolkit, interested parties can access a variety of tools and data streams to help them understand how certain changes in environmental conditions—such as sea level rise and flooding, or droughts and wildfires—may impact their communities.

- *On-the-Ground Partnership with Local Communities.* The Budget provides $4 million to support a Resilience Corps pilot program at the Corporation for National and Community Service. This pilot program will support roughly 200 AmeriCorps members to assist communities in planning for and addressing the impacts of climate change. The Budget also includes $2 million for NOAA to train the Resilience Corps members. In addition to standing up a new Resilience Corps, the Budget also scales up on-the-ground programs that are already at work—such as the Corps of Engineers' Silver Jackets—by providing $31 million for the Corps of Engineers to provide local communities with technical and planning assistance regarding the development and implementation of nonstructural approaches to manage and reduce flood risk. The Budget also provides a total of $50 million, a $40 million increase, for American Indian Tribes and Alaska Native Villages and new funding totaling $7 million for Insular Areas (including territories and freely associated states) for understanding,

Federal Budget Exposure to Climate Risk

The global climate is changing and is projected to continue to change over this century and beyond.[1] Climate change impacts—such as rising sea level and more frequent and intense extreme weather events—will increasingly strain the Federal budget. The ability of policymakers to make smart investment decisions and to steward the Federal budget over the long term is increasingly dependent on understanding the Federal Government's exposure to climate risks.

The Federal Government has broad exposure to escalating costs and lost revenue as a direct or indirect result of a changing climate. For a number of Federal programs, existing climate-related expenditures can be identified. Over the last decade, the Federal Government has incurred over $300 billion in direct costs due to extreme weather and fire alone, including the following:

- *$179 billion for domestic disaster response and relief related to extreme weather.* Models demonstrate that climate-driven changes, such as higher sea levels and changes in hurricane activity, are likely to magnify damages and associated disaster response and relief needs. [2]

- *$24 billion for flood insurance.* While the National Flood Insurance Program is designed to offset losses with premium collections, the program accrued approximately $24 billion in debt to the U.S. Treasury over the last decade. Losses per policy are expected to grow due to climate change.[3]

- *$61 billion for crop insurance.* The Federal Government's total exposure for crop insurance is currently about $110 billion, up from $67 billion in 2007. Climate-driven increases in extreme weather events such as drought and excessive moisture are expected to exacerbate the costs of crop insurance.

- *$34 billion for wildland fire management.* Climate change is contributing to an increase in wildfire frequency and intensity across the western United States and Alaska.[1]

- *Health care.* The effects of climate change will increase risk of asthma attacks and other respiratory illnesses, extreme heat exposure, the spread of infectious diseases, and flood-related health hazards. Already, the United States is spending billions of dollars in Medicaid expenses related to asthma each year.

- *Federal property management.* Federal facilities are directly at risk from the kinds of extreme weather events associated with climate change. For example, a military installation in the Southwest incurred $64 million in damages due to unusual torrential downpours. Another military facility in Alaska will incur $25 million in costs to bolster its seawall and runway against rising seas and thawing permafrost.

- *National security.* National security agencies expect that climate change effects worldwide will drive overseas conflict and associated costs for military and humanitarian operations.

- *Species decline and loss.* Climate change is expected to fundamentally alter ecosystems in ways that are costly to those systems and the people who depend upon and value them. While some species may be able to move to more suitable climates, others may be unable to and could be driven to extinction. As populations decline due to the impacts of existing stressors—such as habitat loss—coupled with climate change, the number of species needing Federal protection and

---

1   Melillo, Jerry M., Terese (T.C.) Richmond, and Gary W. Yohe, Eds., 2014. Climate Change Impacts in the United States: The Third National Climate Assessment. U.S. Global Research Program, 841 pp. doi:10.7930/J0Z31WJ2

2   Kopp, Robert, and Solomon Hsiang, 2014: American Climate Prospectus. Economic Risks in the United States. Rhodium Group, LLC.

3   AECOM, 2013. The Impact of Climate Change and Population Growth on the National Flood Insurance Program through 2100. Prepared for Federal Emergency Management Agency

the costs of Federal species recovery efforts will likely increase. For example, climate change has already brought on a mismatch between the life cycle of the Edith's checkerspot butterfly and the timing of the flowering plants it depends on, causing the butterfly's population to crash along its southern range.

Current projections estimate that unabated climate change would cost the global economy over four percent of global GDP each year by 2100.[4] Such economic losses would translate into lost revenue for the U.S. Government. While the extent of this lost revenue in 2100 is highly uncertain—it could be as much as 0.7 percent of U.S. GDP.[5] For reference, such a loss in 2014 would translate into over $120 billion in lost revenue for the Federal Government.

How we respond to one of the most significant long-term challenges that the Nation and our planet faces speaks volumes about our values. It speaks to who we are as policymakers—if we embrace the challenge of developing pragmatic solutions. It speaks to who we are as Americans—if we seize this moment and lead. It speaks to who we are as parents—if we take responsibility and leave our children a safer planet.

The President has set the United States on an ambitious course to tackle emissions and prepare the Nation's communities for the effects of climate change because he not only believes that we have a moral obligation to do so, but also because climate action is an economic and fiscal imperative.

See *Analytical Perspectives*, Federal Exposure to Climate Risk chapter for more detail.

---

4 Contribution of Working Group II to the Fourth Assessment Report of the Intergovernmental Panel on Climate Change. Parry, M.L., O.F. Canziani, J.P. Palutikof, P.J. van der Linden, and C.E. Hanson (eds.). Cambridge University Press, Cambridge, United Kingdom.

5 Based on 2014 receipts as a share of GDP, estimated by OMB (17.3 percent).

planning for, and implementing actions that support community resilience in the face of a changing climate.

Investing in the Green Climate Fund and Leading International Efforts to Cut Carbon Pollution and Enhance Climate Change Resilience

The President's Climate Action Plan also calls for leadership abroad. To support this objective, the Budget provides $1.29 billion, a significant increase above the 2015 enacted level, to advance the goals of the Global Climate Change Initiative (GCCI) by supporting important multilateral and bilateral engagement with major and emerging economies. This funding includes $500 million for U.S. contributions to the new Green Climate Fund (GCF), which will help developing countries leverage public and private finance and invest in reducing carbon pollution and strengthening resilience to climate change. By reducing the most catastrophic risks of climate change, the GCF will help promote smart, sustainable long-term economic growth and preserve stability and security in fragile regions of strategic importance to the United States. These investments will build on the best practices and lessons learned from the Climate Investment Funds. The United States expects that the GCF will become a preeminent, effective, and efficient channel for climate finance. More broadly, GCCI funding enables the United States to provide international leadership through the Department of State, the U.S. Agency for International Development (USAID), and the Department of the Treasury to expand clean and efficient energy use, to reduce emissions from deforestation and forest degradation and conserve the world's remaining tropical rainforests, to phase down chemicals with high global warming potential, and to support the poorest and most vulnerable communities in their efforts to cope with the adverse impacts of severe weather events and climate change.

Maintaining the Nation's Natural Resources

American forests are a critical resource for the economy. They support thousands of timber and forest product jobs, recreation, hunting and fishing, and help to clean the air we breathe and water we drink. However, in the face of a changing climate and increased risk of wildfire, drought, and pests, the Nation's forests are under increasing pressure and their future health and the jobs they support are at risk. Moreover, pressures to develop forest lands for urban or agricultural uses also contribute to the decline of forest health. Investments in conservation and sustainable management and working lands can help to ensure the forest landowners and dependent communities have sustainable, forest-based economic development opportunities. Such investments also have the benefit of helping to improve soil and water quality, reduce wildfire risk, and otherwise manage forests to be more resilient in the face of climate change. That is

why the Budget invests $83 million, an increase of $13 million over the 2015 enacted level, for the Forest Inventory and Analysis program to deliver landscape scale survey data in all 50 States, including initial surveys and data collection in interior Alaska, to foster terrestrial carbon conservation and retention in land and natural resource management.

Improving the Farm Safety Net through Common Sense Reforms

In the last 15 years, the Crop Insurance program has evolved from a small program with minimal participation to one of the main pillars of farm support. Overly generous benefits have almost eliminated the risk in farming at a cost to taxpayers in the billions. The Budget includes reforms that are designed to reduce the distorting aspects of the program while maintaining its place as an insurance program and a key component of the farm safety net. Specifically, the Budget proposes to reduce the subsidy for the premium on the harvest price protection revenue insurance, and tighten the prevented planting crop insurance rules saving an estimated $16 billion over 10 years.

BUILDING A 21ST CENTURY INFRASTRUCTURE

When we build roads, bridges, ports, communications networks, municipal water systems, and other infrastructure, we are not just putting construction workers and engineers to work—we are also revitalizing communities, protecting public health and safety, connecting people to jobs, empowering entrepreneurs, and making it easier for American businesses to export goods around the world. There is certainly enough work to do, with $2 trillion in deferred maintenance on the Nation's infrastructure. Built by far-sighted investment over generations, America's world-class infrastructure is falling behind the rest of the world. As other nations have sought to compete economically by improving infrastructure, U.S. investment lags behind many of its overseas competitors. In the most recent World Economic Forum rankings, the United States had, in less than a decade, fallen from 7th to 18th overall in

the quality of its roads. Building a durable and reliable 21st Century infrastructure creates good jobs that cannot be outsourced and will provide American workers and businesses with the transportation and communication networks they need to help grow the economy. The Budget includes significant investments to repair the existing infrastructure and build the infrastructure of tomorrow in smart, efficient, and cost-effective ways.

Long-Term Investments in Upgrading America's Transportation Infrastructure

To spur economic growth and allow States and localities to initiate sound multi-year investments, the Budget includes a six-year, $478 billion surface transportation reauthorization proposal.

By reinvesting the transition revenue from pro-growth business tax reform, the President's plan will ensure the health of the Highway Trust Fund for another six years—two years beyond the 2015 Budget GROW AMERICA proposal—and invest in a range of activities to spur and sustain long-term growth. The President's plan to rebuild America will increase spending to repair and modernize the Nation's highways and bridges, as well as injecting much needed investment into the existing transit and intercity passenger rail systems. The President's plan also increases investments to ex-

---

The Case for Investing in Infrastructure in Today's Economy

The Budget proposes to invest in infrastructure through a comprehensive six-year surface transportation reauthorization proposal, as well as tax incentives for State and local infrastructure investment, a new Infrastructure Bank, and other initiatives. The Federal Government plays a vital role in infrastructure investment, and the Nation's roads, bridges, and other surface transportation infrastructure systems are badly in need of upgrades and repairs. For example, 65 percent of America's major roads are rated in less than good condition and one quarter of U.S. bridges need rehabilitation, replacement, or significant maintenance and repair to remain in service or do not meet current design standards and traffic needs. Although the economic recovery has begun to accelerate, the economy is still operating below capacity, and interest rates remain at very low levels. While infrastructure investment will continue to be needed even after the economy reaches full employment, time is running out to make these needed investments under ideal economic conditions.

A recent study published by the International Monetary Fund (IMF)[1] makes a convincing case that "the time is right for a strong infrastructure push" in advanced economies such as the United States. While infrastructure is critical for economic efficiency and growth, the private sector often fails to make sufficient investment in infrastructure for several reasons, such as positive externalities, large start-up costs, and economies of scale. Thus, in many cases, the public sector can provide infrastructure more efficiently.

Public infrastructure investment promotes economic growth by boosting aggregate demand in the short run and improving economic efficiency in the long run. While infrastructure needs to be financed, the IMF study presents statistical evidence that—under the right conditions—the combination of short- and long-term economic gains from infrastructure investment can offset much of its cost. When many workers are unemployed, infrastructure investment increases total employment, as opposed to bidding workers away from other sectors, thus increasing aggregate demand.

The U.S. economy still has unused capacity. While the unemployment rate has declined significantly and more workers are holding full-time jobs, nearly four percent of the workforce is still working part time for the lack of full-time work, and unemployment rates in the construction sector remain higher than in the economy as a whole. Moreover, the Federal Government remains able to borrow at very low interest rates, with the 10-year Treasury rate ending 2014 below two and a half percent. While the Budget proposes to offset the cost of its new infrastructure investments, it would front-load the investments and pay for them over the 10-year budget window. This pro-growth approach has the potential to realize both the short- and long-term gains from investing in infrastructure, with no risk of higher long-run debt.

The IMF study also highlights the importance of choosing high-efficiency infrastructure projects based on rigorous benefit-cost analysis. The United States has a pent up supply of badly needed infrastructure projects that meet these tests, and the President's surface transportation plan would result in larger share of funds being allocated through competitive processes.

---

1   International Monetary Fund, 2014, "Is It Time for an Infrastructure Push? The Macroeconomic Effects of Public Investment," in *World Economic Outlook: Legacies, Clouds, Uncertainties.*

pand new transit projects, link regional economies by funding the development of high-performance rail, and support American exports by improving goods movement within the Nation's freight rail networks. Small businesses particularly depend on the quality of transportation networks to get goods to market competitively, allowing them to win customers, expand operations, and hire new employees. To help spur innovation and economic mobility, the reauthorization proposal would permanently authorize the competitive TIGER grant program to support projects that bring job opportunities to communities across the United States. The proposal would also advance the President's Climate Action Plan by building more resilient infrastructure and reducing transportation emissions by responding to the greater demand and travel growth in public transit. Also, to make sure that Americans are driving vehicles that are safe to operate, the reauthorization proposal includes additional resources for investigating automobile defects, improving data collection to better support Government oversight of auto manufacturers, and making changes to hold auto manufacturers more accountable for reporting and responding to vehicle defects.

Infrastructure Permitting

To further accelerate economic growth and improve the competitiveness of the American economy, the Administration is taking action to modernize and improve the efficiency of the Federal permitting process for major infrastructure projects. In May 2014, the President announced a comprehensive interagency plan with 15 reforms to turn best practices into common practice. To implement this plan, the 2015 Budget proposed a new Interagency Infrastructure Permitting Improvement Center housed at the Department of Transportation to lead the Administration's reform efforts across nearly 20 Federal agencies and bureaus. While waiting for the Congress to act, the Administration set-up an interim interagency team to support reforms, such as moving from separate, consecutive reviews to synchronized, simultaneous reviews. For example, the U.S. Coast Guard, the Corps of Engineers, and the Department of Transportation have launched a new partnership to synchronize their reviews for transportation and other infrastructure projects, such as bridges that cross navigation channels. By developing one environmental analysis that satisfies all three agencies, project timelines can be significantly reduced. Building on these efforts, the Budget supports an expanded, publicly available Permitting Dashboard that tracks project schedules and metrics for major infrastructure projects, further improving the transparency and accountability of the permitting process. To accomplish these goals, the Budget proposes $4 million for the Department of Transportation to expand the Federal Infrastructure Permitting Dashboard and fund staff to lead interagency reforms that accelerate progress and improve outcomes. In addition, the Budget includes $4 million for permitting reforms through a proposal to expand interagency transfer authorities, which would institutionalize capacity to address cross-agency management improvements. The Budget also includes additional funding to expedite the consultations required pursuant to the Endangered Species Act, which also will help accelerate permit review timeframes.

Build America Investment Initiative

The Budget includes support for the Build America Investment Initiative (BAII), a Government-wide, interagency initiative to increase infrastructure investment and promote economic growth by supporting public-private collaboration in major infrastructure sectors such as transportation, water, and telecommunications. As part of the BAII, the Administration has launched investment centers to provide States and municipalities with assistance on securing investment in transportation, water systems, and rural infrastructure. Together, these centers will facilitate direct private investment in U.S. infrastructure and encourage greater public-private collaboration. For example, as part of the BAII, the Department of Transportation established the Build America Transportation Investment Center to serve as a one-stop-shop for cities and States seeking to use innovative financing and partnerships with the private sector to support transportation infrastructure. An Interagency

Infrastructure Finance Working Group, co-chaired by the Secretaries of the Treasury and Transportation, delivered recommendations to the President on how to promote awareness and understanding of innovative financing and increase effective public-private collaboration. Building on those recommendations, the Administration has worked with the private sector to launch two additional investment initiatives that will help leverage existing investments in drinking water and wastewater infrastructure and other infrastructure such as hospitals, schools, local and regional food systems, and broadband expansion throughout rural America. Other Federal agencies are also focusing on using existing authorities to increase the private sector's participation in the financing of public infrastructure. In addition, the Budget proposes to create a new America Fast Forward Bond program that, like its Build America Bond precursor, will provide State and local governments with an optional taxable bond alternative to traditional tax-exempt bonds. The Federal Government will share in the cost of these bonds so they are as affordable to issuers as tax-exempt bonds, proceeds of which can be used to further finance governmental capital projects.

Launching the National Parks Centennial Initiative

For 100 years, National Park Service (NPS) parks and historic sites have preserved and shared America's cultural and historical identity. These places present America's unique history and draw tourists from across the United States and around the world. There is an opportunity to celebrate the centennial anniversary of the Nation's great parks by providing enhanced park services for visitors, and through targeted investments to improve NPS facilities. This opportunity is an historic effort to upgrade and restore national parks, while putting tens of thousands of Americans to work and engaging and inspiring younger generations to carry the Nation's parks into the future.

The Budget proposes $860 million in mandatory and discretionary funding to allow NPS, over 10 years, to make targeted, measurable, and quantifiable upgrades to all of its highest priority non-transportation assets and restore and maintain them to good condition. Addressing the critical needs of these assets avoids deterioration and costs for future generations. The Budget also proposes matching funds to leverage private donations for signature projects and programs at national parks. This significant effort ensures America's national treasures will be preserved over the next hundred years for future generations.

The 1916 Act that created NPS called for parks to be left "unimpaired for the enjoyment of future generations." The Parks Centennial seeks to live up to this call by providing more opportunities for children to interact with natural areas. This targeted effort involves transporting over a million urban youth a year to national and public lands with dedicated youth coordinators to welcome them and their families. Today's investment in the next generation of visitors will help build the stewards of America's national treasures in the future.

This year also marks the 50th anniversary of the Voting Rights Act, which the Budget commemorates by proposing $50 million to restore and highlight key sites across the United States that contributed to the struggle for civil rights. This includes investments in specific NPS sites associated with the 1950s and 1960s civil rights movement, such as the Selma to Montgomery National Historic Trail, Little Rock Central High School National Historic Site, Brown v. Board of Education National Historic Site, and the Martin Luther King, Jr. National Historic Site. State, local, and tribal governments can also apply for historic preservation funds to help them document and preserve stories and sites associated with the struggle.

Smart Investments in Federal Facilities

Investing in the Nation's federally-owned facilities ensures that mission execution is optimized at the lowest possible cost. Funding reductions in recent years have led to facility deterioration, as well as missed opportunities to consolidate and reduce operating costs. The General Services Administration (GSA) is leading the Federal effort to both invest in Federal facilities and consolidate space to reduce costs and optimize efficiency, saving tens of millions in annual lease costs. The Budget will invest more than $2.5 billion in GSA's Federal facilities portfolio, an increase of more than $1.1 billion over the enacted level. GSA will invest $1.25 billion in construction and acquisition priorities, including the next phase of the consolidated Department of Homeland Security Headquarters and the first phase of a Civilian Cyber Campus. GSA will also invest more than $900 million in critical repairs and alterations and consolidation activities. The National Aeronautics and Space Administration and the USDA Forest Service will eliminate operating costs by demolishing unneeded facilities. The Smithsonian Institution and DOI will make

necessary investments to improve the condition of facilities and reduce operational costs. The Budget invests $60 million to continue renovations of USDA headquarters, and $206 million for the Agricultural Research Service to renovate and construct its facilities. The Budget also invests $1.5 billion for construction projects at the Department of Veterans Affairs (VA), an increase of nearly $500 million over the 2015 enacted level. These investments will enhance the Department's mission while providing opportunities for long-term savings, as building upgrades and renovations result in a reduced footprint. Government-wide, agencies will continue their efforts to reduce their space in accordance with the Administration's goal to reduce the Federal footprint. In total, the Budget provides an additional $2.4 billion in capital investment funding over the 2015 enacted level.

HIGH-QUALITY, AFFORDABLE EDUCATION: FROM PRE-K TO COLLEGE

America's education system led the world in the 20th Century—we sent generations to college, and cultivated the most educated workforce in the world, which supported an unparalleled period of economic growth and rising middle class incomes. Since then, other countries have followed our lead to develop globally competitive education systems. America must lead the world in education once again. That requires both reform and investment, and the Budget does both—investing in what works to improve student outcomes. The Budget provides $70.7 billion in discretionary funding for Department of Education programs, an increase of $3.6 billion from the 2015 enacted level.

Significant progress has already been made toward improving educational opportunities. By tying investments to evidence-based reforms and focusing on improving student outcomes, the Administration has worked with States across the Nation to raise their learning standards, improve teacher effectiveness, and use data to ensure students graduate from high school prepared for college and a successful career. These investments have given teachers, school districts, and States the tools to turn around some of the Nation's lowest-performing schools. We are also

on our way to connecting 99 percent of students to next-generation broadband in the classroom through the ConnectED initiative. Progress is being made on the President's goal to prepare 100,000 excellent math and science teachers. Last year, U.S. elementary and middle school students had the highest mathematics and reading scores on record. The high school graduation rate is above 80 percent for the first time in history. More students have been helped to afford college through grants, tax credits, and manageable loans, and today more people are graduating from college than ever before. Further, 1.3 million veterans have been sent to college on the Post-9/11 GI Bill.

Tremendous progress has been made in education, but we still have work to do to make sure we are again leading the world with highly-skilled workers who are able to compete in the global economy and are ready for the jobs of tomorrow. The Budget proposes to do that through improving access to early education; preparing elementary and secondary education students for success; increasing access to quality, affordable higher education; and continuing to build the evidence base for what works to improve student outcomes.

Improving Access to High-Quality, Affordable Early Education

Providing children with access to high-quality, early education enables them to start kindergarten ready to succeed and to realize their full potential. Researchers have established that supporting children during this critical stage yields benefits that far outweigh the costs of the investment. This is particularly true for low-income children, who often start kindergarten far less prepared than their peers.

Preschool for All. The Budget maintains support for the President's landmark Preschool for All proposal to ensure four-year-olds across the Nation have access to high-quality preschool programs. The proposal establishes a Federal-State partnership to provide all low- and moderate-income four-year-olds with high-quality preschool, while providing States with incentives to expand these programs to reach additional children from middle class families, and put in place full-day kindergarten policies. The proposal is paid for through an increase in tobacco taxes that will help reduce youth smoking and save lives. To lay the groundwork for this proposal, the Budget provides $750 million for Preschool Development Grants, a substantial increase of $500 million from the 2015 enacted level. The Department of Education's Preschool Development Grants are currently helping 18 States develop and expand high-quality preschool programs in targeted communities. The Budget also provides $907 million for early intervention and preschool services for children with disabilities, an increase of $115 million from the 2015 enacted level. This proposal includes $15 million for a pay-for-success initiative for early identification of and intervention for learning and developmental delays, with a potential focus on autism, intended to help identify, develop, and scale-up evidence-based practices through innovative public-private partnerships that create incentives for service providers to deliver better outcomes.

Head Start. The Budget makes historic investments in the Department of Health and Human Services' Head Start program by providing more than $1.5 billion in additional funding over the 2015 enacted level, including $650 million to expand access to high-quality early learning settings for tens of thousands of additional children through Early Head Start and the Early Head Start-Child Care Partnerships. The increased Head Start funding will also ensure that children are served in programs that operate for a full school day and a full school year, which recent research shows promotes better outcomes for young children. In addition, the Budget invests $15 billion over the next 10 years to extend and expand evidence-based, voluntary home visiting programs, which enable nurses, social workers, and other professionals to work with current and expecting parents to help families track their children's development, identify any health and development issues and connect them to services to address them, and utilize good parenting practices that foster healthy development and early learning. As with Preschool for All, the proposal is paid for through an increase in tobacco taxes. The program builds on research showing that home visiting programs can significantly improve maternal and child health, child development, learning, and success. As discussed below under Supporting Working Families, the Budget also makes historic investments in expanding access to quality, affordable child care. This investment is designed to meet two important purposes—help parents afford child care so they can work and help children access quality care that can support their healthy development.

Preparing all Students for Success in College and Careers

States and school districts have made significant progress toward expanding opportunity so that all children can meet rigorous, college- and career-ready standards and graduate from high school prepared to succeed in a globally competitive economy. Forty-eight States and the District of Columbia have raised standards for learning in their schools and are supporting the hard work of teachers to enable their students to succeed. Parents, educators, and communities have joined together to transform low-performing schools and embark on a new day of learning for students. School districts are making important strides to connect students to high-speed broadband that will facilitate personalized instruction and link them to a world of learning beyond the classroom. The signs of progress are clear—the high school graduation rate is the highest on record and students are making academic gains. Yet there is a long way to go to ensure that all students, particularly those who are the most disadvantaged, are ready to compete in a global economy.

Title I. The Budget proposes a $1 billion increase from the 2015 enacted level for Title I, the Department's largest K-12 grant program and the cornerstone of its commitment to supporting low-income schools with the funding necessary to provide high-need students access to an excellent education. In addition, the Budget proposes $100 million to support districts that are using their Federal formula funds for evidence-based interventions, and includes a pilot opportunity for districts that distribute funds to schools more equitably to receive relief from Federal reporting and fiscal requirements. The Budget also includes increases for programs that help other students who face academic hurdles meet rigorous academic standards, including $11.7 billion for special education, an increase of $175 million over 2015 funding, and $773 million for English learners, an increase of $36 million.

Support for Teachers. The Budget invests $3 billion in discretionary funding to provide broad support for educators at every phase of their careers, from ensuring they have strong preparation before entering the classroom, to pioneering new approaches to help teachers succeed in the classroom and equipping them with tools and training they need to implement college- and career-ready standards. Recognizing the importance of integrating technology into the classroom, this investment includes $200 million for an improved Education Technology State Grants program focused on providing educators

with training and support to maximize the impact of expanded access to technology to provide high-quality instruction to students.

The Budget also proposes a companion initiative funded at $1 billion annually for five years in mandatory funding that will support State and local efforts to attract more of the best and brightest to the teaching profession and prepare them for the demands of the classroom, while also creating a culture of excellence and professional growth for teachers throughout their careers.

Improving the Nation's High Schools. The Budget establishes a new $125 million competitive program to promote the redesign of America's high schools by integrating deeper learning and student-centered instruction, with a particular focus on science, technology, engineering, and mathematics (STEM)-themed high schools that expand opportunities for girls and other groups underrepresented in STEM fields. The Budget also invests $556 million, a $50 million increase over the 2015 enacted level, in School Improvement Grants, to expand the use of evidence-based approaches to turning around the Nation's lowest performing schools, including high schools with unacceptably low graduation rates.

Replicating Successful Charter School Models. The Budget proposes $375 million for charter schools, a $122 million increase over the 2015 enacted level. This investment includes a significant emphasis on replicating and expanding those charter schools and models that have been shown to significantly improve educational outcomes for disadvantaged students to new areas in need of high-quality schools.

Building Evidence and Fostering Innovation. The Budget funds the Investing in Innovation program at $300 million, a $180 million increase over the 2015 enacted level, to develop and test effective practices and provide better information to States and districts on what works in key areas such as implementing college- and career-ready standards, using data to inform instruction and personalize learning, and improving low-performing schools. Across every dimension, the Budget continues the Administration's efforts to build a much stronger evidence base on what works in education.

Strengthening Opportunities for Native Youth. The Budget supports a comprehensive redesign and reform of the Bureau of Indian Education (BIE) to provide students attending BIE-funded schools with a world-class education, transforming that agency to serve as a capacity-builder and service-provider for Tribes in educating their youth. Investments in the Budget for DOI include funding to: improve opportunities and outcomes in the classroom; provide improved instructional services and teacher quality; promote enhanced language and cultural programs; enhance broadband and digital access; rebuild schools and improve school infrastructure and facilities; and provide grants to incentivize creative solutions to school transformations. The Budget also supports new Native Youth Community Projects at the Department of Education, to provide funding in a select number of Native communities that would support culturally relevant, coordinated strategies to improve the college-and-career readiness of Native children and youth.

Delivering a Quality, Affordable College Education to Millions of Americans

Today, more than ever, Americans need more knowledge and skills to meet the demands of a growing global economy. A college education opens the door to opportunity—for individuals and, in turn, for the Nation as a whole. That is why the President is committed to making a college education affordable and accessible and to undertaking reforms that improve quality and performance, ensuring that the United States once again leads the world in college completion, as it did a generation ago. This effort requires a multi-pronged strategy that includes a strong Pell Grant Program that expands opportunity for low- and moderate-income students; a student loan program that helps students and families make sound financial choices and ensures student debt stays manageable; key investments in

America's higher education system that make two years of college free for responsible students, ensuring affordable, high-quality community college options for students seeking occupational training or a stepping stone to a four-year degree; and a simpler, better targeted tax system that helps families pay for college. But affordability is not enough. Colleges also need to help students from all backgrounds, including disadvantaged and academically underprepared students, to persist and ultimately succeed. A number of leading colleges and States have already begun to successfully meet these challenges and demonstrate what is possible—the Budget builds on these lessons and the steps the Administration has already taken to improve higher education access, affordability, and quality.

Investing in Pell Grants. Over the course of this Administration, the maximum Pell Grant for working and middle class families has gone up by more than $1,000, to nearly $5,800 in award year 2015-16, and the Budget will continue the President's commitment to college affordability by ensuring that Pell Grants keep pace with inflation. The Budget also proposes strengthening academic progress requirements in the Pell Grant program and provides a College Opportunity and Graduation Bonus to successful schools, to ensure that students make progress toward completing their degrees.

Making Two Years of Community College Free for Responsible Students and Strengthening the Quality of Community Colleges. The Budget includes a new proposal to ensure all Americans have the opportunity to pursue and succeed in higher education, with a goal of making two years of college as universal as high school. The new grant program will provide funding to States that agree to waive tuition and fees at community colleges for eligible students, increase their own investment by matching the Federal funds, and undertake a set of reforms to improve the quality of community colleges. In addition, the Budget includes $200 million to create a postsecondary American Technical Training Fund within the Career and Technical Education program, which would create or expand job-training programs with strong employer partnerships to provide accelerated training in in-demand fields.

Making the Tax System Simpler and More Effective at Supporting Families and Students. The Budget proposes to expand, simplify, and better target education tax benefits, building on the Administration's success in creating the American Opportunity Tax Credit.

Making Student Loans Work for Students. The Budget continues to propose reforms to Pay-As-You-Earn, an income-based repayment option, to ensure that the program is well-targeted while making student loan payments manageable. It also supports improvements to the loan programs to ensure that borrowers can make sound choices.

Using Evidence to Improve Higher Education. Through a $200 million investment in the First in the World program, a $140 million increase over the 2015 enacted level, the Administration will scale-up promising evidence-based practices that aim to improve college affordability, persistence, and completion for more of America's students and families. The Budget also includes an additional $20 million for innovative, evidence-based approaches in the TRIO programs.

WALL STREET REFORM

When the President took office in 2009, financial markets were in a tailspin. The crisis left millions of Americans unemployed and resulted in trillions in lost wealth. America's broken regulatory system was the principal cause of that crisis. To ensure financial stability for Americans and businesses, the President fought to reform Wall Street, ultimately signing a bill that represented the most sweeping financial regulatory legislation since the Great Depression. Since that time, Americans are getting back to work and regaining lost equity in their homes. But there is still work to do to protect American consumers and investors, and maintain fairness in the financial system.

In response to the destabilizing 2008 financial crisis, the Administration achieved landmark reform of the Nation's financial system in 2010 with enactment of the Dodd-Frank Wall Street Reform and Consumer Protection Act (Wall Street Reform). In the years since enactment, Federal agencies have helped make home, auto, and short-term consumer loan terms fairer and easier to understand for average consumers, improved visibility for investors into the shadowy corners and complex instruments of financial markets, and increased financial firms' planning for and resilience to future financial downturns. The Budget continues to support Wall Street Reform implementation across agencies, including $1.7 billion for the Securities and Exchange Commission and $322 million for the Commodity Futures Trading Commission (CFTC), representing increases over the 2015 enacted level of 15 percent and 29 percent, respectively. These are the only two Federal financial regulators whose budgets are set through annual appropriations. The Budget also reflects continued support for legislation to enable funding the CFTC through user fees like all other financial regulators. The Administration will continue to oppose efforts to restrict the funding independence of the other financial regulators, including the Consumer Financial Protection Bureau, and will fight other attempts to roll back Wall Street Reform.

To finish addressing the weaknesses exposed by the financial crisis, the Government must reform the housing finance system and move forward to wind down the Government-Sponsored Enterprises (GSEs), which have been in conservatorship since September 2008. A bipartisan bill developed in the Senate last year includes many of the Administration's key housing finance reform principles, including ensuring that private capital is at the center of the housing finance system, and that the new system supports affordable housing through programs such as the Housing Trust and Capital Magnet Funds. The President stands ready to work with Members of Congress in both parties to enact common sense housing finance legislation that embodies these core principles. For additional discussion of the GSEs, see the Credit and Insurance chapter in the *Analytical Perspectives* volume of the Budget.

CREATING OPPORTUNITY AND SUPPORTING WORKING FAMILIES

The economy is growing and businesses are creating a record number of jobs; but in order to truly judge this economy as healthy, more must be done to support America's working families and create opportunity for those striving to reach the middle class. Too many Americans are working harder to get by, not feeling the effects of a growing economy. In addition to creating jobs by investing in manufacturing, R&D, and clean energy development, and expanding opportunity by investing in education from the early years through college, support must also be provided to the Nation's working families and more opportunities provided for hardworking Americans to get ahead. That is why this Budget invests in a series of proposals to help ensure that if you work hard and play by the rules, you can reach the middle class and thrive in it.

Supporting Working Families

The Budget includes the following proposals to support working families, and help them reach their full potential in America's growing economy.

Expanding Access to Quality Child Care for Working Families. Research shows that access to affordable, quality child care can increase parents' employment and earnings, while also promoting healthy child development. The Budget invests $82 billion in mandatory funding over 10 years to ensure that all low- and moderate-income working families with children ages three or younger have access to quality, affordable child care. The Budget also provides a $266 million increase in discretionary funding to help States implement the policies required by the new bipartisan Child Care and Development Block Grant Act of 2014, and designed to improve the safety and quality of care while giving parents the information they need to make good choices about their child care providers. In addition, as described later, the Budget proposes to expand tax credits that help middle class families afford the cost of child care.

To help build a supply of high-quality child care that meets the needs of today's working families, including those with non-traditional schedules, the Budget also provides $100 million to States and local communities to develop, implement, and evaluate new, innovative models of providing care. These pilots will benefit low-income working families by focusing on what they need most—high-quality care that is available in their community and during the hours they work.

Encouraging State Paid Leave Initiatives. Too many American workers must make the painful choice between caring for their families and a paycheck they desperately need. While the Family and Medical Leave Act allows many workers to take job-protected unpaid time off to care for a new baby or sick family member, or tend to their own health during a serious illness, millions of families cannot afford to use unpaid leave.

A handful of States have enacted policies to offer paid leave, and the Federal Government can encourage more States to follow their lead. The Budget includes $2 billion for the Paid Leave Partnership Initiative to assist up to five States that wish to launch paid leave programs, following the example of California, New Jersey, and Rhode Island. States that participate in the Paid Leave Partnership Initiative would be eligible to receive funds for the initial set up and benefit costs of the program for three years. The Budget also includes a $35 million State Paid Leave Fund to provide technical assistance and support to States that are still building the infrastructure they need to launch paid leave programs in the future.

Expanding Paid Family Leave for Federal Employees. The United States is one of only a few countries (and the only industrialized country) that does not offer workers paid maternity leave, although Federal workers do have access to paid sick and annual leave. Evidence shows that the availability of paid maternity leave increases the likelihood that mothers return to their jobs following the birth of a child, in addition to producing better outcomes for the infant. In order to recruit and retain the best possible workforce to provide outstanding service to American taxpayers, the Budget proposes legislation that would offer Federal employees six weeks of paid administrative leave for the birth, adoption, or foster placement of a child. In addition, the proposal would make explicit the ability for mothers and fathers to use sick days to bond with a healthy new child. This proposal is part of a broader effort to expand the availability of paid family leave for the Federal workforce, and establish a Federal family leave policy that is on par with leading private sector companies and other industrialized nations. The proposal complements the President's memorandum in January 2015, directing agencies to offer advanced sick leave in connection with the birth or adoption of a child, foster care placement, or for other sick leave eligible uses, and requiring agencies to consider providing access to affordable emergency backup dependent care service.

Helping Families Care for Aging Relatives. Families are the Nation's primary provider of long-term care, but financial constraints, work and family demands, and the challenges of providing care can place great pressure on family caregivers. Caregiving responsibilities demand time and money from families who too often are already strapped for both. Paid leave policies can provide an important support to workers with caregiving responsibilities. The Budget provides $88 million in additional resources for existing programs that are providing critical help and supports to seniors and caregivers, such as respite care, transportation assistance, and nutrition services. To ensure the continued provision of high-quality and effective supports to older adults and caregivers, the Budget also includes $35 million for these programs to develop and disseminate evidence-based innovations. In 2015, the Administration

will host the sixth White House Conference on Aging to recognize the importance of these, and other key programs for older Americans, as well as to look ahead on how to improve and advance the quality of life for older Americans in the next decade.

Maintaining Strong Support for Worker Protections. The Budget includes nearly $1.9 billion for the Department of Labor's (DOL) worker protection agencies, putting them on sound footing to meet their responsibilities to defend the health, safety, wages, working conditions, and retirement security of American workers. The Administration is also pursuing a combination of executive and legislative actions to strengthen these laws and their enforcement, so workers can earn wages that will allow them to sustain their families, be protected from discrimination, return home safely at the end of a day's work, and retire with dignity. In the Budget, and through its administrative actions, the Administration:

- *Supports Raising the Minimum Wage.* In a Nation as wealthy as the United States, far too many workers are living below the poverty line. Over the past 30 years, modest minimum wage increases have not kept pace with the higher costs of basic necessities for working families. The Administration supports raising the minimum wage so hard-working Americans can earn enough to support their families and make ends meet. Many companies, from small businesses to large corporations, also see higher wages as the right way to boost productivity, reduce turnover, and increase profits. Raising the minimum wage is good for workers, their families, and for the economy. The President took an important step in this effort by signing an Executive Order (EO) to increase the minimum wage to $10.10 for those working on new and replacement Federal contracts, and the Administration recently issued regulations to implement the EO. The Administration is encouraged that 17 States and the District of Columbia have passed increases in their minimum wage since the President called for a minimum wage increase during his State of the Union remarks in February

2013. Those increases will benefit seven million workers. As the President continues to encourage States, cities, and businesses to act, he stands ready to work with the Congress to pass legislation to increase the minimum wage for the rest of the workforce as soon as possible.

- *Enhances Worker Safety and Protections for Whistleblowers.* The Budget provides almost $990 million for the Occupational and Mine Safety and Health Administrations (OSHA and MSHA) to make sure workers are protected from health and safety hazards on the job. In particular, the Budget provides additional resources to enhance safety and security at chemical facilities and improve response procedures when major incidents at these sites occur. The Budget also bolsters OSHA's ability to enforce the more than 20 whistleblower laws that protect workers from discrimination and retaliation when they report unsafe and unscrupulous practices. The Budget also provides MSHA the resources it needs to meet its statutory obligation to inspect every mine and address the risks posed to miners by the Nation's most dangerous mines.

- *Strengthens Penalties Against Employers Who Jeopardize Workers' Health, Safety, Wages, and Retirement Security.* Increased enforcement resources are vital to improving compliance with the Nation's labor and employment laws and protecting American workers. However, many of these laws lack strong civil penalties, which can help deter violations. The Budget proposes to strengthen several of the civil monetary penalties that DOL collects. In addition, the Administration will act on recommendations made by the Government Accountability Office (GAO) and the Administrative Conference of the United States by proposing to improve the Federal Civil Penalties Inflation Adjustment Act, which was established to maintain the deterrent effect of civil monetary penalties Government-wide through timely and predictable inflationary adjustments, but has fallen short because of its structure and implementation.

Creating Pathways to High-Growth Jobs. Last year, the Congress came together and passed important improvements to the Nation's job training system with the bipartisan Workforce Innovation and Opportunity Act. To build on this progress, the Budget provides a $500 million increase over the 2015 enacted level to support in-person employment services for unemployed workers to help them find a good job or the training or services to prepare for one. This investment would reach the one-third of unemployment insurance beneficiaries who are most likely to run out of benefits before getting reemployed, all returning veterans who receive unemployment benefits, and other displaced workers who come into American Job Centers for help getting back to work and onto a new career path. Evidence suggests that these types of services are a cost-effective intervention that get workers back into jobs faster, and help employers to fill their in-demand jobs.

For workers who need job training to get back on their feet, the Budget provides $16 billion over 10 years to double the number of workers receiving training through the workforce development system. This training would focus on industries that are expected to experience significant growth in the coming decades, such as health care, energy, advanced manufacturing, transportation and logistics, cybersecurity, and information technology. The combination of intensive reemployment services and expanded training opportunities will allow the workforce system to provide a suite of services that helps workers obtain stable, high-quality employment. To help improve the quality of training programs and speed the development of credentials that have real labor market value, the Budget provides $500 million for competitive Industry Credentialing and Career Pathways Grants including $300 million specifically targeted at information technology jobs to create employer-validated credentials where they do not yet exist, drive additional employer uptake of existing credentials, and develop curriculum and assessments that help individuals earn credentials. Building on the success of the Trade Adjustment Assistance Community College and Career Training grants, the Budget includes $200 million to fund State expansion of postsecondary programs based on defined competencies for high-demand jobs, with strong employer partnerships. The Budget also looks to the successful "learn-and-earn" approaches of the Nation's European counterparts, investing $2 billion to achieve the goal of doubling Registered Apprenticeships across the United States over the next five years. Apprenticeship is a cost-effective pathway into the middle class. According to DOL data, those who complete registered apprenticeship programs earn median wages of over $50,000 and almost 90 percent are employed after completion. The Budget also provides $3 billion for the Connecting for Opportunity initiative, which provides disconnected youth with additional summer and year-round job opportunities and supports competitive grants to municipalities to reengage these youth and create educational and workforce pathways for them.

The Budget also increases job training and financial incentives for public housing residents to secure greater employment through the Department of Housing and Urban Development's (HUD) Jobs-Plus program. The Budget provides $100 million for Jobs-Plus to target assistance to 20,000 individuals, or approximately 15,000 more than in 2015. This includes up to $15 million to implement a demonstration of the Jobs-Plus model in Indian Country. Jobs-Plus is an evidence-based program that has been shown to boost annual incomes by $1,300 on average.

Promoting Responsible Parenthood by Modernizing Child Support. The Administration is taking steps to modernize the child support program, which touches the lives of one in four American children and half of all poor children. In 2014, the Administration proposed the first comprehensive regulatory overhaul of the child support program in years to ensure that the enforcement tools are strong and effective. The Budget builds on this progress by proposing a comprehensive package of legislative reforms to complement executive actions, including a proposal to make sure more child support

reaches children rather than being retained by the Federal and State governments to "pay back" past assistance the child received.

Promoting Permanency, Safety, and Well-Being for Children and Youth in Foster Care. On any given day, there are 400,000 children and youth in the Nation's foster care system with over 100,000 waiting to be adopted. As part of the Administration's efforts to provide support for stable homes and strong support structures for vulnerable children and youth, the Budget includes a package of proposals to help improve the lives of children and youth in foster care and to help them reach their full potential. The Budget includes funding to provide preventative services to vulnerable families and children to address hardships early, keeping more children out of foster care and with their families. In addition, the Budget provides further support and funding to promote family-based care for children with behavioral and mental health needs to reduce the use of congregate care and ensure it is used only when necessary. The Budget also includes funding for Tribes to build their child welfare infrastructure, and for tribal children and youth removed from their homes to remain in their communities.

Easing Access to Credit for Housing. As the Nation's housing market continues to improve, the Federal Housing Administration (FHA) reduced the annual premiums new borrowers will pay by half of a percent in January 2015. This action is projected to save new FHA homeowners an average of $900 annually and spur 250,000 new homebuyers to purchase their first home over the next three years. Even with this premium reduction, the financial condition of FHA's insurance fund will continue to improve. The FHA actuarial review issued in November found that the fund's economic value increased by $21 billion over the past two years and the Budget projects that the value will continue to grow by at least $7 billion each year.

Supporting Tribal Nation-Building and Opportunities for Native Youth. The United States recognizes a unique Nation-to-Nation relationship with each of the 566 federally recognized Tribes. The Budget strongly supports tribal self-determination and Federal treaty and trust responsibilities to Native Americans. The Budget provides significant increases across a wide range of Federal programs that serve Tribes, including education, justice, health, infrastructure, stewardship of land, water, and other natural resources, and climate resilience, and supports a new "one-stop" approach to improving access to Federal programs and resources particularly focused on youth. The Budget includes key investments to support the launch of Generation Indigenous, a Native youth initiative focused on removing barriers to success. This initiative will take a comprehensive, culturally appropriate approach to help improve the lives and opportunities for Native youth. Multiple agencies, including DOI, the Department of Education, HUD, the Department of Health and Human Services (HHS), USDA, the Department of Commerce (DOC), DOL, and the Department of Justice (DOJ), are working collaboratively with Tribes to implement education reforms and address issues facing Native youth. The Budget enhances this work through new and increased investments, including: 1) $41 million at DOI to extend broadband internet and computer access to all BIE-funded schools and dormitories, with support from DOC's National Telecommunications and Information Administration community broadband outreach program; 2) $10 million at HUD and $8 million at DOI to address teacher housing needs; 3) $50 million at HHS to provide youth-focused behavioral and mental health, and substance abuse services; and 4) a new $50 million program at the Department of Education to support community-driven, comprehensive strategies to improve college and career-readiness of Native youth. These new investments will build on current efforts to better coordinate and demonstrate results from across the Federal Government to serve Native youth.

Equalizing Social Security Benefits for Same-Sex Married Couples. The Budget proposes to amend the Social Security Act to ensure all lawfully married same-sex couples will be eligible to receive Social Security spousal benefits, regardless of where they live. Currently, if a legally married same-sex couple lives in a State that does not recognize the marriage, these Social Security benefits are unavailable under Federal law. This means that for a couple that marries in one State where same-sex marriage is recognized and then moves to another State where it is not, the protection that Social Security spousal benefits provides to families is unavailable. Under this proposal, such married couples would have access to these benefits.

Strengthening Retirement Security

As many as 78 million working Americans—about half the workforce—do not have a retirement savings plan at work. Fewer than 10 percent of those without plans at work contribute to a plan of their own. The Nation needs to do more to help families save and give them better choices to reach a secure retirement. The Budget includes the following proposals that will guarantee that nearly every employee has access to an easy way to save for retirement through their employer. These proposals complement additional proposals, discussed later in the chapter, that would make saving easier for millions of Americans by automatically enrolling workers without employer-based retirement plans in Individual Retirement Arrangements (IRAs) through payroll deposit contributions at their workplace, and by providing tax incentives for small businesses to offer retirement plans, especially with automatic enrollment.

Expanding Retirement Savings Options for Long-Term, Part-Time Workers. Under current law, just 37 percent of part-time workers have access to a retirement plan, as compared to 74 percent of full-time private workers, in part because employers are permitted to exclude part-time workers from a retirement plan they provide for full-time workers. The Budget would make employees who have worked for an employer at least 500 hours per year for at least three years eligible to participate in the employer's existing plan. Employers would not be required to offer matching contributions. This proposal would provide approximately one million individuals with access to retirement plan coverage.

Encouraging State Retirement Savings Initiatives. A number of States have been exploring options for creating automatic retirement accounts for workers in the private sector who do not otherwise have access to a workplace retirement plan. However, concerns about potential conflicts with the Federal law that governs employee benefit plans have slowed those efforts. To better support State efforts, the Budget sets aside $6.5 million at DOL, along with waiver authority, to allow a limited number of States to implement State-based automatic enrollment IRAs or 401(k)-type programs.

Promoting Retirement Savings Options among Servicemembers. The Budget proposes to remove the current statutory bar prohibiting DOD and its armed services branches from automatically enrolling servicemembers in the Thrift Savings Plan. Servicemembers would still have the option to opt out at any point. This would allow the branches to decide to automatically enroll certain groups of members by seniority or pay grade, based on the branches' judgment of which members are the most interested in and likely to benefit from auto enrollment.

A Place-Based Approach to Expanding Opportunity

Too often in the past, innovative efforts to expand opportunity at the State and local level have been stymied by a Federal Government acting too much like a "check the box" regulator and not enough like a partner. In addition, Federal programs too often focus only on the problems in a community, while ignoring the assets on the ground. This is especially true in communities where limited local revenues and capacity make it even more important for the Federal Government to be a strong partner.

Recent research demonstrates that the opportunities and stressors surrounding children in the community where they grow up can have deep and lasting impacts on their educational and economic outcomes—their ability to fulfill their inborn potential. That inequality of opportunity in childhood is not just a moral failure, it is also an economic failure for the Nation's cities and America. Every year, the United States incurs a half trillion dollar cost as a result of allowing millions of America's children to grow up in poverty. Most of these costs are obvious, such as health care. But the single most harmful cost is the lost productivity and potential of so many children. Not only do young people lose when they do not get a fair shot—we all lose.

As the President has said, "real progress does not come from the top down, not just from the government. It comes from people." That is why the Administration has made providing ladders of opportunity to all a top priority and has taken a fundamentally different view of expanding opportunity in distressed communities by: taking a comprehensive approach to community revitalization instead of addressing problems in isolation; working with local leaders to support their vision for their communities; and embracing creative new solutions to old problems, especially in this fiscal environment.

The first step in this work is to ensure that the Federal Government is working well across agencies. The Administration's economic mobility and security efforts have sought to increase collaboration across the Federal Government, serve as a better partner with communities, and to direct resources where evidence suggests they will be most impactful. By creating Federal programs that meet urban and rural communities where they are, and Federal policies that respond to the ways that people live, we can better meet the demands of communities that are striving for a better quality of life. To that end, the Budget proposes to institutionalize the Administration's place-based approach to funding programs that help create opportunity in communities across the Nation. The Budget provides funding to support more Federal agency field staff, who are well-versed in both the community's needs and the Federal resources that can address them, to serve as community coordinators on the ground to help those communities maximize the impact of assistance from all sources. In addition, the Budget includes funding to accelerate the availability of geo-coded Federal spending information, so communities and citizens can better understand the Federal funds available to them and put them to effective, prompt use.

Through initiatives such as the Strong Cities, Strong Communities program, which strengthens towns, cities and regions by growing the capacity of local governments to develop and execute their local vision and strategies, the Administration is proposing holistic solutions to expand opportunity in the Nation's most vulnerable communities. The Budget increases the Administration's place-based efforts through the following investments:

- *The Upward Mobility Project.* The Budget proposes an Upward Mobility Project, which will allow up to 10 communities, States, or a consortium of States and communities more flexibility to use funding from up to four Federal programs for efforts designed to promote self-sufficiency, improve educational and other outcomes for children, and enhance communities' ability to provide opportunities for families. Projects will have to rely on evidence-based programs or be designed to test new ideas, and will have a significant evaluation component that will determine whether they meet a set of robust outcomes. The funding streams that States and communities can use in these projects are currently block grants—the Social Services Block Grant, the Community Development Block Grant, the Community Services Block Grant, and the HOME Program—that share a common goal of promoting opportunity and reducing poverty, but do not facilitate cross-sector planning and implementation as effectively as they could. The Budget also provides $1.5 billion in additional funding over five years that States and communities can apply for to help support their Upward Mobility Projects.

- *The Promise Zone Initiative.* The Budget supports the Administration's Promise Zone

initiative, which targets communities of concentrated poverty and establishes partnerships between the Federal Government, local communities, and businesses to create jobs, increase economic security, expand educational opportunities, increase access to quality, affordable housing, and improve public safety. Communities are chosen through a competitive process, and each puts forward a plan on how they will partner with local business and community leaders to make investments that reward hard work and expand opportunity. In exchange, the Federal Government partners with these communities to help them secure the resources and flexibility they need to achieve their goals. The President announced the first five Promise Zone communities in 2014, and will designate an additional 15 Zones by the end of calendar year 2016. The Budget also includes Promise Zone tax incentives to stimulate growth and investments in targeted communities, such as tax credits for hiring workers and incentives for capital investment within the Zone.

- *Choice and Promise Neighborhoods.* To support the President's vision for Promise Zones, the Budget also expands the Department of Education's Promise Neighborhoods program and HUD's Choice Neighborhoods program, funding approximately 25 new Promise Neighborhoods and eight new Choice Neighborhoods.

- *Rural Initiatives.* According to a 2014 report by USDA's Economic Research Service, rural childhood poverty rates are at their highest point since 1986—one in four rural children live in poverty and deep poverty among children is more prevalent in rural areas (12.2 percent) than in urban areas (9.2 percent). To help alleviate this growing disparity, the Budget provides $20 million for demonstration projects to fight childhood poverty in economically distressed rural areas through targeted technical assistance investments in housing, community facilities, small business, and infrastructure. The Budget includes $50 million to expand the Community Facilities Grant Program to address ongo-

---

Modernizing Unemployment Insurance and Improving Automatic Stabilizers

The Budget proposes a suite of reforms to modernize the Unemployment Insurance (UI) program, which provides critical income support to those who are unemployed through no fault of their own. These reforms would improve the solvency of State programs, reach more workers in need, strengthen the program's connection to work, and make the UI program more responsive to economic downturns.

The UI program is a key stabilizer during economic downturns. It provides an important safety net to workers who lose their jobs, and helps the economy by allowing those workers to maintain economic activity. The Budget proposes reforms to strengthen UI's economic stabilization function. The current Extended Benefits (EB) program, which provides up to 20 additional weeks of benefits in States with high and rising unemployment, does not provide sufficient help during recessions because it provides too few weeks of additional benefits and its triggers (which in most States are based on the insured unemployment rate) are not responsive enough. As a result, the Congress passes ad hoc emergency UI programs that begin too late to provide the early stimulus that could lessen the severity of a recession. The Budget proposes to fix this by creating a new permanent, federally funded EB program that would respond quickly when State unemployment rates rise and provide more robust Federal assistance. This new program would provide up to 52 weeks of additional federally funded benefits, with the greatest number of weeks in States with higher unemployment rates. The proposal would provide up to 13 weeks of additional benefits each time States hit certain unemployment rates triggers—at 6.5 percent, 7.5 percent, 8.5 percent, and 9.5 percent. Under the proposal, these threshold rates can be lower in States where unemployment is increasing especially rapidly. This new program would ensure that the UI program responds quickly to dampen the effects of recessions and provides a critical safety net for unemployed workers in States where jobs are scarce.

For the UI program to be effective, it must be on a strong financial footing. Many States' UI systems are chronically underfunded, requiring them to borrow funds from the Federal Government to cover benefits during the most recent downturn. Currently, 12 States have outstanding Federal loans, and 11 other States have outstanding debt exceeding their trust fund balances, including borrowing from the private market. The Budget proposes to improve system solvency by helping States rebuild their trust fund balances to repay their loans, cover current benefits, and create reserves so they are better prepared for the next downturn. The Budget accomplishes this by broadening the taxable wage base to equal average insured wages and reducing the Federal unemployment tax rate to help States shore up their trust funds, while not raising Federal UI taxes. Although the taxable wage base expansion would have the effect of raising State UI taxes, States would be free to change their tax rate structures to offset this increase.

The Budget also proposes to modernize the UI system by improving its connection to jobs and making sure benefits are available to more workers who need them. To do this, the Budget includes a UI modernization fund that would provide incentive payments to States that adopt measures to expand both program eligibility and work-based learning opportunities and training for unemployed workers. A State can receive incentive payments if it adopts two measures that expand eligibility and two measures that improve connections to training and employment. States that maintain these changes for at least four years would also receive a bonus payment. The Budget also creates a $60 million fund to allow a consortium of States to modernize their outdated UI information technology systems, which would improve administrative efficiency and help businesses and workers interact more easily with the UI system.

---

ing needs and emerging priorities such as Promise Zones, Energy Sector Transition, or Strike Force Communities. These funds will allow USDA to be responsive to new needs in communities across rural American and target them in a flexible way.

Strengthening Social Security and Services for People with Disabilities

Social Security is indispensable to workers, retirees, survivors, and people with disabilities, and is one of the most important and successful programs ever established in the United States. Although current forecasts indicate that the combined Social Security Trust Funds can pay full benefits until 2033, the Administration is committed to ensuring that the program is solvent and viable for the American people, now and in the future, and the President has laid out key principles to achieve this objective. Any reforms should strengthen retirement security for the most vulnerable, including low-income seniors, and should maintain robust disability and survivors' benefits. The Administration will oppose any measures that privatize or weaken the Social Security system and will not accept an approach that slashes benefits for future generations or reduces basic benefits for current beneficiaries.

To address reserve depletion of the Social Security Disability Insurance (DI) Trust Fund, the Budget proposes to reallocate existing payroll tax collections between the Old-Age and Survivors Insurance (OASI) and DI trust funds while a longer-term solution to overall Social Security solvency is developed with the Congress. At various points over the course of Social Security's history, the Congress has passed reallocation legislation as the need arose for reallocating revenue from DI to OASI, and vice versa. This proposed reallocation will have no effect on the overall health of the OASI and DI trust funds on a combined basis.

The Budget also includes initiatives to help people with disabilities remain in the workforce. It builds on the bipartisan support for these efforts in the Consolidated and Further Continuing Appropriations Act, 2015, by providing new authority and $400 million in new resources for the Social Security Administration (SSA), in partnership with other Federal agencies, to test innovative strategies to help people with disabilities remain in the workforce. The cost would be offset by a proposal to better coordinate DI and Federal retroactive disability payments between SSA and the Office of Personnel Management (OPM.) Early-intervention measures, such as supportive employment services for individuals with mental impairments, targeted incentives for employers to help workers with disabilities remain on the job, and incentives and opportunities for States to better coordinate services, have the potential to achieve long-term gains in the employment and the quality of life of people with disabilities, and the proposed demonstrations will help build the evidence base for future program improvements.

To address increasing wait times for a disability appeal decision, the Budget proposes to increase the hiring of Administrative Law Judges (ALJ). SSA's workloads continue to increase as the baby boom generation enters its most disability-prone years. The average wait time for a disability decision before an ALJ reached a record high of 18.5 months in August 2008. SSA was able to reduce the wait time down to a 10-year low of 12 months in 2011 and 2012, but due to funding constraints, the wait time has begun to grow again and is anticipated to rise above 16 months in 2015. Currently there are over one million people waiting for a disability appeals hearing decision from an ALJ. The Budget commits increased resources to hire more ALJs. But resources alone will not be enough. The process for hiring SSA ALJs has not operated efficiently as is needed to fill vacancies even when funding is available. Therefore, the Administration is creating a workgroup led by the Administrative Conference of the United States and OPM, along with SSA, DOJ, and the Office of Management and Budget (OMB) to review the process of hiring ALJs and recommend ways to eliminate roadblocks, which may include proposing administrative reforms or legislative changes.

To continue to strengthen the integrity and accuracy of Social Security, the Budget proposes to establish a dependable source of mandatory funding in 2017 for Continuing Disability Reviews (CDRs) and Supplemental Security Income Redeterminations, which ensure that only those eligible for benefits continue to receive them. SSA estimates that each $1 spent on CDRs would save the Federal Government $9. This proposal,

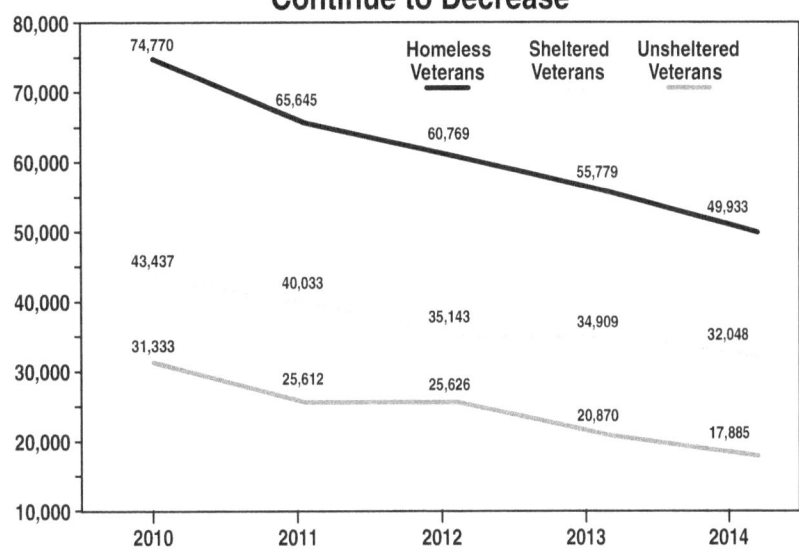

Rates of Homelessness Among Veterans Continue to Decrease

Source: Department of Housing and Urban Development. The 2014 Annual Homeless Assessment Report to Congress, Part 1.

together with discretionary funding proposed for 2016, could produce net savings of $32 billion over 10 years and reduce the current backlog of 906,000 overdue CDRs.

Ending Homelessness

In 2010, the President set ambitious goals to end homelessness across the Nation, and since then significant progress has been made. Major cities have hit important milestones toward the goals including New Orleans, Louisiana, which has ended veteran homelessness, and Salt Lake City, Utah and Phoenix, Arizona, which have ended chronic homelessness among veterans. Over 300 mayors, governors, and county executives have committed to ending veteran homelessness in their communities through the Mayors Challenge to End Veteran Homelessness.

The overall number of veterans experiencing homelessness has declined by 33 percent—nearly 25,000 veterans—since 2010, and with continued focus from Federal, State, and local partners, we are on a path to end veteran homelessness by the end of 2015. The Budget continues to make investments to end chronic homelessness in 2017 and to make significant progress in ending homelessness across all other populations. In addition to targeted increases in HUD's Homeless Assistance Grants, the Budget provides 67,000 new Housing Choice Vouchers to support low-income households, including families experiencing homelessness; survivors of domestic and dating violence; families with children in foster care; youth aging out of foster care; and homeless veterans, regardless of their discharge status.

ENSURING SAFETY, FAIRNESS, AND COMMUNITY TRUST IN THE CRIMINAL JUSTICE SYSTEM

The President has said that if anyone in the American family feels they have been treated unfairly it is a problem for all Americans. That is why the President is committed to ensuring the criminal justice system is safe, fair, and trustworthy for all Americans. In addition to supporting the enhancement of community policing practices across the Nation, the Budget proposes to prioritize DOJ's resources on criminals who pose the most serious threats to American citizens' safety, support Federal reentry programs that help reduce recidivism, and combat violent extremism.

Implementing the Smart on Crime Approach. The Administration continues to advance the DOJ's Smart on Crime initiative, which was announced in 2013, and designed to promote fundamental criminal justice system reforms that will improve public safety, save money, and ensure the fair enforcement of Federal laws. The strategy leverages prevention and reentry programs to reduce recidivism; focuses prosecutorial resources on the most important law enforcement priorities; ensures that punishments for low-level, non-violent offenders are consistent with the offense; and strengthens protections for vulnerable populations. The Budget supports this strategy by providing additional funding for a dedicated Prevention and Reentry Coordinator in each U.S. Attorney's office, while also expanding pre-trial diversion programs, such as reentry and drug courts, that ensure better and more just outcomes for low-level offenders who deserve a pre-incarceration second chance. The Budget also includes funding for research to evaluate the efficacy of these programs using metrics that measure the effects of the Smart on Crime initiative.

Community Policing Initiative. The President's new Community Policing Initiative aims to build and sustain trust between law enforcement and the people they serve. The Budget provides $97 million to expand training and oversight for local law enforcement, increase the use of body-worn cameras, provide additional opportunities for police department reform, and facilitate community and law enforcement engagement in 10 pilot sites, with additional technical assistance and training for dozens of communities and police departments across the Nation.

Reentry Programs. Each year, more than 600,000 people are released from State and Federal prison, while another nine million cycle through local jails. Statistics indicate that more than two-thirds of State prisoners are re-arrested within three years of their release and half are re-incarcerated. High rates of recidivism mean more crime, more victims, and more pressure on an already overburdened criminal justice system. While we must remain vigilant when fighting crime and ensuring the safety of the Nation's communities, there is a substantial and increasing body of evidence showing that reentry programs reduce recidivism by helping individuals transition to their community after they are released. America's Federal criminal justice efforts must also be smarter and more efficient by focusing on prevention and reentry, because whenever a recidivist crime is committed, communities are victimized and less safe; burdens on law enforcement are increased; and already-strained resources are further depleted.

The Administration is committed to a comprehensive strategy to contain incarceration costs over the long term by facilitating inmates' transition into society in order to reduce recidivism rates, increase public safety, and strengthen communities. The Budget reflects these commitments and takes steps to address the cycle of incarceration by investing additional resources in the Bureau of Prisons' (BOP) reentry programs. These investments include $110 million to increase mental health staff, expand sex offender treatment programs, and provide cognitive behavioral treatment and additional residential reentry center beds. The Budget also provides $5 million to support a new broader reentry program that reaches out to offenders' children and families to strengthen familial bonds, which are critical for helping inmates transitioning back home, and $20 million to award innovative reentry programs in BOP facilities. In addition, through State and local assistance programs, the Budget nearly doubles the investment in the Second Chance Act Grant program to reduce recidivism and help those exiting the justice system to rejoin their communities and lead productive lives.

MAINTAINING THE NATION'S SECURITY

The President's Budget includes $612 billion of national defense discretionary funds, a $26 billion, or 4.5 percent, increase from the 2015 enacted level, to provide the resources needed to sustain the President's national security and defense strategies. The Budget reverses the decline in national defense spending of the past five years and proposes to transition enduring overseas contingency operations (OCO) costs to the base budget, to fully fund and account for the costs of keeping the Nation secure. Discretionary national defense function spending has fallen by 18 percent since 2010 as the military has ended its ground combat missions in Iraq and Afghanistan, and adjusted to the sequestration cuts of 2013 and flat base budget funding levels of 2014 and 2015. This spending—which comprises all base and OCO funding for DOD, as well as funding for certain programs in DOE, DOJ, and other Departments and agencies—peaked in 2010 at $714 billion, and has since decreased $128 billion, to the 2015 enacted level of $586 billion. Accounting for the effects of inflation, the decrease over this period is even steeper, at 24 percent.

Part of the decrease reflects the declining costs of OCO-funded operations in Iraq and Afghanistan, as highlighted below. However, sequestration also reduced the base budget significantly in 2013, and the Bipartisan Budget Act essentially straight-lined the defense base budget in 2014 and 2015. These levels required sharp cuts to training, maintenance, and modernization. Combined with a continued demand for U.S. forces to respond to emergent crises while preparing for a widening spectrum of future challenges, reduced budgets contributed to degraded levels of readiness throughout the military, and delays in fielding equipment and technology that will be critical for future security. Going forward, defense base budgets at or near the sequestration level would undermine the military's capacity and capability to respond to contingencies, deter aggression, project power, and decisively win against potential adversaries—leaving it insufficiently prepared to protect and advance U.S. interests.

The President's Budget provides $561 billion in base discretionary funding for national defense (of which $534 billion is for DOD), which is $40 billion, or eight percent, above the 2015 enacted

level. The Budget makes strategic investments to sustain and advance U.S. global leadership while ensuring the Nation's long-term fiscal health. It provides for the training, maintenance, and support needed to restore military readiness over the next several years, and for investment in recapitalization and modernization needed to ensure America's continued technological edge. Along with these funding increases, the Budget provides savings (detailed below) through critical reforms that slow growth in compensation and divest unnecessary overhead, infrastructure, weapons, and end strength. The Budget also increases outyear projections for defense spending across the 2017 to 2020 period to accommodate select investments in key capabilities, such as space security, nuclear deterrence, power projection, and intelligence, surveillance, and reconnaissance. These targeted increases will further enhance the U.S. military's ability to execute the defense strategy as the Nation continues to adapt to a changing threat environment. The Budget presents a responsible alternative to current law, since risks to the Nation would grow significantly if sequestration-level funding returns, if proposed reforms are not accepted, or if uncertainty over budget levels continues.

DOD's OCO request is $51 billion, which is $13 billion, or 21 percent, below the 2015 enacted level. It provides the funding needed to combat diverse terrorist groups, such as the Islamic State of Iraq and the Levant (ISIL); to ensure a responsible transition in Afghanistan, where the United States and international partners will train, advise, and assist Afghan-led operations; and to counter Russia's aggressive actions and reassure allies and partners in Europe. The OCO budget includes certain costs that will endure past these current contingencies, and thus the Budget proposes to transition enduring OCO costs to the base budget, as described later in this chapter.

The President's Budget also provides $53.4 billion for the Department of State and Other International Programs (State/OIP), including $46.3 billion in base funding and $7.0 billion in OCO, which is a $4.0 billion, or eight percent, increase from the 2015 enacted level, excluding emergency Ebola funding. This funding will make strategic investments that will help provide not only for a stronger and safer America, but also for a more stable and prosperous world. The Budget supports sustainable security and shared prosperity at home and abroad through critical investments in diplomacy and development, from life-saving humanitarian assistance to counterterrorism programs aimed at defeating terrorist organizations. It provides strong support for U.S. diplomatic personnel and facilities abroad, security partnerships, global engagement, and development programs that advance economic growth, health, education, and democratic governance. The Budget advances American leadership and engagement at a time when diplomacy is most needed to confront the many challenges facing the world today.

Advancing National Security Priorities

Degrading and Defeating ISIL and Responding to the Syria Crisis. As part of the U.S. effort to degrade and ultimately defeat ISIL, support security and governance, continue efforts in Iraq, support regional partners, and bring stability and promote the conditions for a negotiated settlement to end the conflict in Syria, the Budget proposes $8.8 billion in OCO funds for DOD and State/OIP. ISIL poses an immediate threat to Iraq, Syria, and American allies and partners throughout the region as it seeks to overthrow governments, control territory, terrorize local populations, and attack the United States and coalition partners throughout the world. The ongoing conflict in Syria also continues to threaten regional stability and has displaced over 10 million people. The Budget provides funding for military operations, diplomacy, governance, and humanitarian and security assistance programs to address these challenges. This includes $5.3 billion for DOD to continue Operation Inherent Resolve, which includes conducting airstrikes, collecting intelligence, as well as training, advising, and equipping the Iraqi security forces and properly vetted members of the moderate Syrian opposition. For State/OIP, the Budget provides $3.5 billion to strengthen regional partners, counter ISIL, provide humanitarian assistance,

and strengthen Syria's moderate opposition to advance the conditions for a negotiated political transition.

Ensuring a Responsible Transition in Afghanistan. The Budget continues to support long-term national security and economic interests in Afghanistan and help sustain political, economic, and security gains in the country as the United States draws down its forces, assistance levels gradually decline, and the Afghans assume greater responsibility for securing their country. The Budget includes resources to reinforce Afghanistan's security and development by supporting military training and assistance, as well as health, education, justice, economic growth, governance, and other civilian assistance programs necessary to preserve the gains of the last decade, strengthen diplomatic ties with the international community, and promote stability. The Budget also facilitates the transition of the U.S. military from a combat mission to a mission of training, advising, and assisting the Afghan National Security Forces and maintaining a limited counterterrorism capability to continue targeting the remnants of al Qaeda.

Countering Russian Pressure and Aggressive Action. In response to the Russian Federation's aggressive acts and attempts to constrain the foreign and domestic policy choices of neighboring countries, the Budget includes proposals for political, economic, and military support to NATO allies and partner states in Europe. To increase resilience within the governments and economies most targeted by Russian pressure, the Budget provides an additional $117 million in foreign assistance funds directed specifically toward countering Russian aggressive acts in Ukraine, and $51 million for countering Russian pressure and destabilizing activities in Moldova and Georgia. This assistance will support efforts to bolster democracy and good governance, increase the capabilities of security forces, strengthen the rule of law and anti-corruption measures, and promote European Union integration, trade, and energy security. In addition, through a $16 million investment in U.S. international media activities, the United States will seek to engage vulnerable populations in periphery countries, expand U.S. support to freedom of press and independent journalism in the region, and advance America's foreign policy interests. Building on the $1 billion sovereign loan guarantee provided in 2014 and the forthcoming $1 billion sovereign loan guarantee in 2015, the Budget includes funding that could support an additional loan guarantee providing up to $1 billion in financing in 2016, if conditions warrant, to help Ukraine continue on its path of economic recovery, reforms, and normalized access to international financial markets in the wake of destabilizing Russian actions and violations of Ukrainian sovereignty. To bolster security and reassure NATO allies and partner states in Europe, the Budget provides $789 million to continue the European Reassurance Initiative (ERI). ERI funding will enable the Unites States to continue increased military exercises, training, and rotational presence in Europe, enhance U.S. preparedness to reinforce NATO allies through the prepositioning of equipment, and build the capacity of partner states in Europe to operate alongside the United States and NATO in strengthening regional security.

Strengthening Government-wide Efforts to Combat Terrorism. The Budget provides $2.5 billion for the Counterterrorism Partnerships Fund to support a sustainable and effective approach for combating terrorism, with a focus on enabling and empowering partners facing terrorist threats. The $2.1 billion proposed for DOD would increase partner capacity-building, facilitate partner counterterrorism operations, and enhance DOD's counterterrorism activities. The $390 million proposed for State/OIP would enable the Department to bolster global counterterrorism partnerships, as well as address underlying conditions conducive to terrorism.

Countering Violent Extremism. The Administration has developed a strategy to address recent domestic terror incidents and the emergence of groups attempting to recruit Americans to take part in ongoing conflicts in foreign countries. As part of this effort, DOJ's Countering Violent Extremism (CVE) initiative is an Administration priority and supports the United Nations' efforts to address foreign terrorist fighters. Additional resources are provided to support community led-efforts, including $4 million to conduct research targeted toward developing a better understanding of violent extremism and advancing evidence-based strategies for effective prevention and intervention; $6 million to support flexible, locally-developed CVE models; $2 million to develop training and provide technical assistance; and $3 million for demonstration projects that enhance the ability of law enforcement agencies nationwide to partner with local residents, business owners, community groups, and other stakeholders to counter violent extremism.

Rebalancing to the Asia-Pacific Region. The Budget supports the Presidential priority of advancing security, prosperity, and human dignity across the Asia-Pacific region. Recognizing that security in the Asia-Pacific region underpins regional and global prosperity, the Budget aligns resources and activities to strengthen U.S. alliances, to forge deeper partnerships with emerging powers, and to pursue a productive relationship with China. Building on the President's successful November 2014 trip, the Budget provides resources to help deepen U.S. trade in the region as the United States leads the way in negotiating the high-standard Trans-Pacific Partnership with 11 countries in the Asia-Pacific region, which will boost American exports and create jobs at home by promoting strong rules to protect labor, the environment, and intellectual property. To promote universal and democratic values, the Budget expands education and cultural exchanges and strengthens regional cooperation with organizations such as the Asia-Pacific Economic Cooperation forum and the Association of Southeast Asian Nations. In pursuit of security cooperation, the Budget enhances and modernizes U.S. defense relationships, posture, and capabilities with a focus on maritime security. DOD funding remains consistent with the priorities identified in the 2012 Defense Strategic Guidance and the 2014 Quadrennial Defense Review. To address security, development, and economic challenges, the Budget prioritizes advancing regional and country capabilities. These investments are critical to the Administration-wide effort to promote regional security and economic cooperation.

Investing in Adolescent Girls' Education, Safety, and Health. In collaboration with the Office of the First Lady and building on ongoing U.S. efforts that currently support more than a million adolescent girls worldwide every year, the Budget provides $250 million in new and reallocated funds to broaden opportunities for adolescent girls around the world. This new, expanded Let Girls Learn initiative—building on USAID's initial funding and programs—will improve access to quality education and health care, and help address violence and other barriers to education that adolescent girls face. The Budget also continues support for the President's Emergency Plan for AIDS Relief (PEPFAR) interventions to reduce HIV infections in young women, and expands USAID's programs in support of adolescent girls' education, including expanded investments in educating adolescent girls in Afghanistan. These and other investments will deepen the United States' commitment to adolescent girls, helping girls and young women thrive and play a fuller role in their respective societies and economies.

Maintaining Technological Superiority. Technological superiority enables the United States to project power to dangerous environments, defend against threats in all domains, and continuously adapt, innovate, and prevail as new threats arise. Maintaining this superiority is becoming increasingly challenging as potential adversaries have accelerated their investments in modernizing their militaries, and as disruptive technologies have proliferated, resulting in growing threats where U.S. access had formerly been assured. The Budget makes needed investments in DOD and National Nuclear Security Administration (NNSA) procurement, and research, development, test and evaluation (RDT&E) to address this challenge and maintain technological superiority. Base budget funding for DOD's procurement and RDT&E accounts—which took disproportionate reductions under sequestration to achieve rapid savings in recent years—and funding for NNSA increase to $190

billion, a $22 billion, or 13 percent, increase compared to the 2015 enacted level. With this funding, the Administration is prioritizing investments in cybersecurity; missile defense; nuclear deterrence; space; precision strike; intelligence, surveillance, and reconnaissance; and air and sea capabilities for projecting power and operating in denied environments. In addition, DOD recently announced in November 2014, the establishment of a broad, Department-wide initiative to pursue innovative ways to sustain and advance U.S. military superiority for the 21st Century and improve business operations throughout the Department. The Defense Innovation Initiative will pursue breakthrough technologies and new concepts of operations to enhance the U.S. military's dominance even as the diffusion of disruptive technology to potential adversaries makes the future operating environment more challenging. Scientific discovery and applied research are central to all these efforts, and thus the proposed funding for DOD's RDT&E accounts includes $12 billion for science and technology investments in areas including quantum information science, cognitive neuroscience, nanoscience, synthetic biology, autonomy, cybersecurity, and countering weapons of mass destruction, among other investments.

Strengthening Space Security. Space capabilities are vital to U.S. national security and the ability to understand emerging threats, project power globally, conduct operations, support diplomatic efforts, and enable global economic prosperity. It is also the shared interest of all nations to act responsibly in space to help prevent mishaps, misperceptions, and mistrust. The Budget supports a variety of measures to help assure the use of space in the face of increasing threats to U.S. national security space systems. The Budget also supports the development of capabilities to defend and enhance the resilience of these space systems. These capabilities help deter and defeat interference with, and attacks on, U.S. space systems.

Addressing Cyber Threats. Cyber threats targeting the private sector, critical infrastructure, and the Federal Government demonstrate that no sector, network, or system is immune to

Transitioning Overseas Contingency Operations Spending

Since 2001, the Nation has financed the incremental costs of overseas conflicts, primarily in Iraq and Afghanistan, outside of the base budget. From 2001 to 2009 these funds were designated for the "Global War on Terror" (GWOT), and from 2009 to the present these funds have been designated for "overseas contingency operations" (OCO). Following the institution of statutory budget caps in the Budget Control Act of 2011, funding designated as OCO/GWOT has remained flexible and separate from base budget constraints, which has enabled the United States to fully fund wartime costs principally associated with these major combat operations.

As the U.S. combat mission in Afghanistan ends, it is time to reconsider the appropriate financing mechanism for costs of overseas operations that are enduring. As the chart below shows, the Administration's transitions in Iraq and Afghanistan have resulted in a $129 billion, or 69 percent, reduction in OCO costs, from their peak of $187 billion in 2008 to the Administration's 2016 request for $58 billion. Beyond 2016, some costs currently funded in the OCO budget will endure. The United States will continue to provide support to its Afghan partners, counter terrorism abroad, maintain a strong forward presence in the Middle East region, and ensure U.S. military forces are ready to respond to a wide range of potential crises. The Nation's fiscal and defense policies must fully plan and account for these costs, and the transition must be accomplished in a manner that protects the defense strategy. Accordingly, early this year the Administration will propose a plan to transition all enduring costs currently funded in the OCO budget to the base budget beginning in 2017 and ending by 2020. This plan will describe which OCO costs should endure as the United States shifts from major combat operations, how the Administration will budget for the uncertainty surrounding unforeseen future crises, and the implications for the base budgets of DOD, the Intelligence Community, and State/OIP. This transition will not be possible if the sequester-level discretionary spending caps remain in place. The Administration continues to support the replacement of sequestration with a balanced package of deficit reduction as described elsewhere in the Budget.

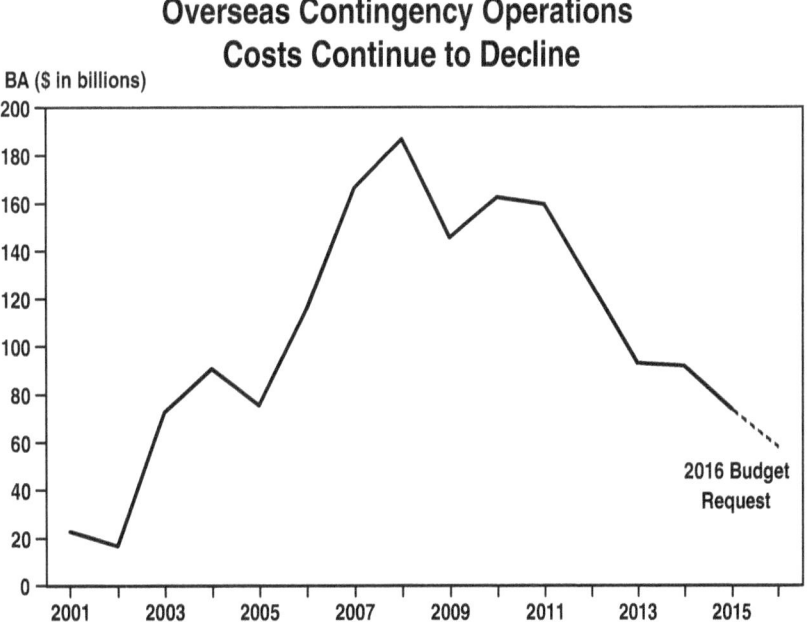

Overseas Contingency Operations Costs Continue to Decline

BA ($ in billions)

2016 Budget Request

infiltration by those seeking to steal commercial or Government secrets and property or perpetrate malicious and disruptive activity. Addressing these threats requires a comprehensive approach that brings all elements of government together with private industry, academia, and the public, while also protecting individual privacy. The Budget identifies and promotes initiatives and priorities, including the deployment of intrusion detection and prevention capabilities and enhancement of Government information sharing capabilities with the private sector so that they can be more vigilant and better protect themselves against emerging threats. It also makes investments in cyber research and development to strengthen U.S. cybersecurity defenses and make cyberspace inherently more secure. In addition, the Budget includes funding to enhance U.S. capabilities to respond to cyber threats and incidents once they have occurred, begin building a civilian cyber campus to better share information on cyber threats and incidents with those being targeted, improve the ability to share evidence of cyber-crimes with other nations, and maintain efforts to increase the Nation's cyber workforce.

As cybersecurity challenges continue to impact Federal agencies, the protection of the Government's information and information systems has become critical to protecting national infrastructure. The Budget funds key investments to enhance the Federal Government's cybersecurity posture. These include Continuous Diagnostics and Monitoring of Federal systems, the EINSTEIN intrusion detection and prevention system, and Government-wide testing and incident response training to mitigate the impact of evolving cyber threats. These resources will allow the Government to more rapidly protect American citizens, systems, and information from cyber threats.

Modernizing Military Compensation. The Budget continues to provide a robust compensation and benefits system that honors the service of the Nation's men and women in uniform and their families. For 2016, the Budget provides a 1.3 percent increase to basic pay, a 1.5 percent increase in the Basic Allowance for Housing, and a 3.4 percent increase in the Basic Allowance for Subsistence. In addition, the Budget proposes to modernize the TRICARE Program and continues to pursue commissary operational efficiencies and revenue generating enhancements. These proposals will ensure that DOD continues to

recruit and retain a high quality All-Volunteer Force, while addressing costs in a responsible and balanced manner. In addition to these proposals, the Administration looks forward to reviewing the report from the Military Compensation and Retirement Modernization Commission, and working with the Congress to ensure a strong and sustainable military compensation and retirement system.

Promoting Defense Reforms. The defense strategy depends on investing every dollar where it will have the greatest effect, which the Budget will accomplish through critical reforms that divest unneeded force structure, slow growth in compensation, and reduce wasteful overhead. To direct investments toward a ready, technologically superior force, the military must shed unnecessary force structure now that ground combat missions in Iraq and Afghanistan have ended. Venerable weapons systems, such as the A-10 aircraft, have performed decades of service, yet would now face survivability challenges against a technologically advanced adversary. Therefore, the Budget reproposes the retirement of this and other systems, and directs the money saved toward investment in the most capable, versatile, and survivable systems to perform their missions. The Budget also reduces overhead and waste by continuing the initiative to reduce DOD's major headquarters' operating budgets by 20 percent, pursuing acquisition reform through the Better Buying Power initiative, and proposing another round of Base Realignment and Closure (BRAC) to free resources currently consumed by maintaining unneeded facilities. The need to reduce unneeded facilities is so critical that, in the absence of authorization of a new round of BRAC, the Administration will pursue alternative options to reduce this wasteful spending.

Suitability and Security. It is critical to the safe and effective operation of the Federal Government to ensure that Federal employees continue to be good stewards of sensitive information and worthy of the public trust their positions require. In order to protect against threats from individuals within the Government, and drive increased efficiency of the security clearance processes, the Administration is pursuing several reforms in the personnel security, suitability, and credentialing mission space.

Following the Washington Navy Yard shooting, the President directed OMB to conduct a comprehensive review of Federal procedures for background investigations and security clearances. The Performance Accountability Council delivered a Report to the President (120 Day Report), which was approved in March 2014. The Report established a set of recommendations to increase the availability of critical information, reduce risk inherent in the system, and increase oversight and accountability. The Administration established an interagency Program Management Office focused on implementing the Report's recommendations. The immediate and meaningful progress to date includes:

- *Continuous Evaluation.* The Administration is committed to shifting security and suitability evaluations to a continuous evaluations approach, allowing agencies to gather real-time information that may be relevant to these clearances. In the past year, initial pilots have successfully demonstrated the effectiveness of more frequent investigations of cleared personnel. The Budget provides funding in DOD and the Office of the Director of National Intelligence to expand these initial pilots and move to making "Continuous Evaluation" a Government-wide practice. While agencies transition to Continuous Evaluation, the Federal Investigative Standards has already established a new five-year re-investigation requirement for all individuals with a security clearance.

- *Improved Access to Law Enforcement Records.* The National Defense Authorization Act-mandated Records Access Task Force report provided recommendations for improving information sharing among State, local, and Federal law enforcement entities when conducting background investigations. The Budget continues to invest in improving agencies' information technology (IT) systems to enhance data sharing between the Federal Government and State and local

entities.

- *Access to Classified Information.* The Director of National Intelligence issued a requirement for all agencies to validate whether each individual identified as eligible for access to classified information still required eligibility. Through this process, the Administration achieved its objective to reduce the total number of security-cleared individuals by 10 percent. This reduction will allow agencies to better deploy resources to priority activities, such as completing periodic reinvestigations for the most sensitive populations.

Honoring America's Commitment to Veterans

The Budget includes $70.2 billion in discretionary 2016 resources for the Department of Veterans Affairs (VA), a 7.8-percent increase over 2015. The Budget also includes an advance appropriation request of $63.3 billion for 2017 medical care, a 5.5-percent increase over the 2016 request. This funding will ensure continued investment in the five pillars the President has outlined for supporting the Nation's veterans: providing the resources and funding they deserve; ensuring high-quality and timely health care; getting veterans their earned benefits quickly and efficiently; ending veteran homelessness; and helping veterans and their families get good jobs, education, and access to affordable housing.

Implementing the Veterans Access, Choice, and Accountability Act of 2014. On August 7, 2014, the President signed into law the Veterans Access, Choice, and Accountability Act of 2014 (Veterans Choice Act). The Budget supports implementation of the Veterans Choice Act and the Administration's goal of providing timely, high-quality health care for the Nation's veterans. The Veterans Choice Act provided $5 billion in mandatory funding to increase veterans' access to health care by hiring more physicians and staff and improving VA's physical infrastructure. It also provided $10 billion in mandatory funding through 2017 to establish a temporary program (Veterans Choice Program) improving veterans' access to health care by allowing eligible veterans who meet certain wait-time or distance standards to use health care providers outside of the VA system. The Veterans Choice Program provides a measure of short-term relief from the pressure of escalating health care requirements as current patients in the VA system elect to receive their care through the program. These investments, together with the Budget request of $70.2 billion, will provide authorities, funding, and other tools to enhance service to veterans in the short term while strengthening the underlying VA system to better serve veterans in the future. However, more resources will be required to ensure that the VA system can provide timely, high-quality health care into the future. In the coming months, the Administration will submit legislation to reallocate a portion of Veterans Choice Program funding to support essential investments in VA

system priorities in a fiscally-responsible, budget-neutral manner.

Speeding the Processing of Disability Compensation Claims. VA has made tremendous progress reducing the veteran disability claims backlog. The Budget provides additional funding to continue investment in the Veterans Claims Intake Program and paperless claims, helping provide faster and more accurate benefits claims processing decisions. The Budget also includes funding to hire additional employees to address the growth in related claims and improve the VA's timeliness in resolving appeals. Further, the Budget funds efforts to ensure consistent, personalized, and accurate information about services and benefits, especially in the delivery of compensation and pension claims processing.

TAX REFORM THAT PROMOTES GROWTH AND OPPORTUNITY

A simpler, fairer, and more efficient tax system is critical to achieving many of the President's fiscal and economic goals. At a time when middle class and working parents remain anxious about how they will meet their families' needs, the tax system does not do enough to reward hard work, support working families, or create opportunity. After decades of rising income and wealth inequality, the tax system continues to favor unearned over earned income, and a porous capital gains tax system lets the wealthy shelter hundreds of billions of dollars from taxes each year. In a period where an aging population will put increasing pressure on the Federal budget, a wide range of inefficient tax breaks prevent the tax system from raising the level of revenue the Nation needs. While commerce around the world is increasingly interconnected, an out-of-date, loophole-ridden business tax system puts U.S. companies at a disadvantage relative to their competitors, while also failing to encourage investment in the United States.

The Budget addresses each of these challenges. It reforms and simplifies tax incentives that help families afford child care, pay for col-

lege, and save for retirement, while expanding tax benefits that support and reward work. It pays for these changes by reforming the system of capital gains taxation and by imposing a new fee on large, heavily-leveraged financial firms. It raises revenue for deficit reduction by curbing high-income tax benefits and closing loopholes and reforms the business tax system to make it fairer and more pro-growth. It also reinvests in the Internal Revenue Service (IRS), reversing the sharp funding reductions of recent years and improving customer service and tax enforcement.

Supporting Middle Class and Working Families through the Tax Code

The President's tax proposals would simplify and improve tax benefits that help middle class families afford quality child care, pay for college, and save for retirement, as well as tax benefits that support work and keep millions of children from growing up in poverty. The Budget also proposes the creation of a new "second earner" tax credit benefiting middle-income couples where both spouses work.

Expanding Access to Affordable Child Care. The cost of child care is a major barrier to work for many parents, especially parents of young children, and can put a real strain on the budgets of working families. Through a combination of tax credits and direct subsidies, the Budget would make a major investment in quality, affordable child care for infants and toddlers. Specifically, the Budget would triple the maximum Child and Dependent Care Tax Credit (CDCTC) for families with children under age five. It would also make the full CDCTC available to families with incomes of up to $120,000, benefiting families with young children, older children, and elderly or disabled dependents. Meanwhile, the Budget would eliminate tax preferences for flexible spending accounts for child care expenses, which are poorly targeted and complex, reinvesting the savings in the improved CDCTC. The child care tax reforms would benefit 5.1 million families, helping them cover costs for 6.7 million children. They would complement a proposal, described above, to make direct child care subsidies universally available for young children in lower-income working families.

Simplifying and Improving Education Tax Benefits. A significant portion of Federal spending on higher education occurs through the tax code. But navigating current higher education tax benefits is so complicated that the GAO found that 27 percent of families who claimed one benefit would have been better off claiming another, while 14 percent of eligible families failed to claim any benefit at all. Higher education tax benefits also do not provide enough help for low- and middle-income families that struggle to afford college. Building on bipartisan congressional reform proposals, the Budget proposes to simplify and better target higher education tax benefits, including by consolidating six education tax benefits into just two. The Budget would repeal or let expire duplicative and less effective provisions, including the Lifetime Learning Credit, the tuition and fees deduction, the student loan interest deduction (for new borrowers), and Coverdell accounts (for new contributions), and it would roll back a portion of the subsidy for 529 savings plan (for new

contributions). Meanwhile, it would make permanent and expand the American Opportunity Tax Credit, including by indexing the maximum credit amount for inflation, making the credit available for a fifth year of higher education, providing a partial credit to part-time students, and increasing the amount of the credit available to low-income students without income tax liability. To help struggling borrowers, the Budget would also eliminate tax on debt forgiven under Pay-as-You-Earn or other income-based repayment plans. Overall, these reforms would cut taxes for 8.5 million families and students and simplify taxes for more than 25 million families and students that claim education tax benefits.

Expanding Access to Workplace Savings Opportunities. Workers with an easy way to save for retirement through their employer overwhelmingly do so, while tens of millions of American workers without such access by and large do not. Small business and part-time employees are especially unlikely to have access to an employer retirement plan. The Budget proposes to automatically enroll workers without access to employer-based retirement plans in IRAs through payroll deposit contributions at their workplace (with an option to opt out). This proposal would give 30 million more workers access to a workplace saving opportunity. The Budget also proposes to expand the tax credits available to small businesses who set up automatic enrollment IRAs, set up 401(k)s or other employer plans, or start automatically enrolling workers in their existing retirement plans.

Supporting Work and Addressing the Challenges of Dual-Earner Couples. Two earner couples face unique challenges in the workforce. When both spouses work, the family incurs additional costs: commuting; professional expenses; child care; and increasingly, elder care. On top of explicit Federal and State taxes, these work-related costs can be quite burdensome and can contribute to a sense that work is not worth it. To address these challenges, the Budget proposes a new second earner credit of up to $500 for families where both spouses work. The new credit would benefit 24 million couples.

Expanding the Earned Income Tax Credit (EITC) for Workers without Children and Non-Custodial Parents. The EITC is among the Nation's most effective tools for reducing poverty and encouraging people to enter the workforce. But because the EITC available to them is so small, workers without children and non-custodial parents miss out on these anti-poverty and employment effects of the EITC. The Budget would double the "childless worker" EITC and make the credit available to workers with earnings up to about 150 percent of the poverty line. It would also expand eligibility to workers age 21-24 and age 65-66, so that the EITC can encourage employment and on-the-job experience for young adults, as well as to older workers, harmonizing the EITC rules with ongoing increases in the Social Security full retirement age. The proposal would directly reduce poverty and hardship for 13.2 million low-income workers struggling to make ends meet, and would encourage and support work.

Continuing EITC and Child Tax Credit (CTC) Improvements that Benefit 16 Million Working Families with Children. The Budget starts from a baseline that makes permanent the improvements to the EITC and Child Tax Credit enacted in 2009 and extended in 2010 and 2013. The baseline also makes permanent the American Opportunity Tax Credit, discussed above. The EITC and CTC provisions benefit 16 million families with 29 million children and have likely encouraged thousands of parents to enter or remain in the workforce. In addition to their direct effects in reducing poverty and supporting work, the EITC and the Child Tax Credit have also been found to improve health and educational outcomes for the children whose families receive them. For example, recent research suggests that the 2009 EITC and Child Tax Credit expansions may have boosted college enrollment by two to three percentage points for high school seniors in eligible families.

Reforming Capital Gains Taxation, Imposing a Fee on Large Financial Firms, and Closing Tax Loopholes

Since the 1970s, income concentration in the United States has surged. In the most recent decade and for the highest income groups, much of that surge resulted from growing concentration of capital income and wealth. Today, the top one percent holds more than 40 percent of the Nation's wealth, and the top 0.1 percent holds more than 20 percent—levels not seen since the 1930s. Meanwhile, the bottom 90 percent has lost ground, with its share of wealth falling since the mid-1980s, and its average wealth falling sharply in the last decade.

A contributing factor in these shifts has been falling tax rates on capital income. While the fiscal cliff deal raised the total capital gains and dividend tax rates to 23.8 percent for high-income households, that is still well below tax rates on earned income and tax rates on capital gains and dividends in earlier decades. Meanwhile, current rules let substantial capital income escape tax altogether.

One of the largest holes in the existing system is what is known as "stepped-up basis." Under current law, capital gains on assets held until death are never subject to income taxes. Not only do bequests to heirs go untaxed, but the basis of inherited assets is immediately increased ("stepped up") to the value at the date of death. For example, suppose an individual bequeaths stock worth $50 million to an heir, who immediately sells it. When purchased, the stock was worth $10 million, so the capital gain is $40 million. However, the heir's basis in the stock is the $50 million when he inherited it—so he owes no tax on the sale.

Each year, hundreds of billions in capital gains escape income tax due to the non-taxation of gains on bequests. Stepped-up basis perpetuates inequality of wealth and opportunity, since the vast majority of the tax benefits accrue to the wealthiest of decedents and their heirs. It also creates a more basic inequity. Retirees who need to spend down their assets in retirement pay tax on their capital gains. But the small minority that can afford to hold onto appreciated assets until death can pass them onto their heirs tax-free.

The Budget would reform the taxation of capital income through two important changes. First, it would increase the capital gains and dividend rate to 28 percent (inclusive of the net investment income tax), the rate at which capital gains were taxed under President Reagan, for the highest-income households. Second, it would end stepped-up basis by treating bequests and gifts as realization events that would trigger tax liability for capital gains. To ensure the proposal creates neither tax nor compliance burdens for middle class families, decedents would be allowed a $200,000 per couple ($100,000 per individual) exclusion for capital gains income, along with a $500,000 per couple ($250,000 per individual) exclusion for personal residences. Tangible personal property other than art and similar collectibles (e.g., bequests or gifts of furniture or other household items) would also be excluded. In addition, family members that inherited small, family-owned and operated businesses would not owe tax on the gains unless and until the asset were sold, and closely-held businesses would have the option to pay tax on gains over 15 years.

The proposed capital income reforms would raise $208 billion over the first 10 years, with larger revenue gains when fully implemented. Not only is the proposal highly progressive, with 99 percent of the revenue coming from the top 1 percent, it would also improve the efficiency of the tax system. By letting very wealthy investors make their capital gains disappear for tax purposes at death, stepped-up basis creates strong "lock-in" incentives to hold onto assets for generations, even when resources could be invested more productively elsewhere. Eliminating stepped-up basis would reduce lock-in and promote higher productivity and growth by encouraging more efficient capital allocation.

The Budget would also impose a new fee on large, highly-leveraged financial institutions.

Specifically, the Budget would raise $112 billion over 10 years by imposing a seven basis point fee on the liabilities of large U.S. financial firms—the roughly 100 firms with assets over $50 billion. This fee will complement other Administration policies aimed at preventing future financial crises and making the economy more resilient. Even with the end of "too big to fail," excessive leverage still creates risks for the broader economy. Alongside capital requirements and other tools that help rein in excessive leverage, a financial fee would improve economic stability by attaching a direct cost to leverage for large firms. The fee will also satisfy the statutory requirement for the President to propose a means to recoup any remaining costs of assistance provided through the Department of the Treasury's Troubled Asset Relief Program.

The Budget would also close a number of inefficient, unintended, and unfair tax loopholes in the individual tax code. For example, it would end a loophole that lets some high-paid professional avoid Medicare and Social Security payroll taxes, costing the Trust Funds almost $10 billion a year by the end of the decade. It would also prevent wealthy individuals from using loopholes to accumulate huge amounts in tax-favored retirement accounts. While tax-preferred retirement plans are intended to help middle class workers prepare for retirement, loopholes in the tax system have let some wealthy individuals convert these accounts into tax shelters. The Budget would prohibit contributions to and accruals of additional benefits in tax-preferred retirement plans and IRAs once balances are about $3.4 million, enough to provide an annual income of $210,000 in retirement.

The combination of the capital gains reform package, the financial fee, and closing tax loopholes would pay for the pro-middle class, pro-work tax reforms described above, as well as for the complementary investments in child care access and quality, and for the Budget's proposal to partner with States to make community college free for responsible students.

Making Sure Everyone Pays Their Fair Share and Reducing the Deficit

As described in the first chapter, the President's Budget takes a number of steps to put the Nation on a sound fiscal footing. Building on the Affordable Care Act (ACA), it introduces additional health reforms that will help maintain the historic slow-down in health care cost and price growth over the last several years. It proposes comprehensive immigration reform that reduces deficits and strengthens Social Security, while also boosting growth by raising productivity. Even with proposed new investments, discretionary spending would still reach its lowest level on record as a share of GDP.

But even with slower health care cost growth, immigration reform, and spending restraint, an aging population will put increasing pressures on the budget over the next several decades. For example, by the end of the 10-year budget window in 2025, the ratio of retirees to workers will be almost 50 percent higher than it was at the beginning of the 2000s, and it will increase further over the subsequent decade. Given these demographic shifts, the reality is that additional revenue is needed to maintain the Nation's commitments to seniors without shortchanging investment in future generations.

In addition to raising revenue to pay for tax reforms that help middle class families and support work, as described above, the Budget would also raise an additional $638 billion in revenue for deficit reduction. Rather than obtaining this additional revenue by raising tax rates, the President's tax reform proposals would reduce the deficit by reforming tax breaks and closing loopholes, making the tax code fairer, simpler and more efficient. Specifically, the Budget would:

- *Limit the Value of Itemized Deductions and Other Tax Preferences to 28 Percent.* Currently, a millionaire who deducts a dollar of mortgage interest enjoys a tax benefit that is more than twice as generous as that received by a middle class family. The Budget would limit the value of most tax deductions and exclusions to 28 cents on the dollar, a limitation that would affect only couples with incomes over about $250,000 (singles with incomes over about $200,000). The limit would apply to all itemized deductions, as well as other tax benefits, such as tax-exempt interest and tax exclusions for retirement contributions and employer-sponsored health insurance.

- *Observe the "Buffett Rule."* As in past years, the Budget proposes to institute the Buffett Rule, requiring that wealthy millionaires pay no less than 30 percent of income—after charitable contributions—in taxes. This proposal will act as a backstop to prevent high-income households from using tax preferences to reduce their total tax bills to less than what many middle class families pay.

Fixing America's Broken Business Tax System and Rebuilding Its Infrastructure

In February 2012, the President proposed a framework for business tax reform that would help create jobs and spur investment, while eliminating loopholes that let companies avoid paying their fair share. Consistent with that framework, the Budget includes a reserve for long-run revenue neutral reform, while detailing a number of specific proposals that the President believes should be part of reform, including a detailed international tax reform plan that is new to this year's Budget.

Key features of the President's plan include:

- *Cutting the Corporate Tax Rate and Broadening the Tax Base.* The Budget would lower the corporate tax rate to 28 percent, with a 25 percent effective rate for domestic manufacturing, putting the United States in line with major competitor countries and encouraging greater investment here at home. The rate reduction would be paid for by eliminating dozens of inefficient tax expenditures and through additional structural reforms—addressing accelerated depreciation and reducing the tax preference for debt financed investment. Together, these reforms would help achieve more neutral tax treatment of different industries, types of investment, and means of financing, improving capital allocation and contributing to economic growth.

- *Improving Incentives for Research and Clean Energy.* The Budget would make permanent—and pay for—important research and clean energy incentives that the Congress routinely extends on a year-to-year basis, including the Research and Experimentation Tax Credit, the Production Tax Credit, and the Investment Tax Credit. It would also reform these incentives to make them simpler and more efficient, for example by creating a single formula for calculating the Research and Experimentation Tax Credit and making the renewable energy Production Tax Credit refundable so innovative, growing firms can fully benefit.

- *Simplifying and Cutting Taxes for Small Business.* The Budget includes new proposals to make tax filing simpler for small businesses and entrepreneurs so that they can focus on growing their business rather than filling out their tax returns. Building on bipartisan proposals, the Budget would let businesses with gross receipts of less than $25 million—more than 99 percent of all businesses—dispense with many of the tax system's most complex rules and instead pay tax based on simpler, "cash" accounting. The Budget would also permanently extend and enhance Section 179 expensing to let small businesses write off up to $1 million of investments in equipment up front, so that the vast majority of firms would not have to deal with depreciation rules. The net result is that almost all small businesses would pay taxes based on an income measure much closer to their bank statement: deducting their expenses—including funds reinvested in their businesses—and paying tax based on their cash flow profits.

- *Reforming the International Tax System.* The Budget details the President's full plan for reforming and modernizing the international business tax system. The core of the President's proposal is a 19 percent minimum tax on foreign earnings that would require U.S. companies to pay tax on all of their foreign earnings when earned—with no loopholes or opportunities for deferral—after which earnings could be reinvested in the United States without additional tax. Other proposals in the international reform plan would prevent U.S. companies from avoiding tax through "inversions"—transactions in which U.S. companies buy smaller foreign companies, then reorganize the combined firm to reduce U.S. tax liability—and prevent foreign companies operating in the United States from using excessive interest deductions to "strip" earnings out of the United States and avoid U.S. tax. The Department of the Treasury has taken initial steps to reduce the economic benefits of inversions, but the President has been clear that the only way to fully address the issue of inversions is through action by the Congress, preferably as part of broader tax reform.

- *Devoting One-Time Savings from International Reform to Investment in Infrastructure.* As part of transitioning to a reformed international tax system, the Budget would impose a one-time transition toll charge of 14 percent on the up to $2 trillion of untaxed foreign earnings that U.S. companies have accumulated overseas. As explained above, the Budget would devote the one-time revenue from this toll charge to the Highway Trust Fund, financing the President's six-year Surface Transportation Reauthorization proposal. Devoting one-time transition revenue to infrastructure investments is both pro-growth (see above, The Case for Investing in Infrastructure in Today's Economy) and fiscally responsible, since—unlike using this temporary revenue for permanent tax cuts or spending increases—devoting it to one-time investments will not increase long-term deficits.

Investing in a High-Performing Internal Revenue Service

Middle class families and small businesses deserve a simpler tax system. But they also deserve an IRS with the resources to answer the phone when they call, promptly issue new guidance clarifying laws and regulations, and ensure that those who try to cheat the system are held accountable. Likewise, reforms to the business and—especially—international tax system depend on an IRS that is capable of going toe-to-toe with high-paid tax lawyers and accountants to enforce the law and make sure corporations, the wealthiest, and ordinary American workers all play by the same rules.

Unfortunately, congressional Republicans have insisted on cutting the IRS budget by about 10 percent since 2010 (adjusted for inflation), severely compromising both customer service and enforcement. The Budget would reinvest in taxpayer services, as well as other IRS responsibilities. Specifically, the Budget's $12.9 billion investment in the IRS would greatly improve services for taxpayers, including through investments for digital services that will fundamentally change how taxpayers interact with the IRS, such as by creating new online tax filing status and payment options. It also makes investments for the IRS to adequately and fairly administer the tax code. More than $650 million of the Budget's IRS total is provided through a program integrity cap adjustment for tax enforcement activities that return six times their value in increased revenue.

FIXING AMERICA'S BROKEN IMMIGRATION SYSTEM

On November 20, 2014, the President announced a series of executive actions to begin to fix the Nation's broken immigration system. These executive actions crack down on illegal immigration at the border; prioritize deporting felons, not families; and allow certain undocumented immigrants who register and pass criminal and national security background checks to start paying their fair share of taxes and temporarily stay in the United States without fear of deportation. These actions are only a first step toward reform of the system, and the Administration continues to count on the Congress for the more comprehensive reform that only legislative changes can provide.

The comprehensive reform supported by the President and passed by the Senate in 2013 would fix the Nation's broken immigration system by continuing to strengthen U.S. border security, cracking down on employers who hire undocumented workers, modernizing the Nation's legal immigration system, and providing a pathway to earned citizenship for hardworking men and women who pay a penalty and taxes, learn English, pass background checks, and go to the back of the line.

In addition to contributing to a safer and more just society, comprehensive immigration reform will also boost economic growth, reduce deficits, and strengthen Social Security. Common sense immigration reform will strengthen the workforce by attracting and retaining the best and brightest students whom are trained at U.S. universities, strengthening capital investment and overall productivity, and increasing the number of entrepreneurs starting companies in the United States, thereby creating more jobs. Moreover, by adding younger workers to the labor force, reforming America's broken legal immigration system will help balance an aging population and improve the economic and budget outlook as the baby boom generation retires.

The Congressional Budget Office has estimated that the immigration bill that passed with bipartisan support in the Senate would reduce the deficit by about $160 billion in the first decade and by almost $1 trillion over 20 years. Meanwhile, the Social Security Actuaries have found that the Senate bill would reduce the Social Security shortfall by $300 billion over the first 10 years and would close eight percent of the 75-year Social Security shortfall.

The Administration supports the bipartisan Senate approach taken in 2013, and calls on the Congress to act on comprehensive immigration reform this year. While the President's executive actions will provide temporary relief while demanding accountability for those whose cases are not an enforcement priority, the Administration urges the Congress to act to permanently fix the Nation's broken immigration system.

Addressing the Root Causes of Migration from Central America

The President's Budget provides $1 billion to support a long-term, comprehensive strategy for Central America to minimize the pressures of illegal immigration on the United States. The Budget will enable concrete progress toward achieving the President's priority of advancing security, prosperity, and economic growth in the region. The Budget provides resources to focused lines of effort that will take on the root causes of the dangerous migration of unaccompanied children and families, where Central American migrants are extremely vulnerable to becoming victims of violent crime or sexual abuse along the journey. These lines of effort are designed to achieve an economically-integrated Central America that provides economic opportunities to its people; more democratic, accountable, transparent, and effective public institutions; and a safe environment for its citizens to build their lives in peace and stability. Investments in the region also will allow the United States to work with its partners to improve the capacity of Central American governments to receive and reintegrate migrants and to target human smugglers. These resources will complement efforts by Central American governments, especially in El Salvador, Honduras, and Guatemala, to accelerate longer-term reforms and improvements in the lives of ordinary citizens. They will allow the United States to increase its coordination with regional governments as well as with international financial institutions, the private sector, civil society, and other international partners, to promote regional prosperity through a sustained, well-coordinated plan to address longstanding challenges to economic growth

in the region. Based on the U.S. Strategy for Engagement in Central America, which focuses on the interlocking themes of prosperity, security, and good governance, the United States is ready to support aspects of the "Alliance for Prosperity" plan developed jointly by the governments of El Salvador, Honduras, and Guatemala, while working with other international stakeholders and the private sector to define and accelerate their support.

Securing the Borders and Enforcing U.S. Immigration Laws

Our long-term investment in border security and immigration enforcement has produced significant and positive results. Under this Administration, the resources that the Department of Homeland Security (DHS) dedicates to security at the Southwest border are at an all-time high. Compared to 2008, today there are 3,000 additional Border Patrol agents along the Southwest border. Border fencing, unmanned aircraft surveillance systems, and ground surveillance systems have more than doubled since 2008. Border apprehensions—a key indicator of border security—are at their lowest levels since the 1970s. Even this summer's influx of unaccompanied children was met with an aggressive, coordinated Federal response focused on heightened deterrence, enhanced enforcement, stronger foreign cooperation, and greater capacity for Federal agencies to ensure that the U.S. border remains secure. As a result of the Administration's efforts at the border, the size of the unauthorized population living in the United States has stopped growing for the first time in 40 years.

The Budget continues the investment in border security by maintaining U.S. Customs and Border Protection (CBP) front line operations, funding additional technology and infrastructure, and expanding and enhancing intelligence and targeting capabilities. The Budget supports 21,370 Border Patrol Agents and 26,075 CBP Officers, including over 2,300 new Officers supported by proposed increases to user fees. The Budget includes over $373 million for the acquisition and sustainment of technology and tactical infrastructure along U.S. borders, an increase of $90 million over the current Continuing Resolution funding levels for DHS and $11 million above the 2015 Budget. This includes $128 million to support the deployment of new technology and tactical infrastructure investments along the Southwest border. These technology investments provide CBP with increased situational awareness on the border, as well as the ability to effectively respond to border incursions. The Budget also provides $97 million for recapitalization of aging non-intrusive inspection equipment at ports of entry, which will help CBP more efficiently detect security threats and facilitate lawful trade and travel. The Budget also funds an increase of $36 million in CBP intelligence and targeting activities that provide cutting-edge analytic support to Agents and Officers in the field.

IMPROVING HEALTH CARE THROUGH ACA AND ADDITIONAL REFORMS

The President's health plan provides hard-working, middle class Americans the economic security they deserve. American families no longer need to worry about losing coverage due to economic setbacks, such as lay-offs or job changes, or due to pre-existing conditions, such as asthma. The ACA also forces insurance companies to play by the rules, prohibiting them from discriminating against anyone with a pre-existing condition, dropping coverage due to illness, billing patients into bankruptcy because of an illness or injury, and limiting annual or lifetime benefits. Further, as discussed in the first chapter, the ACA has taken historic and significant steps toward putting the Nation back on a sustainable fiscal course, while laying the foundation for a higher-quality, more secure health care system. The ACA is improving the quality of care that Americans receive and reducing cost growth by deploying innovative new payment and delivery models that incentivize more efficient, higher-quality care.

Since the full implementation of the ACA began in 2014, millions of people have enrolled in either private insurance through the Health Insurance Marketplace, or coverage through Medicaid and the Children's Health Insurance Program (CHIP). As a result, the number of uninsured Americans has dropped by an estimated 10 million. The ACA is helping to enhance competition among insurance companies, expand coverage choices, and increase affordability, by keeping premiums

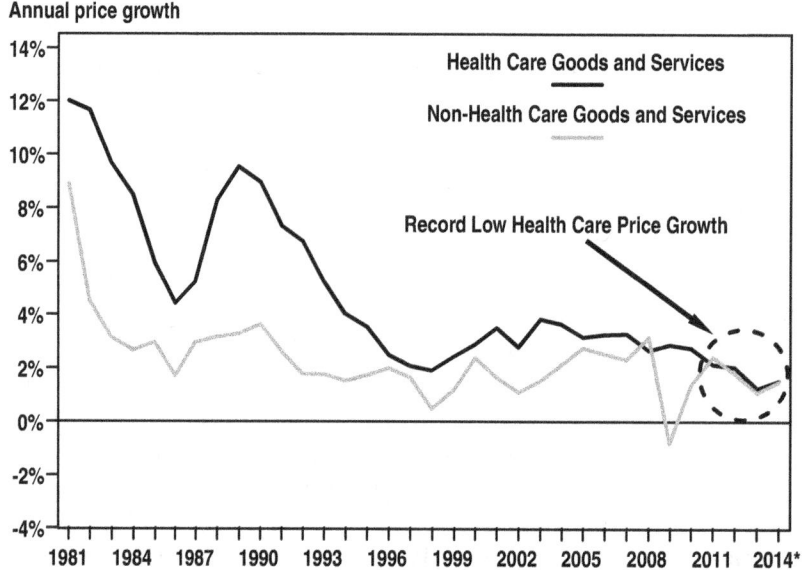

Health Care Costs Are Under Control

*Annualized using data through 2014:Q3
Source: Department of Commerce, Bureau of Economic Analysis; Personal Consumption Expenditures data with OMB calculations.

low and offering tax credits to more Americans to help them purchase coverage.

Supporting Implementation of the Affordable Care Act

The Budget fully funds the ongoing implementation of ACA's health insurance coverage improvements through the operation of Health Insurance Marketplaces and the premium tax credits and cost sharing assistance to help make coverage affordable, drive down long-term health care costs, and improve care for millions of citizens.

Preserving Coverage through CHIP. CHIP currently serves over eight million children of working parents who are not eligible for Medicaid. The Budget proposes to extend funding for CHIP, which ends in 2015, through 2019, ensuring continued, comprehensive, affordable coverage for these children. The proposal is paid for through an increase in tobacco taxes that will help reduce youth smoking and save lives.

Strengthening Medicare and Medicaid

This year will mark the 50th anniversary of the enactment of Medicare and Medicaid. Together, Medicare and Medicaid provide affordable health coverage to support longer, healthier lives and economic security for the Nation's seniors and low-income working Americans and families. Today, Medicare provides about 55 million Americans with dependable medical insurance. State Medicaid programs provide health and long-term care coverage to more than 68 million low income Americans. The ACA and the Budget strengthen the Medicare and Medicaid programs through reforms that expand health coverage in Medicaid, encourage high-quality and efficient care, and continue the progress of reducing cost growth.

Expanding Health Coverage by Improving Access to Medicaid and CHIP Coverage and Services. The Budget gives States the option to streamline eligibility determinations for children in Medicaid and CHIP and to maintain Medicaid coverage for adults by providing one-year of continuous eligibility. The Budget expands access to preventive benefits and tobacco cessation for adults in Medicaid and ensures children in inpatient psychiatric treatment facilities have access to comprehensive benefits.

Promoting Access to Medicaid Long-Term Care Services and Supports (LTSS). The Budget includes proposals that would expand access to Medicaid home and community-based services (HCBS) as an alternative to institutional care for individuals with disabilities and elderly populations. First, the Budget expands and simplifies eligibility to encourage more States to provide HCBS in their Medicaid programs. The Budget also includes a comprehensive long-term care pilot for up to five States to test, at an enhanced Federal match rate, a more streamlined approach to delivering LTSS to support greater access and improve quality of care. In 2015, the Administration will host the sixth White House Conference on Aging to recognize the importance of these, and other key programs for older Americans, as well as to look ahead to how to improve and advance the quality of life for older Americans in the next decade.

Improving Care Delivery for Low-Income Medicare-Medicaid Beneficiaries. The Budget proposes a budget-neutral pilot in a limited number of States to provide qualifying low-income adults, under age 55, benefits under the Program for All-Inclusive Care for the Elderly (PACE), while promoting community services in line with the integration of the landmark Olmstead Supreme Court decision[1], supporting self-determination, serving people with disabilities in the most integrated setting appropriate to their needs, and achieving better health outcomes. Under current law, PACE provides comprehensive long-term services to qualifying individuals age 55 and older. Pilots will test whether PACE programs can effectively serve a younger popula-

---

1 The U.S. Supreme Court's 1999 landmark decision in *Olmstead v. L.C.* (Olmstead) found the unjustified segregation of people with disabilities is a form of unlawful discrimination under the Americans with Disabilities Act. Olmstead requires States to administer programs in the most integrated setting appropriate to the needs of qualified individuals with disabilities.

tion without increasing costs. The Budget also proposes to implement streamlined processes for beneficiary appeals and joint Federal-State review of marketing materials for managed care plans that integrate Medicare and Medicaid payment and services and serve Medicare-Medicaid enrollees. These proposals address the sometimes conflicting requirements in each program. In addition, the Budget proposes to permanently authorize a demonstration that provides retroactive drug coverage for certain low-income Medicare beneficiaries through a single plan, establishing a single point of contact for beneficiaries seeking reimbursement for claims.

Encouraging High-Quality, Efficient Care among Medicare Providers. The Budget continues a set of proposals that build on initiatives included in ACA to help extend Medicare's solvency while encouraging provider efficiencies and improved patient care. This includes a proposal to encourage efficient post-acute care by adjusting payment updates and other payment modifications for certain post-acute care providers. The Budget also proposes to better align certain special payments to hospitals with the cost of care and reduce Medicare bad debt payments in a way that more closely matches private sector standards. Additional proposals to promote efficiency in the Medicare program include: improving payment accuracy for Medicare Advantage; constraining Medicare cost growth; better aligning payments to teaching hospitals with patient care costs; and addressing excess payments for Medicare Part B drugs to hospitals and physicians. Together, these proposals would save approximately $222 billion over 10 years.

Improving Health Outcomes for Children and Youth in Foster Care. The Budget also establishes a new Medicaid demonstration project in partnership with the Administration for Children and Families to encourage States to provide evidence-based psychosocial interventions to address the behavioral and mental health needs of children in foster care and reduce reliance on psychotropic medications, with the goal of improving overall health outcomes.

Reducing Cost Growth by Encouraging Beneficiaries to Seek High-Value Services. The Budget includes structural changes that will encourage Medicare beneficiaries to seek high-value health care services. To help improve the financial stability of the Medicare program, the Budget reduces the Federal subsidy of Medicare costs for those beneficiaries who need that subsidy the least. The Budget includes several modifications for new beneficiaries starting in 2019, such as a modified Part B deductible and a modest copayment for certain home health episodes. Research indicates that beneficiaries with Medigap plans that provide first, or near-first-dollar coverage have less incentive to consider the costs of health care services, thus raising Medicare costs and Part B premiums for all beneficiaries. The Budget applies a premium surcharge for new beneficiaries beginning in 2019 if they choose such Medigap coverage. Together, these proposals would save approximately $84 billion over 10 years.

Improving Quality and Lowering Drug Costs for Federal Health Programs. The Budget includes a number of proposals that lower drug costs, while improving quality and reducing waste in the Medicare Part D program. The Administration is deeply concerned with the rapidly growing prices of specialty and brand name drugs. The Budget proposes to give the Secretary of HHS the authority to negotiate drug prices for biologics and high-cost drugs in Medicare Part D to help ensure access to and affordability of these treatments. This proposal is one of a range of potential solutions to address these growing costs, and the Administration looks forward to working with the Congress on this challenge. The Budget also proposes to close the coverage gap for brand drugs in the Part D benefit by 2017, three years earlier than under current law, by increasing the discounts offered by the pharmaceutical industry. In addition, the Budget proposes to align Medicare payments for drugs with Medicaid policies for low-income beneficiaries. It also provides the Secretary the authority to suspend coverage and payment for questionable Part D prescriptions. The Budget also establishes a program to reduce prescription drug abuse in Medicare.

Together, these proposals will save Medicare $126 billion over 10 years. In addition, the Budget includes two proposals designed to increase access to generic drugs and biologics by stopping companies from entering into anti-competitive deals intended to block consumer access to safe and effective generics, by awarding brand biologic manufacturers seven years of exclusivity, rather than 12 years under current law, and by prohibiting additional periods of exclusivity for brand biologics due to minor changes in product formulations. These two proposals will save the Federal Government $16 billion over 10 years, including savings in Medicare and Medicaid.

Lowering Medicaid Drug Costs for States and the Federal Government. The Budget includes targeted policies to lower drug costs in Medicaid. First, the Budget improves the Medicaid drug rebate program by clarifying the definition of brand drugs, collecting an additional rebate for generic drugs whose prices grow faster than inflation, clarifying the inclusion of certain prenatal vitamins and fluorides in the rebate program, and taking actions to promote the integrity of the rebate program. The Budget also corrects a technical error to a rebate for new drug formulations, limits to 12 quarters the timeframe for which manufacturers can dispute drug rebate amounts, and excludes authorized generic drugs from average manufacturer price calculations for determining manufacturer rebate obligations for brand drugs. In addition, the Budget improves Medicaid drug pricing by calculating Medicaid Federal upper limits based only on generic drug prices. These proposals are projected to save the Federal Government approximately $6.3 billion over 10 years.

Cutting Waste, Fraud, and Abuse in Medicare and Medicaid. The Administration has made targeting waste, fraud, and abuse in Medicare, Medicaid, and CHIP a priority and is aggressively implementing new tools for fraud prevention included in the ACA. In 2013, the Health Care Fraud and Abuse Control program's law enforcement efforts produced a record-breaking $4.3 billion in judgments, settlements, and recovery of taxpayer dollars from individuals trying to defraud Federal health care programs serving seniors and taxpayers. In addition, further development of the CMS Fraud Prevention System, a predictive analytic model similar to those used by private sector experts, continues to support CMS' efforts to identify and prevent wasteful, abusive, and potentially fraudulent billing activities. While these results indicate progress, more remains to be done. Therefore, the Budget proposes a series of policies to build on these efforts that will save nearly $3 billion over the next 10 years. Specifically, the Budget proposes to implement new initiatives to reduce fraud, waste, and abuse in Medicare, Medicaid, and CHIP by:

- Requiring prior authorization for power mobility devices and advanced imaging, which could be expanded to other items and services at high risk of fraud and abuse;

- Directing States to track high prescribers and utilizers of prescription drugs in Medicaid to identify aberrant billing and prescribing patterns;

- Supporting efforts to investigate and prosecute allegations of abuse or neglect of Medicaid beneficiaries in non-institutional health care settings and in the territories; and

- Strengthening the Federal Government's ability to identify and act on fraud, waste, and abuse through Medicaid Integrity Program improvements and investments.

In addition, the Budget would simplify and streamline State program integrity reporting requirements by consolidating redundant error rate measurement programs to create a streamlined audit program with meaningful outcomes, while maintaining the Federal and State government's ability to identify and address improper Medicaid payments.

Health Care Delivery System Reforms

Since passage of the ACA, the Administration has developed an aggressive agenda to reform the Nation's health care delivery system. This means avoiding costly mistakes and readmissions, keeping patients healthy, rewarding quality instead of quantity, and creating the health information technology infrastructure that enables new payment and delivery models to work. Such reforms will help to further slow growth in health care costs, and increase savings for Medicare and Medicaid. Building on the lessons learned and success from existing initiatives, the delivery system reform agenda will continue to improve health care quality and reduce costs using the following three strategies:

- Modify health care payment structures to reward providers for optimal care;

- Support practice redesign and create better capacity to improve care delivery; and

- Improve access to information to encourage data-driven decision-making by consumers, providers, and businesses.

To encourage health care providers who deliver better care and better outcomes for their patients, the Administration has set a goal for 2016 of making 30 percent of Medicare payments through alternative payment models, which link payments to delivery of efficient, high-quality, coordinated health care rather than paying for volume of health care services. By 2018, the Administration's goal is to make 50 percent of Medicare payments to providers through alternative payment models.

To further align incentives and improve care coordination, the Budget includes a proposal to accelerate physician participation in high-quality and efficient health care delivery systems by repealing the Medicare Sustainable Growth Rate formula and reforming Medicare physician payments in a manner consistent with the reforms included in recent bipartisan, bicameral legislation.

The Budget encourages post-acute providers, such as nursing homes and home health agencies, to deliver care efficiently by making a single (bundled) payment for such services. It also includes proposals that will enhance the ability of Accountable Care Organizations to increase quality and reduce costs. In addition, the Budget

improves incentives for providers to deliver care in the most appropriate ambulatory setting and also reduces incentives for physicians to inappropriately order services from which they would financially benefit.

The Budget establishes quality bonuses for the highest rated Part D plans and modifies incentives in the Medicare prescription drug program to encourage patient engagement in health care decisions.

To improve transparency and distribution of information, the Administration has improved access to Federal data through the Open Data Initiative, released Medicare data on cost and quality, and invested in innovative ways to collect and share data, from the way we measure the quality of care to the way health care is documented and communicated to consumers. The Budget increases support to advance interoperable health IT as part of delivery system reform while protecting patient privacy. The Budget supports the Office of the National Coordinator for Health Information Technology (ONC) in developing standards and consensus around policies that will help consumers and providers access electronic health information when and where they need it to make health care decisions, including development of interoperable mobile tools to help consumers use their health information effectively. The Budget also expands Medicare data sharing with qualified entities, which will enable additional third party analysis of data, and may lead to more transparent public discussion of care practices improvement in health care quality and efficiency, and/or reduce fraud, waste, and abuse in the Medicare program.

Public Health, Safety, and Security

The Budget proposes a number of key investments and reforms to improve the Nation's public health system and to promote access to health care services for vulnerable populations. Further, the Budget invests in protecting the Nation's public health system against global health security challenges such as infectious diseases, antibiotic-resistant bacteria, and biohazard threats. Since the first cases of Ebola were reported in West Africa in March 2014, the United States has mounted a Government-wide response to contain and eliminate the epidemic at its source, while also taking prudent measures to protect the American people. Emergency funding appropriated in 2014 in response to the President's proposal will mitigate the epidemic in West Africa, enhance domestic preparedness, speed the procurement and testing of new vaccines and therapeutics, and accelerate the Global Health Security Agenda. These activities will combat the spread of Ebola and will help reduce the potential for future outbreaks of infectious diseases that could follow a similarly devastating, costly, and destabilizing trajectory. The Budget continues to invest in these critical programs to strengthen the Nation's preparedness capabilities.

Prescription Drug and Heroin Abuse. Every day, more than 100 people die as a result of drug overdose, and more than 6,700 are treated in emergency departments. Abuse of prescription and illicit drugs, such as heroin, is an urgent public health concern. The Budget increases funding for programs across the Centers for Disease Control (CDC), the Substance Abuse and Mental Health Services Administration, the Agency for Healthcare Research and Quality, and ONC to decrease the rates of inappropriate prescription drug abuse. The Budget increases funding for every State to expand existing Prescription Drug Monitoring Programs to improve clinical decision making, interoperability, and effective public health interventions. The Budget also includes funding to expand and improve the treatment for people who use heroin and prescription opioids. In addition, the Budget supports increased dissemination of naloxone by first responders in an effort to prevent overdose deaths in high risk communities.

Modernizing the Nation's Food Safety System. CDC has estimated that 48 million foodborne illnesses occur each year from contaminated foods. The Budget includes $1.6 billion in total program resources to bolster food safety activities, including an increase of $301 million

for the Food and Drug Administration to implement new safety measures under the Food Safety Modernization Act for domestic and imported foods.

Investing in Native American Health Care. The Budget provides the Indian Health Service (IHS) with $5.1 billion, an increase of $461 million over the 2015 enacted level, which will expand health care services, and allow IHS to make significant progress toward the construction of health care clinics in Indian Country. The Budget proposes to fund contract support costs through mandatory funds beginning in 2017. The Administration intends to consult broadly with Tribes on this new approach prior to implementation in 2017.

Combating Antibiotic Resistant Bacteria (CARB). The Budget includes an increase of more than $550 million above 2015 enacted levels across the Federal Government to prevent, detect, and control illness and death related to infections caused by antibiotic-resistant (AR) bacteria. These resources will also help support the advancement of therapeutics for the treatment of bacterial infections. The Budget also fully implements the surveillance, prevention, and stewardship activities outlined in the CARB National Strategy. The investments will protect patients and communities by implementing interventions that reduce the emergence and spread of AR pathogens to prevent current antibiotic resistant threats. By 2020, the United States, together with partners, will reduce the incidence of overall Clostridium difficile infection in half and reduce Carbapenem-resistant *Enterobacteriaceae* infections acquired during hospitalization by 60 percent.

Preventing, Detecting, and Responding to Infectious Diseases, Both Abroad and at Home. The Ebola epidemic in West Africa underscores the need to urgently strengthen global health security in countries around the world that are not equipped to handle Ebola, including the most vulnerable countries across Asia, the Middle East and Africa that have poor infrastructure, limited capacity, high population density, and major transport hubs. In addition, recent and ongoing outbreaks of Plague, Marburg, Lassa fever, the Middle East Respiratory Syndrome, and avian influenza clearly demonstrate the need to immediately address global vulnerabilities. The Budget continues to invest in the Global Health Security Agenda, increases funding to eradicate polio and for the U.S. contribution to Gavi, the Vaccine Alliance, and creates a new PEPFAR Impact Fund for targeted global HIV/AIDS efforts. The Budget also increases funding for domestic preparedness efforts to more effectively and efficiently respond to potential, future outbreaks here at home and dedicates funding for States to develop HIV Plans to help them reach the goals of the National HIV/AIDS Strategy.

Strengthening Preparedness for all Health Threats, Including Naturally Occurring Hazards and Intentional Attacks. The Budget includes $522 million to enhance the advanced development of next generation medical countermeasures against chemical, biological, radiological, and nuclear threats. The Budget also more than doubles support for Bioshield by providing $646 million to continue the Federal Government's long-term commitment to the acquisition of new medical countermeasures. The Government response to Ebola has highlighted the importance of sufficient funding and operational capabilities to facilitate an effective and coordinated response to public health crises that may not meet the current criteria for a national disaster or public health emergency declaration, such as those under the Stafford Act. Informed by lessons learned from the Ebola response, the Budget proposes additional funding for HHS to strengthen the Nation's capability to plan for and respond to public health emergencies and enables potential changes in structure and capabilities to improve our public health emergency response.

The Budget includes $110 million to respond to unanticipated public health emergencies through support for domestic or international activities, such as State and local response and emergency staffing, hospital and containment facilities, infection control, laboratory equipment and supplies, data gathering and analysis, countermeasures,

and other potential needs in such an incidence. Within the total, there are resources for staff coordination and training, command and control, and other related logistical needs.

Health Centers and Health Workforce

The Budget helps ensure Americans in need of health care services are able to access them in a timely manner. Health centers are a key component of the Nation's health care safety net that provide Americans with access to affordable comprehensive, high-quality, primary care services regardless of their ability to pay. The Budget also strengthens the primary care workforce by providing increased resources for primary care health care providers who train and practice in areas where they are needed most.

Improving Access to Health Care Services. Across the United States, 1,300 health centers operate over 9,000 primary care sites that serve as high-quality, dependable sources of primary care services in communities. The Budget invests $4.2 billion, including $2.7 billion in new mandatory resources, in the Health Centers program in 2016 to support services for an estimated 28.6 million patients. This funding level will enable health centers to expand services to 1.1 million additional patients. In total, the Budget provides $8.1 billion in new mandatory resources over three years so that health centers can continue to serve their patients.

Improving Access to High-Quality Health Care Providers. The Budget includes new funding to implement innovative policies to train new health care providers and ensure that the future health care workforce is prepared to deliver high-quality and efficient health care services. The Budget invests $810 million in 2016 and $2.1 billion from 2017-2020 in the National Health Services Corps to place and maintain 15,000 health care providers in the areas of the Nation that need them most. To encourage and enhance training of primary care practitioners and other physicians in high-need specialties, the Budget proposes $5.25 billion over 10 years to support 13,000 new medical school graduate residents through a new competitive graduate medical education program that incentivizes high-quality physician training. To continue encouraging provider participation in Medicaid, the Budget extends increased payments for primary care services delivered by certain physicians through 2016, with modifications to expand provider eligibility and better target primary care services.

As discussed in this chapter, the President's Budget makes balanced investments in health care, infrastructure, clean energy, education, innovation, and research to grow the U.S. economy. By investing in the military, the Budget enhances America's national security. These investments will be fully paid for by cutting inefficient spending and by reforming tax benefits to make sure everyone pays their fair share.

The President believes that investments in the economy and national security must be done together. We cannot abandon our security in service of our economy, and we cannot abandon our economy in service of our security because harm to one does harm to the other. That is why the Budget provides a roadmap to make the investments needed both domestically and abroad.

As discussed in the next chapter, A Government of the Future, the Budget also proposes to make Government work better, by investing in effectiveness and efficiency; using Government data to drive economic growth; and supporting the people who work in Government.

A GOVERNMENT OF THE FUTURE

> *"We cannot win the future with the government of the past."*
>
> —President Barack Obama, State of the Union Address, January 25, 2011

The President is committed to creating a Government that makes a significant, tangible, and positive difference in the economy and the lives of the American people, and to driving lasting change in how Government works. This Administration has launched successful efforts to eliminate wasteful information technology (IT) spending, reduce the Federal real property footprint, modernize and improve citizen-facing services, and open tens of thousands of Federal data sets to spur innovation in the private sector. Yet, despite this progress, public trust in government remains low and there is more work to be done.

The Administration is ramping up its efforts to restore this trust through investments that modernize and improve how the Government serves citizens, and through initiatives that maximize the impact of taxpayer dollars. Past investments in management priorities have resulted in a significant return. For example, an $11 million investment funded the development and execution of the PortfolioStat initiative, a data-driven review of agency IT portfolios. This work, along with other OMB and technology reform and implementation efforts, has saved over $2.7 billion in the past three years. This represents a return on investment of nearly $245 for every $1 invested. In 2016, the Administration proposes over $450 million to drive forward progress on cross-agency management priorities. This includes new funding to support the teams leading cross-agen-

cy priority goals and to promote Federal spending transparency. It also increases support for ongoing initiatives—such as the U.S. Digital Service (USDS), PortfolioStat, Freeze the Footprint, and Open Data—that have already had an impact on improving Government operations.

The Budget fully supports the President's Management Agenda, a comprehensive and forward-looking plan to modernize and improve government to ultimately deliver better, faster, and smarter services to citizens and businesses. The President's Management Agenda is built on four pillars: Effectiveness—delivering world-class customer service to citizens and businesses; Efficiency—enhancing productivity and achieving cost savings across the Government; Economic Growth—opening Government-funded data and research to the public to spur innovation, entrepreneurship, economic growth, and job opportunities; and People and Culture—unlocking the full potential of today's Federal workforce and building the workforce needed for tomorrow.

Since launching the Management Agenda last year, the Administration has seen significant initial success in each of these four pillars. The Administration launched the USDS, a small team of our Nation's digital experts working to build the Federal Government's capacity to deliver world-class services to the American people. We stepped up our focus on delivering better customer service, increased agency use of shared services and strategic sourcing, ramped up agency progress and compliance with the Administration's open data policy, and started work on an ambitious plan for Senior Executive Service (SES) reform.

In addition to the Management Agenda, the Budget also supports the President's plan to reorganize the Federal Government so that it does more for less, and is best positioned to assist businesses and entrepreneurs in the global economy.

EFFECTIVENESS: DELIVERING WORLD-CLASS CUSTOMER SERVICE FOR CITIZENS AND BUSINESSES

Government must be able to keep pace with the innovation and user experiences that the American people and businesses expect. Throughout 2014, the Administration piloted new and innovative approaches to increase the Government's ability to drive impact for Americans on national priorities, including initiatives that help veterans find employment and help workers invest in safe and affordable retirement accounts. The Budget invests in scaling those pilot programs and processes that have proven successful. Ultimately, a more effective Government will more efficiently use taxpayer dollars to better deliver for citizens.

Ramping Up Smarter Information Technology Delivery

The Administration has embarked on a comprehensive approach to fundamentally improve the way that the Government delivers technology services to the public. Top technologists and entrepreneurs are being recruited to work within agencies on the highest priority projects. The best processes are being leveraged to increase oversight and accountability for IT spending. In addition, several efforts are being piloted to improve IT procurement and ramp up Government contracting with innovative companies.

People. Getting the best talent working inside of Government is a key component of the Administration's Smarter IT Delivery strategy. In 2014, the Administration piloted the USDS by recruiting a select group of private sector innovators, entrepreneurs, and engineers to Government service. Since standing up, this team of America's best digital experts has worked in collaboration with Federal agencies to implement cutting-edge digital and technology practices on the Nation's

highest impact programs, including the successful re-launch of *HealthCare.gov* in its second year, the Veterans Benefits Management System, and an improved process for online visa applications, among others. In addition to their work on these high priority projects, this small team of technical experts has worked to establish best practices and recruit still more highly-skilled digital service experts and engineers into Government.

Every agency in Government has citizen-facing digital projects that are critical to its mission. Too often, these services have been delivered over budget, behind schedule, and in ways that do not meet citizen needs. Unsurprisingly, since the launch of USDS in 2014, there has been significant demand for its expertise, from project design and development to recruiting technical experts. To address this problem, the Budget scales and institutionalizes this new approach to technology by providing funding to 25 agencies for the development of their own agency digital services teams. These small, high-impact teams will drive the quality and effectiveness of the agencies' most important digital services. USDS will work closely with agencies to stand up these teams by providing support for hiring, training, and procurement.

Process. The Administration has made significant progress encouraging data-driven processes to provide effective oversight of Government IT. By establishing mechanisms such as PortfolioStat, a data-based review of agency IT portfolios, we have not only strengthened Federal IT, but made it significantly more cost effective. PortfolioStat has helped the Government achieve more than $2.2 billion in savings over the past three years while ensuring agencies are efficiently using taxpayer dollars to deliver effective and innovative solutions to the public. PortfolioStat promotes the adoption of new technologies, such as cloud computing and agile development practices. For example, as a result of these continuing efforts, the Federal Government now spends approximately 8.5 percent of its budget on provisioned services such as cloud computing, on par with leading private sector companies.

In addition, agencies involved in PortfolioStat are becoming more effective in rapidly delivering value in IT. For example, agencies have increased their use of agile development practices and are delivering IT capabilities 21 days (11 percent) faster than they were in May 2013. Agile development is an incremental, fast-paced style of software development that better meets evolving user needs. Using agile development ultimately increases the ability to deliver a better product, faster.

In 2016, the Administration will continue to use PortfolioStat to drive efficiencies in these programs, and also will continue to revise and encourage adoption of the TechFAR and Digital Services Playbook, which were released to the public in the fall of 2014. These tools provide clear guidance to agencies on using agile development and innovative contracting practices to deliver IT services that work for 21st Century consumers. Throughout 2016, the Administration will continue to scale up best practices by institutionalizing them within the agency digital service teams.

Companies. The Government must work with private sector innovators to ensure the best use of cutting-edge technologies and practices. Yet, too often, there are barriers to entry that prevent agencies from contracting with these firms. Over the past year, initial steps have been taken to address this challenge. For example, the Administration has piloted FBOpen, a tool that helps small and innovative companies search for opportunities to work with Government, and launched an online national dialogue on procurement reform to solicit ideas for reducing barriers to access. As part of the broader strategy to transform the Federal marketplace, the Administration is piloting new initiatives in IT

acquisition. In 2016, these early pilots will be expanded to increase digital acquisition capability within agencies, train agency personnel in digital IT acquisitions, and test innovative contracting models.

Delivering World-Class Customer Service

The Administration is continuing its efforts to improve the quality, timeliness, and effectiveness of Federal services. A customer service Community of Practice has been established to develop standards, practices, and tools for agencies to improve their customer service. The Federal Customer Service Awards program has also been established to recognize individuals and teams who provide outstanding customer service directly to the American people. The awards will begin in the fall of 2015, and will support innovative practices and provide performance incentives to frontline employees.

Agencies are also increasing their focus on improving the most frequently used Government services, and the Budget supports the introduction and scale-up of these programs. The Internal Revenue Service (IRS) has launched IRS Direct Pay, which provides taxpayers a no-fee electronic payment option and allows them to establish installment agreements; built an e-Authentication tool that provides taxpayers a user-friendly, low-cost way to securely access IRS online tools and applications; and launched IRS2Go, a downloadable app that allows taxpayer self-service access to IRS information and services on any device. Since its release, it has been downloaded more than 5.4 million times. The Transportation Security Administration (TSA) is continuing to improve passenger experience at airports, including continuing to expand and improve TSA Pre-Check, an expedited passenger screening program. TSA is exploring new and innovative ways of collecting and responding to customer feedback to provide the best possible service while keeping U.S. airports safe. Going forward, the Administration will build and expand on this progress by improving the collection and use of customer feedback data across Government to make tangible improvements in customer interactions.

EFFICIENCY: INCREASING QUALITY AND VALUE IN CORE OPERATIONS

Over time, duplicative efforts have made Government less effective, wasting taxpayer dollars and making it harder for the American people to navigate their Government. To address this issue, the President has focused on improving Government efficiency. The Budget invests in expanding shared services, simplifying Federal contracting, continued benchmarking to drive data-driven Federal management, and shrinking the Federal real property footprint.

Expanding Shared Services to Increase Quality and Savings

It will come as no surprise that most Federal agencies have similar administrative functions that require the investment of increasingly scarce resources. Human resources, financial management, and payroll, for example, are common administrative functions that all agencies need, but not all agencies are equally efficient at managing. By creating Shared Service Providers (SSPs), and concentrating the delivery of administrative services within a smaller number of agencies, duplicative efforts can be reduced. Further, by giving this task to agencies with the right expertise, we can free up resources for mission critical activities, and deliver cost-effective support to agencies.

The use of shared services has grown in recent years, with smaller agencies leading the charge. In 2014, cabinet-level agencies took steps to realize the benefit of shared service agreements. For instance, in the Federal Government's largest shared service arrangement to date, the Department of Housing and Urban Development (HUD) has begun transitioning all of its core financial management functions—as well as select administrative and human-resource functions— to the Department of the Treasury, with other cabinet-level agencies expected to follow. To support greater adoption of shared services by all agencies for a broad range of functions, the Office of Management and Budget (OMB), in partnership with the Department of the Treasury's Office of Financial Innovation and Transformation, has developed a new governance model for SSPs that incorporates feedback from early adopters and builds on lessons learned from shared services in private sector companies.

The move to SSPs also supports the ability to modernize agency financial systems to allow for greater spending transparency. It will also allow more efficient implementation and adoption of the Digital Accountability and Transparency Act (DATA Act) of 2014. This Act requires the creation and adoption of standard definitions for Government spending data and the display of that data on *USASpending.gov*. The Budget includes funding that will allow agencies to make progress in implementing the DATA Act and increase Federal spending transparency.

Buying as One through Category Management. Federal contracting is often seen as a highly complex process that ultimately leads to less innovation, higher costs, and weaker performance. Today, proposals for contracts are lengthy, overly prescriptive, and laden with Government-specific requirements. There is also staggering duplication of contracts across Government and very little information sharing between agencies on pricing or other important contractual information. In order to fundamentally improve how taxpayer dollars are used in the Federal contracting space, the Administration is embarking on a comprehensive initiative to enhance collaboration and cooperation and drive greater innovation and improved performance. The category management initiative draws upon private sector best practices to create categories of commonly purchased items such as computers, software licenses, fuel for vehicle fleets, and human capital training services that are each managed with their own set of Government-wide strategies. This new approach will build on the progress made in the strategic sourcing initiative, leveraging the consolidated purchasing power of the Government to buy smarter and reduce duplication. Increased use of strategic sourcing has saved over $417 million since 2010, and reduced some areas of contract duplication by up to 40 percent. The Budget better leverages resources across categories to increase efficiencies, reduce duplicative contracts, and increase cost savings for both Government and industry.

The category management approach is a fundamental shift from the practice of handling purchasing, analyzing pricing, and developing vendor relationships individually within thousands of procurement units across Government. Under category management, the Administration will "buy as one" by creating common categories of products and services across Government, and managing each category as a mini-business with its own set of strategies. Each category will be led by a senior team with expertise in its assigned category, operating out of agencies identified as "centers of excellence." Strategic sourcing will continue to be one effective strategy that a category manager may implement to drive down total costs and improve overall performance for that category. Bringing common spending under management of knowledgeable category leaders, including collecting prices paid and other key performance information to allow easy comparisons, will ensure that agencies get a more competitive price and quality of performance when they are buying similar commodities under similar circumstances. This will also free up agency acquisition personnel to focus on complex agency-specific procurements.

To complement these efforts, the Administration will propose legislation making it easier for vendors seeking to bid on modestly-sized procurements and bringing more new companies into the Federal marketplace. The Administration will request authority to raise the simplified acquisition threshold from $150,000 to $500,000 in order to broaden the range of purchases that can be accomplished with minimal complexity and Government-unique requirements. The Administration will also seek new pilot authority allowing agencies to set aside work for new small businesses and other firms that have limited experience selling to the Government, but can offer cutting-edge technology and more creative solutions to address the Government's needs.

Shrinking the Federal Real Property Footprint

The Federal Government is the largest property owner in the United States. For example, the domestic building inventory contains almost 300,000 buildings requiring approximately $21 billion of annual operation and maintenance expenditures, including approximately $6.8 billion of annual lease costs. As a result, there are numerous opportunities to save by using Federal space more efficiently and disposing of unneeded buildings, land, and structures. In 2012, the Administration issued a "Freeze the Footprint" policy and directed agencies to freeze the growth in their office and warehouse real estate inventory. This led to a 10.2 million square foot reduction in Federal office and warehouse holdings in 2013. In 2015, the Administration will implement a five-year national strategy to continue reducing the size of the portfolio, and agencies will be required to set annual reduction targets for office and warehouse space and annual disposal targets for all building types to further reduce costs.

The Administration is also expanding the General Services Administration (GSA) Consolidation Activities program, first proposed and enacted in 2014. The Administration proposes to use $200 million in annual rental payments collected from agencies, $130 million over the 2015 enacted level, to execute additional office space consolidations. This will allow the Government to more effectively use real property by relocating Federal agencies into more efficient, lower cost or consolidated locations that also enable improved delivery of Government services. More than a dozen consolidations were implemented in 2014, the first year of the program, and the changes begun in that year alone will ultimately yield more than $16 million in annual cost avoidance to the taxpayer each year that the Government leases or owns the properties involved. Over time, this will result in significant avoided cost for this portfolio and will reduce the Federal real property footprint by approximately 500,000 square feet.

In addition to these administrative actions, the Budget includes a $57 million proposal to implement the Civilian Property Realignment Act (CPRA). If enacted, CPRA would create an independent board of private and public sector real estate experts that would perform Government-wide, independent portfolio analysis and make recommendations to the Congress on properties that should be disposed, consolidated, co-located, or reconfigured. Enactment of CPRA would help consolidate Government operations, streamline the disposal process, generate an estimated $1.2 billion in sales proceeds over 10 years, further reduce operations and maintenance costs associated with excess buildings, and provide funds for real property reinvestment.

The Benchmarking Initiative

The Benchmarking initiative is aimed at improving the performance of Federal mission-support functions, and identifying areas that may be ripe for innovative thinking or new efficiencies.

The Administration began the initiative in 2014 by measuring an initial set of five administrative functions—acquisition, financial management, human capital, IT management, and real property—at major bureaus/components within the 24 Chief Financial Officers Act Federal agencies. Agencies were able to see for the first time both how their internal bureaus compared against each other, and how they performed compared to peer agencies and the Government-wide average. Results of this effort are already being realized. For example, some agencies have experienced as much as a 10-percent increase in their reporting of contractor past performance, a vital way in which the Federal Government tracks the performance of its contractors. In 2015 and 2016, the Benchmarking program will be expanded to include customer satisfaction metrics and to make the results part of agency performance reviews and strategic planning exercises.

ECONOMIC GROWTH: INVESTING IN GOVERNMENT ASSETS TO FUEL INNOVATION, JOB CREATION, AND ECONOMIC PROSPERITY

The Budget continues to invest in efforts to open up Government-generated assets, including data and the results of federally funded research and development— such as intellectual property and scientific knowledge—to the public. Through these efforts, the Government can empower citizens and businesses to increase the return on investment with innovation, job creation and economic prosperity gained through their use of open Government data and research results. The use of this data and scientific knowledge has impacted the private sector, including fueling innovative start-up companies and creating American jobs, increasing the transparency of retirement plans, helping consumers uncover fraudulent charges on their credit card bills, assisting potential homebuyers in making informed housing decisions, and creating new life-changing technologies, such as leading-edge vaccines.

Opening Data to Spark Innovation

The Administration places a high priority on opening Government data as fuel for private sector innovation and public use. Since 2009, the Administration has released over 75,000 data sets to the public, while continuing to protect individual privacy, with over 67,000 of these data sets released in the last year alone. These data sets include everything from credit card complaints, to weather and climate measurements, to what different hospitals charge for different procedures. In demonstrating its commitment to open data, the Administration has developed performance metrics to measure agency progress in reaching open data goals, provided tools to make it easier for Federal agencies to publish data, and released guidance to agencies on how to engage with the community to identify priority data sets for release. The Administration continues to invest in and support efforts to unlock Federal data sets with a high potential for economic impact, including in the areas of health care, energy, education, employment, public safety, tourism, and agriculture. In addition, the Administration is committed to fueling the open data ecosystem by taking steps to connect agencies, entrepreneurs, and other innovators. The Budget provides $16 million for E-Government initiatives in GSA's Federal Citizen Services Fund, supporting important IT investments including open data and digital Government initiatives. While emphasizing the opening of Federal data, safeguarding the privacy, confidentiality, and security of sensitive information is of the utmost importance, and agencies are required to do thorough reviews of their data prior to publication to ensure no sensitive information is released.

Accelerating and Institutionalizing Lab-to-Market Practices

As discussed in the chapter on Investing in America's Future, the Budget invests $146 billion in research and development (R&D) across Government. The Federal Government's investment in R&D yields extraordinary long-term economic impact through the creation of new knowledge, new jobs, and ultimately new industries. The Federal R&D enterprise must continue to support fundamental research that is motivated primarily by an interest in expanding the frontiers of human knowledge and diffusing this knowledge through open data and publications. At the same time, economic growth can be accelerated through more effective transition of R&D results from the laboratory to the marketplace, based on close collaboration with industry.

The Budget reflects the Administration's commitment to accelerating the transfer of the results of federally funded research to the commercial marketplace by proposing increased funding for technology transfer from Federal labs in the National Institute of Standards and Technology (NIST) and for the National Science Foundation's (NSF) public-private Innovation Corps (I-Corps) program. In response to the President's 2011 Memorandum on Accelerating Technology Transfer and Commercialization, the Budget proposes an additional $4 million for NIST efforts to accelerate and expand technology transfer across the Federal Government, which will enhance the competitiveness of U.S. industry by sharing innovations and knowledge from Federal laboratories. The Budget also proposes $30 million for the public-private I-Corps program at NSF aimed at bringing together the technological, entrepreneurial, and business know-how necessary to bring discoveries ripe for innovation out of the university lab.

Another example of federally funded R&D powering marketplace innovation can be seen in the Department of Energy's (DOE) Office of Energy Efficiency and Renewable Energy (EERE) Lab-Corps program. This program empowers National Laboratory teams to identify market applications and private sector partners to commercialize high-impact new EERE technologies. The initial Lab-Corps pilot will be completed by the end of 2015, and in 2016, depending on the results of the pilot, DOE will expand the Lab-Corps program to other laboratory partners.

PEOPLE AND CULTURE: UNLOCKING THE FULL POTENTIAL OF TODAY'S FEDERAL WORKFORCE AND BUILDING THE WORKFORCE NEEDED FOR TOMORROW

In his December 2014 address to Federal Senior Executives, President Obama said, "[W]e need the best and brightest of the coming generations to serve. [T]hose of us who believe government can and must be a force for good…we've got to work hard to make sure that government works." Through the Management Agenda's focus on People and Culture, the Administration is committed to undertaking executive actions that will attract and retain the best talent to the Federal workforce and foster a culture of excellence. The Budget supports efforts to reform the Senior Executive Service (SES) and improve employee engagement in order to fully capitalize on the talents in today's Federal workforce at all levels, and recruit and develop the talent needed to continue moving the Federal Government forward in the 21st Century.

Leading America's Workforce

More than half of the Government's SES leaders are currently eligible to retire, and that number will rise to 64 percent by 2016. The impending SES "retirement wave" provides a unique opportunity to train the next generation of leaders. Agencies are piloting a number of reforms to transform the SES in preparation for 21st Century service. For example, the current hiring process for SES can now take almost a year to complete, so one pilot currently underway looks at accelerating hiring speeds. Another pilot focuses on new performance management measures and onboarding procedures to better prepare SES for their new positions and support top performers. In addition, agencies are improving their recruitment techniques to ensure the SES cadre better reflects the diversity of the workforce they lead and the American people they serve. To achieve these goals, the Budget proposes new funding for the Office of Personnel Management (OPM) to strengthen SES hiring and accountability.

The Administration has launched two new efforts that will start in 2015 and continue into 2016 to support SES reform:

White House Advisory Group. In order for SES reform to be successful, it cannot happen in a vacuum. Regular, high-quality feedback is needed from senior executives, the people who are both charged with implementing the reforms and best positioned to evaluate their impact on the ground. The White House Advisory Group on SES Reform was established to provide that direct feedback and advice on the core components of the Administration's efforts to improve the SES corps. The Advisory Group members were selected by their agency leadership as examples of highly effective SES, Senior Level, and Senior Technical professionals, as well as some aspiring SES, and will provide a broad set of advice on the current and future state of the senior career leadership. They will be charged with helping improve the way the Government recruits, hires, develops, and retains senior career leaders. They will also advise on effective performance management and accountability mechanisms for the SES. The breadth of experience of this group, as well as its close connections to SES in the field, will ensure we are getting the best ideas directly from the front lines.

White House Leadership Development Program. As part of the President's continued commitment to training and developing the Government's high performers and strengthening the next generation of SES, the Administration is launching the White House Leadership Development Program. Through this program, top civil servants and SES candidates will participate in rotational assignments to drive progress on Cross-Agency Priority (CAP) Goals and lead change across Departments and programs. Participants in the program will gain valuable experience by playing a key role in addressing critical management challenges facing the Federal Government and will gain valuable experience to bring back to their agencies.

Employee Engagement

In both the private and public sector, an employee's investment in the mission of their organization is closely related to the organization's overall performance. Engaged employees display greater dedication, persistence, and effort in their work, and better serve their customers—whether they are consumers or taxpayers. This makes employee engagement a critical performance measurement for Federal agencies. Overall, employee engagement levels in Government are at 63 percent, below the private sector average. Further, wide variation exists across and within agencies, including among organizations that perform similar functions. The Administration is committed to strengthening employee engagement, and aims to increase engagement levels to 67 percent by 2016. However, there is no single solution that will guarantee positive results. Rather, it takes actions at all levels of an organization to achieve these targets. Recent Budgets have invested in OPM to enhance its ability to measure employee engagement, most notably by making the Federal Employee Viewpoint Survey (EVS) an annual survey. From the EVS, OPM derives the Employee Engagement Index, which measures employees' attitudes toward office leadership, their supervisors, and their workplace experience. This allows agency and administration leadership to closely follow changes in employee engagement Government-wide and within particular organizations. In 2014, OPM released *UnlockTalent. gov*, a dashboard providing managers with deep insight into the data from the EVS results of 21,000 organizations. These data help managers see in minute detail their employees' attitudes toward issues such as leadership, training, and promotion, allowing agency leaders to tailor strategic plans that specifically address employee needs. The Budget funds tools to enhance the value of the EVS through *UnlockTalent.gov* and other mechanisms that communicate this critical information about the Federal workforce to a wider audience.

In December 2014, the Directors of OMB, OPM, and the White House Presidential Personnel Office jointly issued a memorandum laying out the annual cycle for strengthening employee engagement and linking employee engagement to mission outcome. Moving forward, agency Chief Human Capital Officers and other senior officials will facilitate and ensure distribution of EVS results to all executives, supervisors/managers, and employees at the component and office level, within three months of the survey completion date. The Administration has also clarified the roles and responsibilities of agency heads, Deputy Secretaries, component heads, Chief Human Capital Officers, Performance Improvement Officers, SES, and others in advancing employee engagement. For example, component heads will review progress on workforce improvement efforts at least quarterly, and SES will begin to have some aspects of employee feedback incorporated into their performance plans.

Encouraging an Agile Workforce

Part of successfully engaging with employees is ensuring an agile Federal workforce that can put its large store of talent to the best possible use, whether that is within their own office or agency, or to address critical problems at other agencies. To support this and encourage an engaged and flexible workforce, the Administration is building innovative tools to share talent across agencies. For example, the GovConnect workforce agility program allows managers to find employees outside their agencies that have the necessary skills to manage special projects. With GovConnect, managers can assemble virtual teams to work on new projects, or manage in the face of crisis. This project is being piloted throughout 2014 and 2015, and agencies will begin adapting successful pilot models for their own mission needs in 2016.

IMPROVING RESULTS: SETTING GOALS AND TRACKING PERFORMANCE

Improving Performance and Accountability

The Administration is executing the Management Agenda through CAP goals, which are focused on improving coordination across multiple agencies to address key performance improvement priorities. The CAP goals are part of the performance improvement framework developed with the Congress through the Government Performance and Results Act (GPRA) and the GPRA Modernization Act. Performance for each CAP goal is regularly tracked throughout the year and goal teams are held accountable for results, publishing quarterly updates on *Performance.gov*. While impressive progress has been seen on CAP goal priorities, overall performance delivery across agency boundaries remains a challenge, and in many cases significant management improvements require investments that cut across agencies and budget accounts. The Budget proposes authority for the OMB Director, with prior notification to the Congress, to transfer up to $15 million to support these crosscutting management initiatives. This proposal institutionalizes a capability to fund cross-agency efforts, rather than handling the challenges on a case-by-case basis. More details about the Federal Government's specific performance framework can be found on *Performance. gov* and in the *Analytical Perspectives* volume of the Budget. The Government can and should be more effective and efficient, and this proposal will provide a powerful tool to turn management reform ideas into real and lasting results for the American people.

Using Evidence and Evaluation to Drive Innovation and Outcomes

There is growing momentum for evidence-based approaches at all levels of government. The Administration's embrace of evidence-based approaches has resulted in important gains in areas ranging from reducing veterans' homelessness, to improving educational outcomes, to improving the effectiveness of international development programs. The Budget proposes to take additional evidence-based approaches to scale: for example, providing unemployed workers with reemployment services that have been shown to speed job placement; serving substantially more public housing residents through HUD's Jobs-Plus program, which has been shown to boost earnings; and making major investments in high quality early education and quality child care, which have been shown to significantly improve children's outcomes. In addition, Members of Congress from both parties, visionary governors and State legislatures, action-oriented mayors, and the non-profit and research communities are promoting greater use of data and research in policymaking and program management.

To enable future administrations and the Congress—as well as State and local leaders—to drive even more resources to policies backed by strong evidence, the Budget proposes a series of legislative changes and investments to accelerate learning about what programs work and why.

Improving Access to Administrative Data. One major focus of the Budget is increasing availability of data that the Government already collects through administering programs—also known as "administrative data"—to answer important questions about the effectiveness of Federal programs and policies. Through the Administration's Open Data Initiative and recent efforts to increase the use of administrative data

for statistical purposes, Federal agencies have made notable progress. However, significant challenges remain, including the need to update both the legal framework around data access and many agencies' data infrastructure.

The Budget addresses these challenges through a series of initiatives. First, it proposes immediate action to improve access to Federal data sets, most notably national Unemployment Insurance (UI) earnings data, while adhering to a robust framework of privacy, confidentiality, and security protections. Among other benefits, expanding access to UI data will make it possible to create consistent employment outcome "scorecards" for federally-subsidized job training providers, a goal of both the Administration's job training review and the bipartisan Workforce Innovation and Opportunity Act. Earnings data can also be used to rigorously evaluate the effects of other program changes and interventions on employment, wages, and upward mobility. Another Budget proposal would expand statistical agency access to business tax data, improving the quality and consistency of economic statistics from the U.S. Census Bureau (Census), the Bureau of Economic Analysis, and the Bureau of Labor Statistics. Second, the Budget makes data infrastructure investments at Census, the Department of Education, and elsewhere. These investments will allow the Federal Government to measure outcomes and test new approaches more easily and cheaply across a range of Federal programs. For example, the Census investments would help Census work with States to obtain access to data from State-administered programs, such as the Supplemental Nutrition Assistance Program (SNAP) or the Special Supplemental Nutrition Program for Women, Infants, and Children (WIC), allowing new analysis of how these programs are used and their effects; Census would also improve its infrastructure for linking data sets together. Finally, the Budget embraces a proposal by Representative Paul Ryan and Senator Patty Murray to establish a Commission on Evidence-Based Policymaking, which will advise the Congress on additional ways to improve access to data, while protecting privacy.

Coupling Flexibility with Accountability to Learn What Works. The Budget expands the use of innovative, outcome-focused grant designs that focus Federal dollars on effective practices while also encouraging innovation in service delivery. As discussed in the Investing in America's Future chapter, a new initiative, the Upward Mobility Project, will allow up to 10 communities, States, or consortia of States and communities to combine funds from up to four block grant programs currently designed to promote opportunity and economic development. Upward Mobility Projects would test and validate promising and evidence-based approaches to help families become more self-sufficient, improve children's outcomes, and revitalize communities so they can provide more opportunities for their residents. The Budget provides $1.5 billion in additional competitive funding over five years to help support Upward Mobility Projects. This initiative builds on prior Administration evidence building and place-based efforts by coupling greater flexibility in a discrete set of grant programs with requirements to utilize evidence-based strategies or rigorously test innovative approaches to evaluate their effectiveness.

Consistent with the focus on linking flexibility and accountability, the Budget would also authorize up to 10 new Performance Partnership Pilots for Disconnected Youth. Building on provisions included in 2014 and 2015 appropriations bills, this would create a third round of pilots letting States, localities, and Tribes blend funding and receive waivers under multiple youth-serving programs in order to build evidence about more effective ways to help vulnerable youth.

Doubling Down on Evidence-Building Efforts. The Budget also doubles down on Administration evidence efforts that are starting to produce results, such as "tiered evidence" competitive grant programs. Tiered evidence programs focus resources on practices with strong evidence, promote innovation by providing smaller grants to test new, promising ideas, and build evidence on both existing and new practices. The Budget provides significant funding for tiered evidence programs and other efforts that seek to expand our evidence base in important areas. Examples of these efforts include:

- *Innovating to Improve Education Outcomes.* The Budget invests $300 million for the Investing in Innovation Fund (i3), more than double the 2015 investment, to provide better information to States and school districts on what works in key K-12 education areas such as implementing college- and career-ready standards, improving low-performing schools, and improving the performance of students in science, technology, engineering, and mathematics (STEM). The Budget also triples funding to $200 million for First in the World, which focuses on building the evidence base in higher education, with particular emphasis on college completion.

- *Energy Assistance Innovation Fund.* The Budget requests $200 million for a Low Income Home Energy Assistance Program Innovation Fund to support State and utility partnerships that test innovative strategies for serving low-income beneficiaries. The competitive funds may include strategies related to reducing energy burden, supporting more efficient and clean energy sources, and improving households' ability to pay utility costs.

- *Using Data and Evidence to Reduce Global Poverty.* The Budget provides $1.25 billion over two years for the Millennium Challenge Corporation, which uses competition, evidence-based interventions, and evaluation to target international aid funding to where it can have the largest impact.

- *Building Evidence to Inform Conservation Programs.* The Budget includes $10 million over two years to build evidence on the incremental effect incentive payments and outreach efforts have on farmers' willingness to adopt conservation practices and to leverage data and evidence to improve the efficiency of private lands conservation programs.

- *Supporting Federal Employees with Innovative Ideas.* At the Department of Health and Human Services (HHS), the "Idea Lab" provides the support, resources and recognition for agency employees with promising new ideas for improving agency functions to pilot and develop their proposals. Funding in the Budget would enable the Departments of Commerce, Education, the Treasury, GSA, and the Small Business Administration (SBA) to create their own versions of an Idea Lab to drive the development of a culture of innovation that yields results.

The Budget also continues support for State and local Pay for Success initiatives, where philanthropic and private investors provide up-front financing for effective preventive services, and Government pays only if and when results are achieved. The Budget reproposes a $300 million Pay for Success Incentive Fund at the Department of the Treasury, similar to bipartisan legislation introduced in the House and Senate last year. It will encourage innovation and accelerate the use of evidence-based approaches by lowering and sharing the risk associated with initial private investments and by enabling State and local governments to attract additional investment in services that result in Federal, State, and local government savings. The Budget also proposes to allocate up to $64 million of appropriations for the Departments of Education and Justice and the Corporation for National and Community Service to support their Pay for Success projects.

Increasing Federal Evaluation Capacity. The Budget proposes significant increases in evaluation capacity to support key priorities. The Budget's major investments in preschool and child care are accompanied by more than $60 million for early childhood research and evaluation at HHS, the creation of a new National Education Research and Development Center for early education, and the launch of a new round of the Early Childhood Longitudinal Study focused on birth

to kindergarten entry, both at the Department of Education. These investments will yield crucial information on children's early life experiences and help determine which models and practices are most effective at improving child outcomes. In addition, the Administration's Native youth initiative, "Generation Indigenous," environmental conservation initiatives, child support reforms, and health proposals are paired with investments in high-quality evaluation. The Budget also reproposes $400 million for the Social Security Administration, in partnership with other Federal agencies, to test innovative strategies to help people with disabilities remain in the workforce. Building on an initial $35 million provided for this purpose in 2015, this proposal will help build the evidence base for future program improvements.

The Budget also supports the expansion of the White House Social and Behavioral Sciences Team (SBST), which is coordinated by the Office of Science and Technology Policy and based at GSA. SBST is already helping over a dozen Federal agencies test the impact of behaviorally-informed interventions on program impact and efficiency using rapid, rigorous, and low-cost randomized control trials. For example, SBST helped the Department of Education to test alternative approaches to informing student loan borrowers about their repayment options. This expansion will allow the team to recruit additional experts and expand services to more agencies. Also, to improve the quality of Federal evaluations and reduce waste from inefficient procurement processes, the Budget provides expanded legislative flexibilities for certain agencies to spend funds over longer periods of time for evaluations and surveys. These flexibilities will allow agencies to better target funds to reflect changing circumstances on the ground.

REORGANIZING GOVERNMENT: REFORMING THE GOVERNMENT TO WIN
IN THE GLOBAL ECONOMY

The President is renewing his request for the Congress to revive the reorganization authority given to nearly every President from Herbert Hoover to Ronald Reagan. This authority would allow the Administration to submit plans to consolidate and reorganize Executive Branch Departments and agencies for fast track consideration by the Congress, but only so long as the result would be to reduce the size of Government or cut costs, a new requirement for this type of authority.

The following represents an ambitious set of cross-Government consolidations intended to serve as a blueprint for reorganizing and reforming the Government. The Administration will continue to work with the Congress and stakeholders to identify opportunities to make the Government more efficient and effective.

Economic Competitiveness

As the President first indicated in 2012, if he is given Presidential reorganization authority, he would propose to consolidate a number of agencies and programs into a new department focused on fostering economic growth and driving job creation. This proposal would consolidate six primary business and trade agencies, as well as other related programs, integrating the Government's core trade and competitiveness functions into one new department. Specifically, the department would include the Department of Commerce's core business and trade functions, SBA, the Office of the U.S. Trade Representative, the Export-Import Bank, the Overseas Private Investment Corporation, and the U.S. Trade and Development Agency.

By bringing together the core tools to expand trade and investment, grow small businesses, and support innovation, the new department would coordinate these resources to maximize the benefits for businesses and the economy. With more effectively aligned and deployed trade promotion resources, strengthened trade enforcement capacity, streamlined export finance programs, and enhanced focus on investment in the United States, the Government could more effectively implement a strong, pro-growth trade policy. This reorganization would also bring together the core tools to help American businesses compete in the global economy, expand exports, and create more jobs at home. Businesses will more easily and seamlessly be able to access services in support of exports, domestic competitiveness, and job creation.

Absent this authority, the Administration has already taken numerous steps to begin streamlining Federal trade, business, and export-related programs. This includes initiatives simplifying the export control system to improve the competitiveness of U.S. businesses while maintaining strong national security protections; encouraging foreign investment into the United States; providing a one-stop online platform consolidating information on business- and export-related programs, resources, and services from across the Federal Government; and improving the ability of private companies to adapt Federal research for use in the marketplace by increasing Government-private sector partnerships and simplifying licensing procedures. Agencies have also begun to reorganize business-related offices and staff to maximize the effectiveness of limited Federal resources and focus on increasing export opportunities for American businesses, particularly small businesses.

Food Safety

While the U.S. food safety system is among the safest in the world, consolidating food safety functions is an essential step to reforming the Federal food safety system overall. More than a dozen agencies are involved in overseeing the safety of the Nation's food supply, implementing at least 30 statutes governing some part of food safety. The Department of Agriculture's (USDA) Food Safety and Inspection Service (FSIS) and food safety-related components of the Food and Drug Administration (FDA) at HHS represent approximately 80 percent of the Nation's total food safety system, and exemplify the fragmented Federal system. While FDA is responsible for most foods, FSIS is responsible for meat and poultry. While FSIS oversees processed egg products, FDA oversees shell eggs. FDA is responsible for seafood, but FSIS is responsible for catfish. FDA and FSIS can each have jurisdiction over the same category of food at different points in the food chain: a cheese pizza and its ingredients are regulated solely by FDA, but both agencies play roles in regulating the components and manufacturing of a pepperoni pizza. FSIS inspects manufacturers of packaged open-face meat or poultry sandwiches, while FDA inspects manufacturers of closed-face meat or poultry sandwiches.

Under FSIS jurisdiction, meat and poultry products must be approved prior to marketing, requiring continuous, visual inspection. In contrast, FDA conducts risk-based inspections to enforce prevention-oriented food safety standards. Fractured oversight and disparate regulatory approaches are confusing. This division of responsibilities was not deliberately designed, but rather evolved as the Congress passed laws to address specific food safety concerns. The Administration has taken the lead on food safety issues. The Administration partnered with the Congress to transform food safety oversight, and the President signed into law the Food Safety Modernization Act (FSMA), which strengthened FDA's mandate to set and enforce modern standards for preventing food safety problems, ensure the safety of imported food, and make more effective, risk-based use of resources. The FSMA provided FDA mandatory recall authority, in addition to a number of new authorities and enforcement tools, to strengthen the ability to swiftly remove contaminated food from the market.

Food safety and the prevention, mitigation, and response to foodborne illness outbreaks are public health concerns, consistent with the larger mission of HHS. The Budget proposes to consolidate the FSIS and the food safety related components of the FDA to create a single new agency within HHS. This new agency would be independent from FDA and have primary responsibility for food safety inspections, enforcement, applied research, and outbreak response and mitigation. The new agency would be charged with pursuing a modern, science-based food safety regulatory regime drawing on best practices of both agencies, with strong enforcement and recall mechanisms, expertise in risk assessment, and enforcement and research efforts across all food types based on scientifically supportable assessments of threats to public health. The agency would also serve as the central point for coordinating with State and local entities and food safety stakeholders.

A single Federal food safety agency would provide focused, centralized leadership, a primary voice on food safety standards and compliance with those standards, and clear lines of responsibility and accountability that will enhance both prevention of and responses to outbreaks of foodborne illnesses. It would rationalize the food safety regulatory regime and allow the Federal Government to better allocate resources and responsibilities.

Science, Technology, Engineering, and Mathematics

The Nation's competitiveness depends on the ability to improve and expand STEM learning in the United States. Over the past two years, the Administration has made considerable progress toward creating a more cohesive framework for delivering STEM education. Guided by the Federal STEM Education Five-Year Strategic Plan and a significant reorganization of programs, agencies are increasing coordination, strengthening partnerships, and identifying ways to leverage existing resources to improve the reach of agency assets. The number of different STEM programs has been cut from over 220 to just under 140. The Budget builds on these efforts and continues to reduce fragmentation, ensuring that investments are aligned with the Strategic Plan and support effective programs with strategic approaches to evaluation. The Budget invests $3 billion in 113 programs including $200 million for K-12 education in the Department of Education's

Math and Science Partnerships, $338 million for graduate fellowships, $62 million for graduate traineeships, and $135 million for improving undergraduate education at the NSF.

Reforming the Tennessee Valley Authority

Since its creation in the 1930s during the Great Depression, the federally-owned and operated Tennessee Valley Authority (TVA) has been producing electricity and managing natural resources for a large portion of the Southeastern United States. TVA's power service territory includes most of Tennessee and parts of Alabama, Georgia, Kentucky, Mississippi, North Carolina, and Virginia, covering 80,000 square miles and serving more than nine million people. TVA is a self-financing Government corporation, funding operations through electricity sales and bond financing. Since the Administration announced in the 2014 President's Budget its intentions to undertake a strategic review of options for addressing TVA's financial situation, the agency has taken significant steps to improve its operating and financial performance and has committed to resolve its capital financing constraints. The Administration supports TVA's ongoing initiatives and will continue to monitor TVA's performance, including the achievement of critical milestones contemplated in TVA's long-term financial plan and the pursuit of efforts to enhance governance and increase transparency of TVA's decision-making on important agency actions. While the strategic review of TVA has concluded, the Administration continues to believe that reducing or eliminating the Federal Government's role in programs such as TVA, which have achieved their original objectives, can help mitigate risk to taxpayers.

Other Actions

In addition to the high-profile reforms described above, the Budget highlights a wide va-riety of agency-level reforms and reorganizations designed to drive efficiency and accountability across Government. For instance, the Budget includes $200 million for GSA's Consolidation Activities program to fund small projects that save money by reducing or economizing space (as discussed earlier in this chapter), and $15 million for DOE's Federal Energy Efficiency Fund, which leverages Federal capital investments to increase renewable energy use and decrease energy consumption across the Federal Government. As in previous years, the Budget proposes the National Preparedness Grant Program, which would strengthen and consolidate the Federal Emergency Management Agency's current fragmented preparedness grants into a streamlined program that emphasizes collaboration and reduces the burden on State, local, and tribal partners. The Budget proposes reforms to the Senior Community Service Employment Program to better target the program to those most in need, promote long-term unsubsidized employment for program participants in the private sector, and drive improved performance outcomes through competition. The Department of Homeland Security again proposes to transfer the Emergency Food and Shelter Program to HUD, reducing fragmentation and synchronizing efforts to reduce homelessness. The Department of Defense continues to pursue efficiencies, including a 20-percent reduction to management and headquarters staff, divestiture of legacy platforms no longer required to execute the defense strategy, and ongoing efforts to shutter unneeded facilities, including administrative actions and requested legislative authority for another round of Base Realignment and Closure. Taken together with the larger-scale reorganization proposals, these efforts represent the President's ongoing commitment to promoting Government efficiency, preventing duplication, and making Government work better and smarter for the American people.

CUTS, CONSOLIDATIONS, AND SAVINGS

As part of the President's Management Agenda, the Administration will continue to build upon successful efforts to maximize the value of every taxpayer dollar by enhancing productivity and efficiency and achieving cost savings across the Government.

Consistent with the Management Agenda, the Budget continues efforts such as reducing administrative overhead, increasing the use of shared services, increasing strategic sourcing and category management, cutting improper payments, saving on real estate costs, reforming military acquisition, and consolidating data centers.

The Budget also continues efforts to reorganize and consolidate Federal programs to reduce duplication and improve efficiency. The President is renewing his request for the Congress to revive the reorganization authority given to nearly every President from Herbert Hoover to Ronald Reagan. In effect, the President is asking to have the same authority that any business owner has to reorganize or streamline operations to meet changing circumstances and customer demand. The Budget outlines a set of ambitious cross-Government consolidations intended to serve as a blueprint for reorganizing and reforming Government, including consolidating the six primary business and trade agencies into a single agency responsible for fostering economic growth; combining the two largest food-safety related agencies into a single agency responsible for inspections, enforcement, and outbreak prevention; and continuing efforts to streamline science, technology, engineering, and mathematics (STEM) programs across Government.

Further detail on all of these initiatives is provided in the chapter titled A Government of the Future.

The Budget also continues to target unnecessary or lower priority programs for reduction or elimination. In the President's first six Budgets, the Administration identified, on average, more than 150 cuts, consolidations, and savings averaging more than $23 billion each year. Many of these proposals have now been implemented, and the Budget builds on this success by including 101 cuts, consolidations, and savings proposals projected to save over $14 billion in 2016. While the Budget proposes increases in discretionary budget caps to make room for a range of domestic and security investments, it still includes discretionary cuts, consolidations, and savings proposals totaling $3.6 billion to further make room for investments to help move the Nation forward. Savings from mandatory and program integrity proposals total $10.6 billion in 2016 and $609 billion over 10 years; about 70 percent of these savings are from health reform proposals. The Budget shows that we can avoid the harmful spending cuts known as sequestration, and instead invest in economic growth, mobility, and national security, while still putting the Nation on a sustainable fiscal path. Overall the Budget achieves about $1.8 trillion in deficit reduction, primarily from reforms in health programs, the tax code, and immigration.

Discretionary and mandatory cuts, consolidations, and savings proposals in this year's Budget are detailed on the following tables. Savings from the Administration's program integrity proposals, totaling $110 billion through 2025, are detailed in the Budget Process chapter of the *Analytical Perspectives* volume.

Discretionary Cuts, Consolidations, and Savings
(Budget authority in millions of dollars)

	2015	2016	2016 Change from 2015
Cuts			
317 Immunization Program, Department of Health and Human Services	611	561	−50
Access to Recovery, Department of Health and Human Services	38	....	−38
Area Health Education Centers, Department of Health and Human Services	30	....	−30
Beach Grants, Environmental Protection Agency	10	....	−10
Centers for Disease Control and Prevention, Direct Healthcare Screenings, Department of Health and Human Services	263	209	−55
Clean Water and Drinking Water State Revolving Funds (SRFs), Environmental Protection Agency	2,356	2,302	−54
Community Development Block Grant - Formula Funds, Department of Housing and Urban Development	3,000	2,800	−200
Community Economic Development Program, Department of Health and Human Services[1]	30	....	−30
Diesel Emissions Reduction Grant Program, Environmental Protection Agency[1]	30	10	−20
Divestiture of the A–10 Fleet, Department of Defense	810	428	−382
Economic Impact Grants, Department of Agriculture[1]	10	....	−10
Education Research Centers and Agricultural Research, Department of Health and Human Services[1]	51	....	−51
Federal Prisoner Detention, Department of Justice[1]	1,407	1,384	−23
Foreign Military Financing, Department of State	5,881	5,807	−74
Global Fund to Fight AIDS, Tuberculosis, and Malaria, Department of State	1,350	1,107	−244
Grants for Abstinence-Only Programs, Department of Health and Human Services	5	....	−5
Grants-In-Aid for Airports, Department of Transportation[1]	3,350	2,900	−450
Great Lakes Restoration Initiative, Environmental Protection Agency	300	250	−50
Harry S. Truman Scholarship Foundation	1	....	−1
Health Care Services Grant Program, Department of Agriculture[1]	3	....	−3
Health Information Technology Research, Department of Health and Human Services	28	23	−5
High Energy Cost Grants, Department of Agriculture[1]	10	....	−10
High Intensity Drug Trafficking Areas, Office of National Drug Control Policy[1]	245	193	−52
Impact Aid - Payments for Federal Property, Department of Education[1]	67	....	−67
Innovative Approaches to Literacy (in Funds for the Improvement of Education Programs of National Significance), Department of Education[1]	25	....	−25
International Forestry, Department of Agriculture[1]	8	4	−4
International Narcotics Control and Law Enforcement, Department of State	1,296	1,194	−102
Joint Standoff Weapon (JSOW), Department of Defense	108	21	−87
Low Priority Studies and Construction, Corps of Engineers	1,762	1,269	−493
Mutual Self-Help Housing Grants, Department of Agriculture	25	10	−15
National Heritage Areas, Department of the Interior[1]	20	11	−9
National Wildlife Refuge Fund, Department of the Interior[1]	13	....	−13
Operation and Maintenance Work, Corps of Engineers	2,909	2,710	−199
Preventive Health and Health Services Block Grant, Department of Health and Human Services[1]	160	....	−160
PRIME Technical Assistance, Small Business Administration[1]	5	....	−5
REACH, Department of Health and Human Services	51	....	−51
Research, Education and Extension Grants, Department of Agriculture:			
Animal Health (Sec. 1433)[1]	4	....	−4
Capacity Building: Non-Land Grant Colleges[1]	5	....	−5
Farm Business Management and Benchmarking[1]	1	....	−1
Food Animal Residue Avoidance Database[1]	1	....	−1
Methyl Bromide Transition Program[1]	2	....	−2
Potato Breeding Research (Competitive)[1]	1	....	−1
Rural Health and Safety[1]	2	....	−2
Sungrants[1]	3	....	−3
Supplemental and Alternative Crops[1]	1	....	−1
Rural Access to Emergency Devices, Department of Health and Human Services	5	....	−5

Discretionary Cuts, Consolidations, and Savings—Continued

(Budget authority in millions of dollars)

	2015	2016	2016 Change from 2015
Rural Community Facilities, Department of Health and Human Services[1]	7	....	−7
Rural Hospital Flexibility Grant Programs, Department of Health and Human Services	42	26	−16
Rural Multifamily Housing Preservation Grants, Department of Agriculture[1]	4	....	−4
State Criminal Alien Assistance Program, Department of Justice	185	....	−185
State Indoor Radon Grant Program, Environmental Protection Agency	9	....	−9
Targeted Airshed Grants, Environmental Protection Agency	10	....	−10
Urban and Community Forestry, Department of Agriculture	28	24	−4
Water and Wastewater and Community Facilities Loan Guarantees, Department of Agriculture[1]	4	....	−4
Water Quality Research and Support Grants, Environmental Protection Agency[1]	17	....	−17
Women in Apprenticeship in Non-Traditional Occupations, Department of Labor[1]	1	....	−1
Total, Discretionary Cuts	**26,600**	**23,242**	**−3,358**
Consolidations			
National Preparedness Grant Program (NPGP), Department of Homeland Security	1,266	1,043	−223
Science, Technology, Engineering, and Mathematics (STEM) Reorganization, Multi-Agency			
Consolidated and Eliminated Programs Total - 20 Programs			
Department of Agriculture - 4 Programs	*[11]*	....	
Department of Commerce - 6 Programs	*[14]*	....	
Department of Defense - 1 Program	*[25]*	....	
Department of Energy - 2 Programs	*[5]*	....	
Department of Health and Human Services - 2 Programs	*[15]*	....	
Environmental Protection Agency - 2 Programs	*[11]*	....	
National Science Foundation - 1 Program	*[6]*	....	
Nuclear Regulatory Commission - 2 Programs	*[15]*	....	
Section 4 and Rural Capacity Building, Department of Housing and Urban Development	40	20	−20
Teacher and Principal Pathways, Department of Education	....	[139]	
Transition to Teaching	*[14]*	....	
School Leadership	*[16]*	....	
Teacher Quality Partnerships	*[41]*	....	
Total, Discretionary Consolidations	**1,306**	**1,063**	**−243**
Savings			
Office of National Drug Control Policy, Executive Office of the President	23	20	−3
Senate Campaign Finance Reports Electronic Submission, Federal Election Commission	....	....	....
Total, Discretionary Savings	**23**	**20**	**−3**
Total, Discretionary Cuts, Consolidations, and Savings	**27,929**	**24,325**	**−3,604**

[1] This cut has been identified as a lower priority program activity for purposes of the GPRA Modernization Act, at 31 U.S.C. 1115(b)(10). Additional information regarding this proposed cut is included in the respective agency's Congressional Justification submission, where applicable.

Mandatory Cuts and Savings
(Outlays and receipts in millions of dollars)

	2016	2017	2018	2019	2020	2016–2020	2016–2025
Cuts							
Coal Tax Preferences, Department of Energy							
Domestic Manufacturing Deduction for Hard Mineral Fossil Fuels[1]	−45	−48	−50	−53	−54	−250	−561
Expensing of Exploration and Development Costs[1]	−40	−68	−70	−74	−77	−329	−694
Percent Depletion for Hard Mineral Fossil Fuels[1]	−183	−299	−288	−278	−266	−1,314	−2,450
Royalty Taxation[1]	−27	−54	−53	−54	−55	−243	−547
Crop Insurance Program, Department of Agriculture	−1,129	−1,374	−1,560	−1,614	−1,650	−7,327	−15,999
Geothermal Payments to Counties, Department of the Interior[2]	−4	−4	−4	−5	−5	−22	−47
Gulf of Mexico Energy Security Act (GOMESA) Payments to States, Department of the Interior[2]	....	....	−367	−375	−376	−1,118	−3,069
Oil and Gas Company Tax Preferences, Department of Energy							
Increase Geological and Geophysical Amortization Period for Independent Producers to Seven Years[1]	−91	−341	−537	−532	−440	−1,941	−2,876
Repeal Credit for Oil and Gas Produced from Marginal Wells[1]	....	....	....	....	....	....	....
Repeal Deduction for Tertiary Injectants[1]	−7	−10	−10	−10	−10	−47	−97
Repeal Domestic Manufacturing Tax Deduction for Oil and Natural Gas Companies[1]	−647	−1,115	−1,139	−1,173	−1,208	−5,282	−11,904
Repeal Enhanced Oil Recovery Credit[1]	....	....	....	....	....	....	....
Repeal Exception to Passive Loss Limitations for Working Interests in Oil and Natural Gas Properties[1]	−9	−17	−19	−20	−20	−85	−185
Repeal Expensing of Intangible Drilling Costs[1]	−2,267	−3,182	−2,351	−1,867	−1,566	−11,233	−15,495
Repeal Percentage Depletion for Oil and Natural Gas Wells[1]	−1,118	−1,790	−1,669	−1,585	−1,498	−7,660	−13,253
Offset Disability Benefits for Period of Concurrent Unemployment Insurance Receipt[2]	....	−35	−172	−253	−252	−712	−2,019
Unrestricted Abandoned Mine Lands Payments, Department of the Interior[2]	−48	−35	−28	−34	−36	−181	−295
Total, Mandatory Cuts	**−5,615**	**−8,372**	**−8,317**	**−7,927**	**−7,513**	**−37,744**	**−69,491**
Savings							
FECA Reform, Department of Labor	−19	−9	−14	−21	−29	−92	−336
Federal Employee Health Benefits Program Reforms, Office of Personnel Management	....	−57	−139	−187	−238	−621	−2,987
Health Care (Medicaid Proposals), Department of Health and Human Services	−582	−857	−917	−962	−1,012	−4,328	−13,895
Health Care (Pharmaceuticals), Department of Health and Human Services[3]	−810	−840	−1,020	−1,350	−1,630	−5,650	−16,040
Medicare Provider Payment Modifications, Department of Health and Human Services[3, 4]	−3,640	−12,420	−22,460	−28,000	−35,170	−101,690	−396,959
Total, Mandatory Savings	**−5,051**	**−14,183**	**−24,550**	**−30,520**	**−38,079**	**−112,381**	**−430,217**
Total, Mandatory Cuts and Savings	**−10,666**	**−22,555**	**−32,867**	**−38,447**	**−45,592**	**−150,125**	**−499,708**

[1] This cut has been identified as a lower priority program activity for purposes of the GPRA Modernization Act, at 31 U.S.C. 1115(b)(10). Additional information regarding this proposed cut is included in the Governmental Receipts chapter of the Analytical Perspectives volume.

[2] This cut has been identified as a lower priority program activity for purposes of the GPRA Modernization Act, at 31 U.S.C. 1115(b)(10). Additional information regarding this proposed cut is included in the respective agency's Congressional Justification submission, where applicable.

[3] Medicare savings estimates do not include interactions.

[4] In addition to the savings reported on this table, the Budget includes investments to reform Medicare physician payments and improve access to inpatient psychiatric facility services, as well as an additional $83.8 billion in 10-year savings for Medicare Structural Reforms, as detailed on table S–9.

SUMMARY TABLES

Table S–1. Budget Totals

(In billions of dollars and as a percent of GDP)

	2014	2015	2016	2017	2018	2019	2020	2021	2022	2023	2024	2025	Totals 2016-2020	Totals 2016-2025
Budget Totals in Billions of Dollars:														
Receipts	3,021	3,176	3,525	3,755	3,944	4,135	4,332	4,525	4,746	4,986	5,236	5,478	19,692	44,664
Outlays	3,506	3,759	3,999	4,218	4,423	4,653	4,886	5,126	5,372	5,621	5,875	6,165	22,180	50,338
Deficit	485	583	474	463	479	518	554	600	626	635	639	687	2,488	5,674
Debt held by the public	12,780	13,506	14,108	14,705	15,315	15,959	16,635	17,349	18,085	18,830	19,577	20,371		
Debt net of financial assets	11,455	12,038	12,512	12,974	13,453	13,970	14,524	15,124	15,749	16,384	17,022	17,709		
Gross domestic product (GDP)	17,244	17,985	18,819	19,709	20,617	21,540	22,476	23,454	24,474	25,539	26,649	27,808		
Budget Totals as a Percent of GDP:														
Receipts	17.5%	17.7%	18.7%	19.1%	19.1%	19.2%	19.3%	19.3%	19.4%	19.5%	19.6%	19.7%	19.1%	19.3%
Outlays	20.3%	20.9%	21.3%	21.4%	21.5%	21.6%	21.7%	21.9%	21.9%	22.0%	22.0%	22.2%	21.5%	21.7%
Deficit	2.8%	3.2%	2.5%	2.3%	2.3%	2.4%	2.5%	2.6%	2.6%	2.5%	2.4%	2.5%	2.4%	2.5%
Debt held by the public	74.1%	75.1%	75.0%	74.6%	74.3%	74.1%	74.0%	74.0%	73.9%	73.7%	73.5%	73.3%		
Debt net of financial assets	66.4%	66.9%	66.5%	65.8%	65.3%	64.9%	64.6%	64.5%	64.4%	64.2%	63.9%	63.7%		

Table S–2. Effect of Budget Proposals on Projected Deficits

(Deficit increases (+) or decreases (–) in billions of dollars)

	2015	2016	2017	2018	2019	2020	2021	2022	2023	2024	2025	Totals 2016–2020	Totals 2016–2025
Projected deficits in the adjusted baseline[1]	578	535	547	556	666	739	785	947	973	981	1,151	3,044	7,880
Percent of GDP	3.2%	2.8%	2.8%	2.7%	3.1%	3.3%	3.3%	3.9%	3.8%	3.7%	4.1%	2.9%	3.4%
Proposals in the 2016 Budget:[2]													
Tax reforms and investments to support working families:													
Middle-class and pro-work tax reforms	3	10	26	28	28	28	29	31	31	32	33	120	277
Child care for all low- and moderate-income families with young children		3	4	5	6	7	8	9	11	12	14	24	78
Partner with States to provide tuition-free quality community college		*	1	2	3	5	6	8	9	12	13	12	60
Capital gains tax reform	–4	–9	–21	–18	–21	–22	–22	–22	–23	–24	–25	–91	–208
Financial fee		–6	–11	–11	–11	–11	–12	–12	–12	–13	–13	–50	–112
Proposals to address high-income tax avoidance[3]		–6	–8	–9	–9	–10	–10	–11	–12	–13	–12	–42	–101
Debt service	–*	–*	–*	–1	–1	–1	–1	–1	–1	–1	–1	–3	–8
Total, tax reforms and investments to support working families	–1	–8	–9	–4	–6	–4	–1	1	3	6	10	–31	–13
Additional investments in growing the economy and creating opportunity:													
Surface transportation reauthorization		3	10	15	17	18	19	16	10	6	4	61	116
Transition revenue from business tax reform[4]		–35	–56	–54	–52	–50	–20	....	....	....	....	–248	–268
Investments in early education and children's health[5]		*	5	8	10	8	10	11	12	12	11	31	88
Tobacco tax financing		–8	–11	–11	–11	–10	–10	–9	–9	–8	–8	–51	–95
Additional investments in education, innovation, infrastructure, and security	–1	37	54	56	56	48	40	–20	–47	–59	–68	252	96
Additional mandatory and tax proposals	1	–30	–12	15	–28	–33	–38	–93	–46	–2	–53	–89	–322
Debt service	*	–*	–1	–1	–1	–1	–2	–4	–7	–10	–13	–4	–39
Total, additional investments	*	–33	–12	28	–9	–22	–1	–100	–88	–62	–127	–48	–425
Additional deficit reduction from health, tax, and immigration reform:													
Health savings[6]	5	6	–6	–17	–26	–35	–45	–54	–64	–75	–86	–78	–402
Reforms to high-income tax expenditures[7]		–35	–46	–52	–58	–63	–68	–72	–77	–82	–86	–253	–638
Immigration reform		6	–1	–10	–15	–17	–18	–20	–23	–29	–31	–37	–158
Debt service	*	–*	–1	–3	–7	–11	–16	–22	–29	–37	–46	–22	–173
Total, additional deficit reduction	5	–23	–54	–82	–106	–127	–147	–169	–193	–223	–249	–391	–1,371
Subtotal, tax reforms, investments, and additional deficit reduction	4	–63	–75	–58	–121	–152	–149	–268	–278	–278	–367	–470	–1,809
Other changes to deficits:													
Reductions in Overseas Contingency Operations	–*	–11	–29	–41	–48	–51	–53	–71	–81	–85	–87	–180	–557
Replacement of mandatory sequestration		11	18	18	19	20	21	21	27	29	1	86	185

Table S–2. Effect of Budget Proposals on Projected Deficits—Continued

(Deficit increases (+) or decreases (−) in billions of dollars)

	2015	2016	2017	2018	2019	2020	2021	2022	2023	2024	2025	Totals 2016–2020	Totals 2016–2025
Proposed Budget Control Act cap adjustment for disaster relief and wildfires	*	2	3	3	3	3	1	1	1	1	1	12	18
Debt service and indirect interest effects	*	*	–*	–1	–1	–2	–4	–5	–7	–10	–13	–4	–43
Total, other changes to deficits	*	3	–9	–20	–28	–33	–35	–54	–60	–65	–97	–86	–397
Total proposals in the 2016 Budget	4	–61	–84	–77	–148	–185	–184	–321	–338	–343	–464	–556	–2,206
Resulting deficits in 2016 Budget	583	474	463	479	518	554	600	626	635	639	687	2,488	5,674
Percent of GDP	3.2%	2.5%	2.3%	2.3%	2.4%	2.5%	2.6%	2.6%	2.5%	2.4%	2.5%	2.4%	2.5%
Memorandum:													
Debt held by the public in the adjusted baseline	13,502	14,159	14,828	15,505	16,286	17,134	18,018	19,066	20,140	21,216	22,459		
Percent of GDP	75.1%	75.2%	75.2%	75.2%	75.6%	76.2%	76.8%	77.9%	78.9%	79.6%	80.8%		
Debt held by the public in the 2016 Budget	13,506	14,108	14,705	15,315	15,959	16,635	17,349	18,085	18,830	19,577	20,371		
Percent of GDP	75.1%	75.0%	74.6%	74.3%	74.1%	74.0%	74.0%	73.9%	73.7%	73.5%	73.3%		

* $500 million or less.

[1] See Tables S–4 and S–7 for information on the adjusted baseline.

[2] For total deficit reduction since January 2011, see Table S–3.

[3] Includes proposals to limit the total accrual of tax-favored retirement benefits and conform SECA taxes for professional service businesses.

[4] Business tax reform transition revenue finances the $126.5 billion in budget authority for new surface transportation investments (the PAYGO portion of the reauthorization proposal) plus $111.9 billion of cash transfers necessary to ensure Transportation Trust Fund solvency for all programs proposed to be funded via the Transportation Trust Fund over the six-year reauthorization period, leaving an additional $29.7 billion for deficit reduction.

[5] Includes proposals to support Preschool for All, extend the Maternal, Infant, and Early Childhood Home Visiting program, and extend CHIP funding through 2019.

[6] Includes all HHS health savings and OPM FEHBP savings.

[7] Includes proposals to reduce the value of certain tax expenditures and implement the Buffett Rule by imposing a new "Fair Share Tax."

Table S–3. Cumulative Deficit Reduction

(Deficit reduction (–) or increase (+) in billions of dollars)

	2016–2025
Deficit reduction achieved through January 2015, excluding Overseas Contingency Operations (OCO):	
Enacted deficit reduction excluding pending Joint Committee enforcement:	
Discretionary savings [1]	–1,634
Mandatory savings	–97
Revenues	–776
Debt service	–848
Subtotal, enacted deficit reduction excluding pending Joint Committee enforcement	–3,355
Pending Joint Committee enforcement: [2]	
Discretionary cap reductions	–532
Mandatory sequestration	–185
Debt service	–172
Subtotal, pending Joint Committee enforcement	–888
Total, deficit reduction achieved, excluding OCO	–4,243
Tax reforms and investments to support working families:	
Tax reform and investment proposals [3]	–5
Debt service	–8
Total, tax reforms and investments to support working families	–13
Additional investments in growing the economy and creating opportunity:	
Investment proposals and offsets [4]	–386
Debt service	–39
Total, additional investments	–425
Additional deficit reduction from health, tax, and immigration reform:	
Health savings	–402
Reforms to high-income tax expenditures	–638
Immigration reform	–158
Debt service	–173
Total, additional deficit reduction	–1,371
Subtotal, tax reforms, investments, and additional deficit reduction	**–1,809**
Other changes to deficits: [1]	
Replacement of mandatory sequestration	185
Proposed Budget Control Act cap adjustment for disaster relief and wildfires	18
Debt service and indirect interest effects	41
Total, other changes to deficits	244
Grand total, achieved and proposed deficit reduction excluding OCO	**–5,808**

Table S–3. Cumulative Deficit Reduction—Continued

(Deficit reduction (–) or increase (+) in billions of dollars)

	2016–2025
Memorandum, revenue and outlay effects of achieved and proposed deficit reduction:	
Enacted outlay reductions and 2016 Budget spending proposals	–3,438
Enacted receipt increases and 2016 Budget tax proposals	–2,212
Immigration reform	–158
Memorandum, savings in Overseas Contingency Operations (OCO):	
Enacted reduction in OCO funding	–1,016
Proposed reductions in OCO	–557
Debt service	–354
Total, savings in overseas contingency operations (OCO)	–1,927

[1] Excludes savings from reductions in OCO.
[2] Consists of mandatory sequestration for 2016–2024 and discretionary cap reductions for 2016–2021.
[3] See Table S–2 for details on tax reform and investment proposals.
[4] See Table S–2 for details on additional investment proposals.

Table S–4. Adjusted Baseline by Category [1]

(In billions of dollars)

	2014	2015	2016	2017	2018	2019	2020	2021	2022	2023	2024	2025	Totals 2016-2020	Totals 2016-2025
Outlays:														
Appropriated ("discretionary") programs:														
Defense	596	589	631	659	665	673	687	699	717	734	752	770	3,315	6,987
Non-defense	525	558	563	568	569	576	585	595	607	621	635	650	2,860	5,968
Subtotal, appropriated programs	1,121	1,147	1,194	1,227	1,234	1,248	1,271	1,293	1,324	1,355	1,388	1,420	6,174	12,955
Mandatory programs:														
Social Security	845	891	938	991	1,051	1,116	1,184	1,253	1,325	1,402	1,483	1,569	5,280	12,312
Medicare	505	529	585	596	608	675	727	782	875	906	934	1,038	3,190	7,725
Medicaid	301	329	344	364	382	403	423	447	473	501	531	567	1,916	4,434
Other mandatory programs	504	627	680	672	690	739	767	797	843	845	848	899	3,549	7,781
Subtotal, mandatory programs	2,156	2,375	2,548	2,623	2,730	2,932	3,101	3,278	3,516	3,654	3,797	4,073	13,934	32,252
Net interest	229	229	283	364	429	493	560	619	681	744	801	857	2,129	5,832
Adjustments for disaster costs [2]	....	2	6	8	8	9	9	10	10	10	10	10	40	90
Joint Committee enforcement [3]	....	....	–67	–97	–103	–106	–107	–108	–55	–38	–33	–3	–479	–716
Total outlays	3,506	3,753	3,964	4,124	4,299	4,577	4,834	5,093	5,477	5,725	5,963	6,357	21,798	50,412
Receipts:														
Individual income taxes	1,395	1,477	1,610	1,707	1,814	1,915	2,026	2,146	2,271	2,400	2,529	2,661	9,072	21,078
Corporation income taxes	321	342	433	434	441	448	455	466	481	496	510	521	2,212	4,686
Social insurance and retirement receipts:														
Social Security payroll taxes	736	766	797	839	880	920	958	1,010	1,060	1,107	1,159	1,208	4,395	9,939
Medicare payroll taxes	224	234	244	257	270	284	295	311	326	341	357	372	1,351	3,058
Unemployment insurance	55	56	55	54	53	50	51	52	53	57	57	58	262	539
Other retirement	9	9	9	10	11	11	11	12	13	13	14	15	53	119
Excise taxes	93	96	100	105	107	109	112	115	118	121	125	129	533	1,141
Estate and gift taxes	19	20	21	23	24	26	27	29	30	32	34	36	121	283
Customs duties	34	37	39	42	45	48	50	53	56	58	62	65	224	517
Deposits of earnings, Federal Reserve System	99	94	77	48	39	41	46	52	56	61	65	68	251	553
Other miscellaneous receipts	37	45	43	59	58	60	63	63	65	67	70	72	282	619
Total receipts	3,021	3,175	3,430	3,577	3,743	3,910	4,094	4,308	4,530	4,753	4,981	5,206	18,755	42,532
Deficit	**485**	**578**	**535**	**547**	**556**	**666**	**739**	**785**	**947**	**973**	**981**	**1,151**	**3,044**	**7,880**
Net interest	229	229	283	364	429	493	560	619	681	744	801	857	2,129	5,832
Primary deficit	**256**	**349**	**251**	**183**	**127**	**173**	**180**	**165**	**266**	**229**	**180**	**294**	**915**	**2,049**
On-budget deficit	514	590	532	535	527	617	662	692	833	829	809	943	2,872	6,978
Off-budget deficit / surplus (–)	–30	–12	3	12	30	49	78	93	114	144	173	208	171	902

Table S–4. Adjusted Baseline by Category[1]—Continued

(In billions of dollars)

	2014	2015	2016	2017	2018	2019	2020	2021	2022	2023	2024	2025	Totals 2016-2020	Totals 2016-2025
Memorandum, budget authority for appropriated programs:[4]														
Defense	606	586	642	657	671	686	701	716	734	752	770	789	3,357	7,117
Non-defense	523	529	537	547	559	572	584	596	611	626	641	657	2,798	5,930
Total, appropriated funding	1,129	1,115	1,179	1,203	1,230	1,257	1,285	1,313	1,345	1,377	1,411	1,446	6,155	13,046

[1] See Table S-7 for information on adjustments to the Balanced Budget and Emergency Deficit Control Act (BBEDCA) baseline.
[2] These amounts represent a placeholder for major disasters requiring Federal assistance for relief and reconstruction. Such assistance might be provided in the form of discretionary or mandatory outlays or tax relief. These amounts are included as outlays for convenience.
[3] Consists of mandatory sequestration for 2016-2024 and discretionary cap reductions for 2016-2021.
[4] Excludes discretionary cap reductions for Joint Committee enforcement.

Table S–5. Proposed Budget by Category

(In billions of dollars)

	2014	2015	2016	2017	2018	2019	2020	2021	2022	2023	2024	2025	Totals 2016-2020	Totals 2016-2025
Outlays:														
Appropriated ("discretionary") programs:														
Defense	596	589	605	594	582	581	588	595	608	621	633	646	2,951	6,053
Non-defense	525	558	563	581	586	592	594	599	594	597	608	619	2,916	5,933
Subtotal, appropriated programs	1,121	1,146	1,168	1,175	1,169	1,172	1,182	1,194	1,202	1,218	1,241	1,265	5,867	11,986
Mandatory programs:														
Social Security	845	891	938	992	1,051	1,115	1,182	1,251	1,323	1,400	1,481	1,566	5,278	12,298
Medicare	505	530	583	584	585	645	689	735	820	842	857	954	3,086	7,294
Medicaid	301	333	351	364	382	404	427	450	476	504	534	567	1,928	4,459
Other mandatory programs	504	628	662	723	785	800	825	860	858	907	959	962	3,796	8,342
Allowance for immigration reform	....	....	8	11	18	24	28	29	35	41	48	56	89	298
Subtotal, mandatory programs	2,156	2,381	2,543	2,674	2,822	2,988	3,151	3,325	3,511	3,693	3,879	4,105	14,177	32,691
Net interest	229	229	283	361	424	483	544	597	649	700	744	785	2,096	5,571
Adjustments for disaster costs[1]	....	2	6	8	8	9	9	10	10	10	10	10	40	90
Total outlays	3,506	3,759	3,999	4,218	4,423	4,653	4,886	5,126	5,372	5,621	5,875	6,165	22,180	50,338
Receipts:														
Individual income taxes	1,395	1,478	1,646	1,770	1,887	2,000	2,118	2,244	2,374	2,508	2,643	2,781	9,421	21,972
Corporation income taxes	321	342	473	500	503	507	513	493	490	505	519	530	2,496	5,033
Social insurance and retirement receipts:														
Social Security payroll taxes	736	766	801	844	885	926	964	1,017	1,067	1,114	1,166	1,215	4,420	9,999
Medicare payroll taxes	224	234	245	259	273	287	298	314	330	345	361	376	1,362	3,088
Unemployment insurance	55	56	56	60	60	57	58	59	64	66	68	70	291	619
Other retirement	9	9	9	10	11	11	11	12	13	13	14	15	53	119
Excise taxes	93	96	112	120	122	124	126	129	131	134	137	141	605	1,278
Estate and gift taxes	19	20	21	30	33	36	39	42	46	49	54	59	159	409
Customs duties	34	37	38	42	45	47	50	52	55	58	61	64	222	514
Deposits of earnings, Federal Reserve System	99	94	77	48	39	41	46	52	56	61	65	68	251	553
Other miscellaneous receipts	37	45	43	59	59	60	63	64	66	68	70	72	285	625
Allowance for immigration reform	....	....	2	12	28	39	45	47	55	64	77	87	126	456
Total receipts	3,021	3,176	3,525	3,755	3,944	4,135	4,332	4,525	4,746	4,986	5,236	5,478	19,692	44,664
Deficit	**485**	**583**	**474**	**463**	**479**	**518**	**554**	**600**	**626**	**635**	**639**	**687**	**2,488**	**5,674**
Net interest	229	229	283	361	424	483	544	597	649	700	744	785	2,096	5,571
Primary deficit / surplus (–)	**256**	**353**	**191**	**102**	**55**	**34**	**10**	**4**	**-23**	**-65**	**-106**	**-99**	**392**	**103**
On-budget deficit	514	595	477	454	453	475	484	516	521	501	476	488	2,342	4,844
Off-budget deficit / surplus (–)	-30	-13	-3	9	26	43	70	84	105	134	162	199	146	830

Table S–5. Proposed Budget by Category—Continued

(In billions of dollars)

	2014	2015	2016	2017	2018	2019	2020	2021	2022	2023	2024	2025	Totals 2016-2020	Totals 2016-2025
Memorandum, budget authority for appropriated programs:														
Defense	606	586	612	573	584	592	598	610	622	635	648	661	2,959	6,135
Non-defense	523	528	543	565	575	584	590	601	586	599	612	625	2,856	5,878
Total, appropriated funding	1,129	1,114	1,155	1,138	1,159	1,176	1,188	1,211	1,208	1,234	1,260	1,286	5,815	12,013

[1] These amounts represent a placeholder for major disasters requiring Federal assistance for relief and reconstruction. Such assistance might be provided in the form of discretionary or mandatory outlays or tax relief. These amounts are included as outlays for convenience.

Table S–6. Proposed Budget by Category as a Percent of GDP

(As a percent of GDP)

	2014	2015	2016	2017	2018	2019	2020	2021	2022	2023	2024	2025	Averages 2016-2020	Averages 2016-2025
Outlays:														
Appropriated ("discretionary") programs:														
Defense	3.5	3.3	3.2	3.0	2.8	2.7	2.6	2.5	2.5	2.4	2.4	2.3	2.9	2.7
Non-defense	3.0	3.1	3.0	2.9	2.8	2.7	2.6	2.6	2.4	2.3	2.3	2.2	2.8	2.6
Subtotal, appropriated programs	6.5	6.4	6.2	6.0	5.7	5.4	5.3	5.1	4.9	4.8	4.7	4.5	5.7	5.3
Mandatory programs:														
Social Security	4.9	5.0	5.0	5.0	5.1	5.2	5.3	5.3	5.4	5.5	5.6	5.6	5.1	5.3
Medicare	2.9	2.9	3.1	3.0	2.8	3.0	3.1	3.1	3.3	3.3	3.2	3.4	3.0	3.1
Medicaid	1.7	1.9	1.9	1.8	1.9	1.9	1.9	1.9	1.9	2.0	2.0	2.0	1.9	1.9
Other mandatory programs	2.9	3.5	3.5	3.7	3.8	3.7	3.7	3.7	3.5	3.6	3.6	3.5	3.7	3.6
Allowance for immigration reform	....	*	*	0.1	0.1	0.1	0.1	0.1	0.1	0.2	0.2	0.2	0.1	0.1
Subtotal, mandatory programs	12.5	13.2	13.5	13.6	13.7	13.9	14.0	14.2	14.3	14.5	14.6	14.8	13.7	14.1
Net interest	1.3	1.3	1.5	1.8	2.1	2.2	2.4	2.5	2.7	2.7	2.8	2.8	2.0	2.4
Adjustments for disaster costs[1]	....	*	*	*	*	*	*	*	*	*	*	*	*	*
Total outlays	20.3	20.9	21.3	21.4	21.5	21.6	21.7	21.9	21.9	22.0	22.0	22.2	21.5	21.7
Receipts:														
Individual income taxes	8.1	8.2	8.7	9.0	9.2	9.3	9.4	9.6	9.7	9.8	9.9	10.0	9.1	9.5
Corporation income taxes	1.9	1.9	2.5	2.5	2.4	2.4	2.3	2.1	2.0	2.0	1.9	1.9	2.4	2.2
Social insurance and retirement receipts:														
Social Security payroll taxes	4.3	4.3	4.3	4.3	4.3	4.3	4.3	4.3	4.4	4.4	4.4	4.4	4.3	4.3
Medicare payroll taxes	1.3	1.3	1.3	1.3	1.3	1.3	1.3	1.3	1.3	1.3	1.4	1.4	1.3	1.3
Unemployment insurance	0.3	0.3	0.3	0.3	0.3	0.3	0.3	0.3	0.3	0.3	0.3	0.3	0.3	0.3
Other retirement	0.1	0.1	0.1	0.1	0.1	0.1	0.1	0.1	0.1	0.1	0.1	0.1	0.1	0.1
Excise taxes	0.5	0.5	0.6	0.6	0.6	0.6	0.6	0.5	0.5	0.5	0.5	0.5	0.6	0.6
Estate and gift taxes	0.1	0.1	0.1	0.2	0.2	0.2	0.2	0.2	0.2	0.2	0.2	0.2	0.2	0.2
Customs duties	0.2	0.2	0.2	0.2	0.2	0.2	0.2	0.2	0.2	0.2	0.2	0.2	0.2	0.2
Deposits of earnings, Federal Reserve System	0.6	0.5	0.4	0.2	0.2	0.2	0.2	0.2	0.2	0.2	0.2	0.2	0.2	0.2
Other miscellaneous receipts	0.2	0.2	0.2	0.3	0.3	0.3	0.3	0.3	0.3	0.3	0.3	0.3	0.3	0.3
Allowance for immigration reform	....	*	*	0.1	0.1	0.2	0.2	0.2	0.2	0.3	0.3	0.3	0.1	0.2
Total receipts	17.5	17.7	18.7	19.1	19.1	19.2	19.3	19.3	19.4	19.5	19.6	19.7	19.1	19.3
Deficit	**2.8**	**3.2**	**2.5**	**2.3**	**2.3**	**2.4**	**2.5**	**2.6**	**2.6**	**2.5**	**2.4**	**2.5**	**2.4**	**2.5**
Net interest	1.3	1.3	1.5	1.8	2.1	2.2	2.4	2.5	2.7	2.7	2.8	2.8	2.0	2.4
Primary deficit / surplus (–)	**1.5**	**2.0**	**1.0**	**0.5**	**0.3**	**0.2**	*	*	**-0.1**	**-0.3**	**-0.4**	**-0.4**	**0.4**	**0.1**
On-budget deficit	3.0	3.3	2.5	2.3	2.2	2.2	2.2	2.2	2.1	2.0	1.8	1.8	2.3	2.1
Off-budget deficit / surplus (–)	-0.2	-0.1	–*	*	0.1	0.2	0.3	0.4	0.4	0.5	0.6	0.7	0.1	0.3

Table S–6. Proposed Budget by Category as a Percent of GDP—Continued

(As a percent of GDP)

	2014	2015	2016	2017	2018	2019	2020	2021	2022	2023	2024	2025	Averages 2016-2020	Averages 2016-2025
Memorandum, budget authority for appropriated programs:														
Defense	3.5	3.3	3.3	2.9	2.8	2.7	2.7	2.6	2.5	2.5	2.4	2.4	2.9	2.7
Non-defense	3.0	2.9	2.9	2.9	2.8	2.7	2.6	2.6	2.4	2.3	2.3	2.2	2.8	2.6
Total, appropriated funding	6.6	6.2	6.1	5.8	5.6	5.5	5.3	5.2	4.9	4.8	4.7	4.6	5.7	5.3

*0.05 percent of GDP or less.

[1] These amounts represent a placeholder for major disasters requiring Federal assistance for relief and reconstruction. Such assistance might be provided in the form of discretionary or mandatory outlays or tax relief. These amounts are included as outlays for convenience.

Table S–7. Proposed Budget in Population- and Inflation-Adjusted Dollars

(In billions of constant dollars, adjusted for population growth)

	2016	2017	2018	2019	2020	2021	2022	2023	2024	2025
Outlays:										
Appropriated ("discretionary") programs:										
Defense	605	577	548	530	520	510	505	500	495	489
Non-defense	563	564	552	540	525	513	493	481	475	469
Subtotal, appropriated programs	1,168	1,141	1,100	1,069	1,045	1,023	998	981	970	958
Mandatory programs:										
Social Security	938	963	989	1,017	1,045	1,071	1,099	1,127	1,157	1,187
Medicare	583	567	551	588	609	630	681	678	670	723
Medicaid	351	354	360	368	377	386	396	406	418	430
Other mandatory programs	662	702	739	730	729	737	712	731	749	729
Allowance for immigration reform	8	11	17	22	25	25	29	33	38	42
Subtotal, mandatory programs	2,543	2,596	2,656	2,725	2,785	2,849	2,917	2,975	3,031	3,111
Net interest	283	351	399	441	481	511	539	564	581	595
Adjustments for disaster costs[1]	6	7	8	8	8	8	8	8	8	8
Total outlays	3,999	4,095	4,163	4,243	4,319	4,392	4,462	4,528	4,590	4,672
Receipts:										
Individual income taxes	1,646	1,719	1,776	1,824	1,872	1,922	1,972	2,021	2,065	2,108
Corporation income taxes	473	485	473	463	453	423	407	407	405	402
Social insurance and retirement receipts:										
Social Security payroll taxes	801	819	833	844	852	871	886	898	911	921
Medicare payroll taxes	245	251	257	261	264	269	274	278	282	285
Unemployment insurance	56	59	56	52	51	51	53	53	53	53
Other retirement	9	10	10	10	10	10	10	11	11	11
Excise taxes	112	117	115	113	112	110	109	108	107	107
Estate and gift taxes	21	30	31	33	34	36	38	40	42	44
Customs duties	38	41	42	43	44	45	46	47	48	49
Deposits of earnings, Federal Reserve System	77	46	37	37	41	44	47	49	51	51
Other miscellaneous receipts	43	58	55	55	56	55	55	54	55	55
Allowance for immigration reform	2	12	26	36	40	40	46	52	60	66
Total receipts	3,525	3,646	3,712	3,771	3,829	3,877	3,943	4,017	4,091	4,152
Deficit	**474**	**449**	**451**	**472**	**490**	**514**	**520**	**511**	**499**	**520**
Net interest	283	351	399	441	481	511	539	564	581	595
Primary deficit / surplus (−)	**191**	**99**	**51**	**31**	**9**	**3**	**−19**	**−52**	**−82**	**−75**
On-budget deficit	477	440	427	433	428	442	433	403	372	370
Off-budget deficit / surplus (−)	−3	9	24	39	62	72	87	108	127	151

Table S–7. Proposed Budget in Population- and Inflation-Adjusted Dollars—Continued

(In billions of constant dollars, adjusted for population growth)

	2016	2017	2018	2019	2020	2021	2022	2023	2024	2025
Memorandum, budget authority for appropriated programs:										
Defense	612	556	550	540	529	523	517	512	506	501
Non-defense	543	548	541	533	521	515	487	482	478	474
Total, appropriated funding	1,155	1,105	1,091	1,073	1,050	1,037	1,003	994	984	974
Memorandum, index of population growth and inflation .	1.00	1.03	1.06	1.10	1.13	1.17	1.20	1.24	1.28	1.32

[1] These amounts represent a placeholder for major disasters requiring Federal assistance for relief and reconstruction. Such assistance might be provided in the form of discretionary or mandatory outlays or tax relief. These amounts are included as outlays for convenience.

Table S–8. Bridge from Balanced Budget and Emergency Deficit Control Act (BBEDCA) Baseline to Adjusted Baseline

(Deficit increases (+) or decreases (–) in billions of dollars)

	2014	2015	2016	2017	2018	2019	2020	2021	2022	2023	2024	2025	Totals 2016-2020	Totals 2016-2025
BBEDCA baseline deficit	485	565	544	594	617	711	785	835	945	953	956	1,093	3,253	8,034
Adjustments for current policy:														
Continue tax benefits provided under the American Taxpayer Relief Act [1]					1	22	24	24	24	24	24	24	47	166
Prevent reduction in Medicare physician payments		5	9	5	7	9	11	12	13	13	14	15	41	108
Reflect incremental cost of funding existing Pell maximum grant award			1	3	1	1	1	1	1	1	1	1	7	11
Reflect Postal Service default on retiree health benefit payments		6	6	–1	–1	–1	–1	–1	–1	–1	–1	–1	3	–1
Subtotal		11	15	7	9	32	35	36	37	37	38	38	99	285
Adjustments for provisions contained in the Budget Control Act:														
Set discretionary budget authority at cap levels [2]			28	34	36	36	35	33	32	32	33	34	169	333
Reflect Joint Committee enforcement [3]			–56	–89	–103	–106	–107	–108	–55	–38	–33	–3	–461	–698
Subtotal			–28	–56	–67	–70	–72	–75	–22	–6	–*	31	–292	–365
Adjustments for emergency and disaster costs:														
Remove non-recurring emergency costs [4]			–3	–6	–9	–12	–12	–13	–13	–14	–14	–14	–42	–110
Add placeholder for future emergency costs [4]		2	6	8	8	9	9	10	10	10	10	10	40	90
Reclassify surface transportation outlays:														
Remove outlays from appropriated category	–57	–58	–60	–60	–59	–59	–59	–59	–60	–62	–63	–64	–296	–604
Add outlays to mandatory category	57	58	60	60	59	59	59	59	60	62	63	64	296	604
Subtotal														
Total program adjustments		13	–10	–47	–59	–41	–40	–42	11	28	33	64	–196	–101
Debt service on adjustments		*	*	–*	–2	–4	–6	–8	–9	–9	–8	–6	–13	–52
Total adjustments		13	–9	–47	–61	–45	–46	–50	2	19	26	58	–209	–154
Adjusted baseline deficit	485	578	535	547	556	666	739	785	947	973	981	1,151	3,044	7,880

* $500 million or less.

[1] The baseline permanently continues the tax benefits provided to individuals and families that were extended only through taxable year 2017 under ATRA.

[2] Includes adjustments for discretionary program integrity funding and associated mandatory benefit savings.

[3] Consists of mandatory sequestration for 2017-2024 and discretionary cap reductions for 2016-2021.

[4] These amounts represent a placeholder for major disasters requiring Federal assistance for relief and reconstruction.

Table S–9. Mandatory and Receipt Proposals

(Deficit increases (+) or decreases (–) in millions of dollars)

	2015	2016	2017	2018	2019	2020	2021	2022	2023	2024	2025	Totals 2016-2020	Totals 2016-2025
Mandatory Initiatives and Savings:													
Agriculture:													
Reduce premium subsidies for harvest price revenue protection and improve prevented planting coverage	....	-1,129	-1,374	-1,560	-1,614	-1,650	-1,675	-1,709	-1,739	-1,773	-1,776	-7,327	-15,999
Reauthorize Secure Rural Schools	178	190	105	61	37	8	....	....	....	....	....	401	401
Enact Food Safety and Inspection Service (FSIS) fee	....	-4	-4	-4	-5	-5	-5	-5	-5	-5	-5	-22	-47
Enact biobased labeling fee	....	....	....	....	....	....	....	....	....	....	....	....	....
Enact Grain Inspection, Packers, and Stockyards Administration (GIPSA) fee	....	-30	-30	-30	-30	-30	-30	-30	-30	-30	-30	-150	-300
Enact Animal Plant and Health Inspection Service (APHIS) fee	....	-20	-27	-27	-28	-29	-30	-31	-32	-33	-34	-131	-291
Enact NRCS Conservation user fee	....	....	....	....	....	....	....	....	....	....	....	....	....
Establish RHS Guaranteed Underwriting System fee	....	....	....	....	....	....	....	....	....	....	....	....	....
Increase funding for Supplemental Nutrition Assistance Program (SNAP) Employment & Training[1]	....	....	13	25	25	25	25	25	25	25	25	88	213
Create State option to improve SNAP access for elderly	....	9	21	34	41	48	54	60	67	74	80	153	488
Outyear mandatory effects of discretionary changes to the Conservation Stewardship Program	....	....	-54	-54	-54	-54	-54	-54	-54	-54	-54	-216	-486
Total, Agriculture	178	-984	-1,350	-1,555	-1,628	-1,687	-1,715	-1,744	-1,768	-1,796	-1,794	-7,204	-16,021
Commerce:													
Enact Scale-Up Manufacturing Initiative	....	....	163	365	365	365	....	....	....	....	....	1,258	1,258
Expand National Network of Manufacturing Institutes	....	....	90	190	280	390	390	290	200	100	....	950	1,930
Total, Commerce	....	....	253	555	645	755	390	290	200	100	....	2,208	3,188
Education:													
Support Preschool for All	....	130	1,235	3,110	5,456	7,360	8,773	9,787	10,560	10,275	9,356	17,291	66,042
Enact Teaching for Tomorrow	....	50	250	550	850	1,000	950	750	450	150	....	2,700	5,000
Partner with States to provide tuition-free quality community college	....	41	951	2,401	3,477	4,822	6,408	7,653	9,443	11,914	13,175	11,692	60,285
Extend Pell CPI Increase	....	....	....	226	1,104	2,055	3,044	4,095	5,208	6,389	7,624	3,385	29,745
Reform student loan Income-Based Repayment plans[2]	....	-1,143	-678	-940	-1,331	-1,612	-1,683	-1,703	-1,727	-1,850	-1,910	-5,704	-14,577
Reform and expand Perkins loan program	....	-418	-1,138	-944	-830	-736	-652	-623	-602	-584	-560	-4,066	-7,087
Enact student aid reforms	....	-16	-57	-58	-83	-73	-50	-21	14	37	61	-287	-246
Implement College Opportunity and Graduation Bonus Program	....	123	360	481	671	684	692	702	709	719	727	2,319	5,868
Total, Education	....	-1,233	923	4,826	9,314	13,500	17,482	20,640	24,055	27,050	28,473	27,330	145,030

Table S–9. Mandatory and Receipt Proposals—Continued

(Deficit increases (+) or decreases (–) in millions of dollars)

	2015	2016	2017	2018	2019	2020	2021	2022	2023	2024	2025	Totals 2016-2020	Totals 2016-2025
Energy:													
Enact nuclear waste management program	....	....	....	....	90	170	400	520	760	–1,394	764	260	1,310
Reauthorize special assessment from domestic nuclear utilities [3]	....	–204	–208	–213	–218	–223	–228	–233	–238	–244	–249	–1,066	–2,258
Establish Southwestern Power Administration Purchase Power Drought Fund	....	–15	–15	5	–15	–2				24	–15	–42	–33
Total, Energy	....	–219	–223	–208	–143	–55	172	287	522	–1,614	500	–848	–981
Health and Human Services:													
HHS health savings:													
Medicare providers:													
Encourage delivery system reform:													
Reform Medicare physician payments to promote participation in high-quality and efficient health care delivery systems	260	430	770	980	1,720	5,190	5,660	6,420	6,680	6,980	9,160	9,090	43,990
Make permanent the Medicare primary care incentive payment in a budget neutral manner	....	....	....	....	....	....	....	....	....	....	....	....	—
Encourage efficient care by improving incentives to provide care in the most appropriate ambulatory setting	....	....	–430	–1,160	–2,050	–3,100	–3,730	–4,130	–4,520	–4,950	–5,430	–6,740	–29,500
Allow ACOs to pay beneficiaries for primary care visits up to the applicable Medicare cost sharing amount	....	....	....	....	....	....	....	....	....	....	....	....	....
Allow CMS to assign beneficiaries to Federally Qualified Health Centers and Rural Health Clinics participating in the Medicare Shared Savings Program	....	....	....	....	–10	–10	–10	–10	–10	–10	–20	–20	–80
Expand basis for beneficiary assignment for Accountable Care Organizations to include Nurse Practitioners, Physician Assistants, and Clinical Nurse Specialists	....	....	....	....	....	–10	–10	–10	–10	–10	–10	–10	–60
Establish quality bonus payments for high-performing Part D plans	....	....	....	....	....	....	....	....	....	....	....	....	....
Implement bundled payment for post-acute care	....	....	....	....	....	–430	–1,020	–1,690	–1,890	–2,040	–2,190	–430	–9,260

Table S–9. Mandatory and Receipt Proposals—Continued

(Deficit increases (+) or decreases (–) in millions of dollars)

	2015	2016	2017	2018	2019	2020	2021	2022	2023	2024	2025	Totals 2016-2020	Totals 2016-2025
Implement value-based purchasing for skilled nursing facilities (SNFs), home health agencies (HHAs), ambulatory surgical centers (ASCs), hospital outpatient departments (HOPDs), and community mental health centers (CMHCs)	......											......	......
Establish a hospital-wide readmissions measure	......											......	......
Extend accountability for hospital-acquired conditions	......											......	......
Expand sharing Medicare data with qualified entities	......											......	......
Improve beneficiary access:													
Eliminate the 190-day lifetime limit on inpatient psychiatric facility services	......	400	400	450	450	450	500	550	550	600	650	2,150	5,000
Expand coverage of dialysis services for beneficiaries with acute kidney injury	......	–10	–20	–20	–20	–20	–20	–20	–20	–20	–30	–90	–200
Bad debts:													
Reduce Medicare coverage of bad debts	......	–370	–1,250	–2,440	–3,100	–3,370	–3,590	–3,840	–4,100	–4,360	–4,660	–10,530	–31,080
Graduate medical education:													
Better align graduate medical education payments with patient care costs	......	–1,000	–1,270	–1,390	–1,470	–1,570	–1,680	–1,790	–1,910	–2,030	–2,150	–6,700	–16,260
Better align payments to rural providers with the cost of health care:													
Reduce Critical Access Hospital (CAH) payments from 101% of reasonable costs to 100% of reasonable costs	......	–110	–130	–150	–150	–170	–180	–190	–200	–220	–230	–710	–1,730
Prohibit CAH designation for facilities that are less than 10 miles from the nearest hospital	......	–50	–60	–70	–70	–70	–80	–80	–90	–100	–100	–320	–770
Cut waste, fraud, and improper payments in Medicare:													
Reduce waste, fraud, and abuse in Medicare	......	110	112	34	–102	–226	–298	–329	–348	–375	–399	–72	–1,821
Drug rebates and additional Part D savings:													
Align Medicare drug payment policies with Medicaid policies for low-income enrollees	......	......	–3,630	–8,680	–9,480	–11,000	–12,730	–14,100	–16,480	–19,200	–20,830	–32,790	–116,130

Table S–9. Mandatory and Receipt Proposals—Continued

(Deficit increases (+) or decreases (−) in millions of dollars)

	2015	2016	2017	2018	2019	2020	2021	2022	2023	2024	2025	Totals 2016-2020	Totals 2016-2025
Accelerate manufacturer discounts for brand drugs to provide relief to Medicare beneficiaries in the coverage gap	......	......	−110	−430	−700	−1,250	−1,360	−1,470	−1,380	−1,250	−1,480	−2,490	−9,430
Suspend coverage and payment for questionable Part D prescriptions and incomplete clinical information	......	......	......	......	......	......	......	......	......	......	......	......	......
Establish authority for a program to prevent prescription drug abuse in Medicare Part D	......	......	......	......	......	......	......	......	......	......	......	......	......
Require mandatory reporting of other prescription drug coverage	......	−10	−30	−40	−40	−50	−50	−60	−60	−70	−70	−170	−480
Allow the Secretary to negotiate prices for biologics and high cost prescription drugs	......	......	......	......	......	......	......	......	......	......	......	......	......
Encourage efficient post-acute care:													
Adjust payment updates for certain post-acute care providers	......	−1,600	−3,400	−4,970	−6,690	−8,510	−10,600	−13,270	−15,590	−17,390	−20,050	−25,170	−102,070
Encourage appropriate use of inpatient rehabilitation hospitals (IRFs) by requiring that 75 percent of IRF patients require intensive rehabilitation services	......	−170	−200	−210	−210	−220	−230	−240	−240	−250	−260	−1,010	−2,230
Additional provider efficiencies:													
Exclude certain services from the in-office ancillary services exception	......	......	−350	−540	−590	−640	−680	−730	−780	−830	−880	−2,120	−6,020
Modify the documentation requirement for face-to-face encounters for durable medical equipment, prosthetics, orthotics, and supplies (DMEPOS) claims	......	......	......	......	......	......	......	......	......	......	......	......	......
Modify reimbursement of Part B drugs	......	−320	−570	−620	−660	−710	−770	−830	−890	−970	−1,040	−2,880	−7,380
Improve payment accuracy for Medicare Advantage (MA):													
Increase the minimum MA coding intensity adjustment	......	......	−440	−1,060	−2,020	−3,260	−4,730	−5,470	−5,900	−6,360	−7,000	−6,780	−36,240
Align employer group waiver plan payments with average MA plan bids	......	......	−530	−680	−740	−780	−810	−840	−870	−920	−990	−2,730	−7,160
Other Medicare:													
Clarify calculation of the late enrollment penalty for Medicare Part B premiums	......	......	......	......	......	......	......	......	......	......	......	......	......

Table S-9. Mandatory and Receipt Proposals—Continued

(Deficit increases (+) or decreases (−) in millions of dollars)

	2015	2016	2017	2018	2019	2020	2021	2022	2023	2024	2025	Totals 2016-2020	Totals 2016-2025
Clarify the Medicare Fraction in the Medicare DSH statute	......	......	......	......	......	......	......	......	......	......	......	......	......
Strengthen the Independent Payment Advisory Board (IPAB) to reduce long-term drivers of Medicare cost growth	......	......	......	......	......	......	−752	−1,059	−4,311	−5,693	−9,065	......	−20,880
Total, Medicare providers	260	−2,700	−11,138	−20,996	−25,932	−29,756	−37,170	−43,188	−52,369	−59,468	−67,074	−90,522	−349,791
Medicare structural reforms:													
Increase income-related premiums under Medicare Parts B and D	......	......	......	......	−2,090	−5,790	−7,870	−9,450	−11,350	−13,600	−16,260	−7,880	−66,410
Modify the Part B deductible for new beneficiaries	......	......	......	......	−50	−70	−280	−400	−860	−990	−1,090	−120	−3,740
Introduce a Part B premium surcharge for new beneficiaries who purchase near first-dollar Medigap coverage	......	......	......	......	−90	−220	−370	−530	−710	−910	−1,140	−310	−3,970
Introduce home health co-payments for new beneficiaries	......	......	......	......	−20	−50	−80	−110	−150	−190	−230	−70	−830
Encourage the use of generic drugs by low-income beneficiaries	......	......	−550	−770	−850	−920	−990	−1,070	−1,150	−1,230	−1,330	−3,090	−8,860
Total, Medicare structural reforms ...	......	......	−550	−770	−3,100	−7,050	−9,590	−11,560	−14,220	−16,920	−20,050	−11,470	−83,810
Interactions	......	45	93	153	633	858	1,776	1,225	4,525	2,903	6,137	1,782	18,348
Medicaid and other:													
Medicaid:													
Limit Medicaid reimbursement of durable medical equipment based on Medicare rates	......	−305	−330	−355	−380	−410	−435	−465	−495	−530	−565	−1,780	−4,270
Rebase future Medicaid Disproportionate Share Hospital (DSH) allotments	......	......	......	......	......	......	......	......	......	......	−3,290	---	−3,290
Reduce waste, fraud, and abuse in Medicaid	......	−54	−85	−116	−116	−115	−111	−111	−111	−107	−112	−486	−1,038
Strengthen the Medicaid Drug Rebate program	......	−247	−467	−482	−502	−522	−552	−592	−657	−722	−817	−2,220	−5,560
Exclude brand-name and authorized generic drug prices from Medicaid Federal upper limit (FUL)	......	−30	−60	−80	−80	−80	−90	−90	−90	−90	−90	−330	−780
Increase access to and transparency of Medicaid drug pricing data	......	6	6	6	6	6	......	......	......	......	......	30	30
Create demonstration to address over-prescription of psychotropic medications for children in foster care	......	114	206	219	226	233	91	−11	−11	−9	−6	998	1,052
Allow States to develop age-specific health home programs	......	200	100	90	90	90	80	90	90	90	90	570	1,010

Table S–9. Mandatory and Receipt Proposals—Continued

(Deficit increases (+) or decreases (–) in millions of dollars)

	2015	2016	2017	2018	2019	2020	2021	2022	2023	2024	2025	Totals 2016-2020	Totals 2016-2025
Improve and extend Money Follows the Person Rebalancing Demonstration through 2020	....	....	....	....	....	....	....	....	....	....	....	....	---
Provide home and community-based services (HCBS) to children eligible for psychiatric residential treatment facilities	....	....	79	165	172	180	188	196	205	214	224	596	1,623
Allow full Medicaid benefits for individuals in a home and community-based services (HCBS) state plan option	....	1	2	4	4	4	4	4	5	5	5	15	38
Expand eligibility for the 1915(i) HCBS State plan option	....	26	54	85	119	156	163	171	180	189	198	440	1,341
Expand eligibility under the Community First Choice option	....	238	255	296	319	343	368	395	424	455	488	1,451	3,581
Pilot comprehensive long-term care State plan option	....	....	....	748	782	816	851	888	....	....	....	2,346	4,085
Permanently extend Express Lane Eligibility (ELE) for children	....	30	65	105	160	105	115	130	145	150	165	465	1,170
Create State option to provide 12-month continuous Medicaid eligibility for adults [3]	....	299	238	723	410	378	455	519	574	537	580	2,048	4,713
Allow pregnant women choice of Medicaid eligibility category	....	....	....	....	....	....	....	....	....	....	....	....	---
Expand State flexibility to provide benchmark benefit packages	....	....	....	....	....	....	....	....	....	....	....	....	---
Require full coverage of preventive health and tobacco cessation services for adults in traditional Medicaid	....	95	92	87	81	76	71	67	64	61	60	431	754
Require coverage of EPSDT for children in inpatient psychiatric treatment facilities	....	30	35	35	40	40	45	45	50	50	55	180	425
Extend Qualified Individuals (QI) program through CY 2016	370	775	200	....	....	....	....	....	....	....	....	975	975
Extend Transitional Medical Assistance (TMA) program through CY 2016	825	1,075	730	20	....	....	....	....	....	....	....	1,825	1,825
Total, Medicaid	1,195	2,253	1,120	1,550	1,331	1,300	1,243	1,236	373	293	–3,015	7,554	7,684
Medicare-Medicaid enrollees:													
Ensure retroactive Part D coverage of newly-eligible low-income beneficiaries	....	....	....	....	....	....	....	....	....	....	....	....	---
Establish integrated appeals process for Medicare-Medicaid enrollees	....	....	....	....	....	....	....	....	....	....	....	....	---

Table S–9. Mandatory and Receipt Proposals—Continued

(Deficit increases (+) or decreases (–) in millions of dollars)

	2015	2016	2017	2018	2019	2020	2021	2022	2023	2024	2025	Totals 2016-2020	Totals 2016-2025
Create pilot to expand PACE eligibility to individuals between ages 21 and 55												---	---
Allow for Federal/State coordinated review of Duals Special Need Plan marketing materials												---	---
Total, Medicare-Medicaid enrollees												---	---
Pharmaceutical savings:													
Prohibit brand and generic drug manufacturers from delaying the availability of new generic drugs and biologics		–810	–870	–930	–1,010	–1,090	–1,170	–1,260	–1,350	–1,460	–1,560	–4,710	–11,510
Modify length of exclusivity to facilitate faster development of generic biologics			30	–90	–340	–540	–640	–690	–760	–760	–740	–940	–4,530
Total, pharmaceutical savings		–810	–840	–1,020	–1,350	–1,630	–1,810	–1,950	–2,110	–2,220	–2,300	–5,650	–16,040
Allow CMS to reinvest civil monetary penalties recovered from home health agencies		1	1	1	1	1	1	1	1	1	1	5	10
Allow CMS to assess a fee on Medicare providers for payments subject to the Federal Levy Program												---	---
Invest in CMS quality measurement		30	30	30								90	90
Reauthorize Special Diabetes Program		180	266	291	116	34	9	4				887	900
Extend Health Centers		1,350	2,538	2,619	1,323	162	81	27				7,992	8,100
Total, Medicaid and other	1,195	3,004	3,115	3,471	1,421	–133	–476	–682	–1,736	–1,926	–5,314	10,878	744
Medicare appeals:													
Provide Office of Medicare Hearings and Appeals and Department Appeals Board authority to use RAC collections		127	127	127	127	127	127	127	127	127	127	635	1,270
Establish Medicare appeals refundable filing fee													
Remand appeals to the redetermination level with the introduction of new evidence													
Sample and consolidate similar claims for administrative efficiency													
Increase minimum amount in controversy for administrative law judge (ALJ) adjudication of claims to equal amount required for judicial review													
Establish magistrate adjudication for claims with amount in controversy below new ALJ amount in controversy threshold													

Table S–9. Mandatory and Receipt Proposals—Continued

(Deficit increases (+) or decreases (−) in millions of dollars)

	2015	2016	2017	2018	2019	2020	2021	2022	2023	2024	2025	Totals 2016-2020	Totals 2016-2025
Expedite procedures for claims with no material fact in dispute	....	....	....	....	....	....	....	....	....	....	....	....	....
Total, Medicare appeals	....	127	127	127	127	127	127	127	127	127	127	635	1,270
Health workforce investments:													
Create a competitive, value-based graduate medical education program	....	40	165	280	398	465	487	515	538	565	587	1,348	4,040
Extend the Medicaid primary care payment increase through CY 2016 and include additional providers	3,660	5,010	1,280	....	....	....	....	....	....	....	....	6,290	6,290
Invest in the National Health Service Corps	....	262	487	508	518	524	262	37	16	5	....	2,299	2,619
Total, health workforce investments	3,660	5,312	1,932	788	916	989	749	552	554	570	587	9,937	12,949
Provide CMS Program Management implementation funding	....	25	300	75	....	....	....	....	....	....	....	400	400
Provide CMS Program Management implementation funding for Physician Payment Reform	....	60	180	210	90	30	30	....	....	....	....	570	600
Total, HHS health savings [4]	5,115	5,873	−5,941	−16,942	−25,845	−34,935	−44,554	−53,526	−63,119	−74,714	−85,587	−77,790	−399,290
Provide mandatory funding for tribal contract support costs:													
PAYGO effects	....	....	69	180	340	....	....	....	....	....	....	589	589
Nonscoreable reclassification	....	....	731	745	760	775	790	806	822	839	856	3,011	7,124
Total, provide mandatory funding for tribal contract support costs	....	....	800	925	1,100	775	790	806	822	839	856	3,600	7,713
Annual reduction to discretionary spending limits (non-add)	....	....	*−731*	*−745*	*−760*	*−775*	*−790*	*−806*	*−822*	*−839*	*−856*	*−3,011*	*−7,124*
Extend CHIP funding through 2019 [3]	....	130	4,049	4,018	4,159	−625	150	....	....	....	....	11,731	11,881
Promote Family Based Care	....	78	43	19	1	−19	−29	−39	−41	−43	−38	122	−68
Provide enhanced funding for Tribes to implement Title IV-E programs	....	27	30	28	5	4	4	4	4	4	4	94	114
Establish Title IV-E funding for prevention and permanency services	....	30	41	41	51	57	58	56	61	84	108	220	587
Expand eligibility through age 23 for Chafee Foster Care Independence Program	....	....	....	....	....	....	....	....	....	....	....	....	....
Modernize child support and create a Child Support Research Fund	....	150	169	269	290	360	396	438	436	433	305	1,238	3,246
Reauthorize Family Connection Grants	....	....	10	3	1	....	....	....	....	....	....	14	14
Repurpose Temporary Assistance for Needy Families (TANF) Contingency Fund to support Pathways to Jobs initiative	....	....	....	....	....	....	....	....	....	....	....	....	....
Reauthorize the Personal Responsibility Education Program (PREP)	....	2	24	57	74	75	73	51	18	1	....	232	375
Reauthorize Health Profession and Opportunity Grants	....	4	47	78	85	81	39	7	....	....	....	295	341

Table S–9. Mandatory and Receipt Proposals—Continued

(Deficit increases (+) or decreases (−) in millions of dollars)

	2015	2016	2017	2018	2019	2020	2021	2022	2023	2024	2025	Totals 2016-2020	Totals 2016-2025
Support demonstration to address over-prescription of psychotropic drugs for children in foster care (funding in Administration for Children and Families)	......	1	20	55	71	52	28	16	6	1	1	199	251
Expand access to high-quality, affordable care for young children	......	2,969	3,889	4,632	5,599	6,639	7,709	9,205	10,787	12,476	14,422	23,728	78,327
Establish LIHEAP Contingency Fund	......	825	1,049	919	800	726	694	697	713	729	745	4,319	7,897
Fund Upward Mobility Project	......	300	300	300	300	300						1,500	1,500
Provide researcher access to National Directory of New Hires (NDNH)	......												......
Extend and expand the Maternal, Infant, and Early Childhood Home Visiting Program	......	20	105	395	555	895	1,055	1,395	1,555	1,895	2,055	1,970	9,925
Total, Health and Human Services	5,115	10,409	4,635	−5,203	−12,754	−25,615	−33,587	−40,890	−48,758	−58,295	−67,129	−28,528	−277,187
Homeland Security:													
Reform the aviation passenger security user fee to more accurately reflect the costs of aviation security	......	−195	−200	−350	−600	−625	−650	−675	−680	−690	−700	−1,970	−5,365
Increase customs user fees	......											......	......
Increase immigration inspection user fees	......											......	......
Increase Express Consignment Courier fees	......											......	......
Total, Homeland Security	......	−195	−200	−350	−600	−625	−650	−675	−680	−690	−700	−1,970	−5,365
Housing and Urban Development:													
Provide funding for grants to reduce local barriers to housing development	......	6	30	45	81	81	51	6	......	......		243	300
Interior:													
Provide a fair return to taxpayers for the use of public resources:													
Enact Federal oil and gas management reforms	......	−50	−120	−125	−150	−170	−185	−200	−215	−225	−240	−615	−1,680
Reform hardrock mining on public lands	......		−2	−4	−5	−5	−6	−6	−11	−17	−24	−16	−80
Repeal geothermal payments to counties	......	−4	−4	−4	−5	−5	−5	−5	−5	−5	−5	−22	−47
Enact offshore revenue reform	......			−367	−375	−376	−378	−380	−385	−393	−415	−1,118	−3,069
Total, provide a fair return to taxpayers for the use of public resources	......	−54	−126	−500	−535	−556	−574	−591	−616	−640	−684	−1,771	−4,876
Ensure industry is held responsible for legacy pollution and risks to safety:													
Establish an abandoned mine lands (AML) hardrock reclamation fund [3]	......	......	−200	−150	−100	−50						−500	−500
Increase coal AML fee to pre-2006 levels [3] ...	......	−49	−36	−27	−17	−9	−1	51	37	27	16	−138	−8
Terminate AML payments to certified States ..	......	−34	−26	−35	−36	−30	−27	−25	−10	−1	......	−161	−224
Fund AML reclamation and economic revitalization	......	55	95	140	170	200	145	105	60	30	......	660	1,000

Table S-9. Mandatory and Receipt Proposals—Continued

(Deficit increases (+) or decreases (–) in millions of dollars)

												Totals	
	2015	2016	2017	2018	2019	2020	2021	2022	2023	2024	2025	2016-2020	2016-2025
Total, ensure industry is held responsible for legacy pollution and risks to safety	....	–28	–167	–72	17	111	117	131	87	56	16	–139	268
Conserve natural resources for future generations and provide recreation access to the public:													
Establish dedicated funding for Land and Water Conservation Fund (LWCF) programs	....	156	522	1,000	969	914	900	900	900	900	900	3,561	8,061
Reauthorize the Federal Land Transaction Facilitation Act of 2000 (FLTFA)	....	–5	–6	–10	–12	–3	....	....	....	....	....	–36	–36
Permanently reauthorize the Federal Lands Recreation Enhancement Act (FLREA)	....	....	....	....	....	....	....	....	....	....	....	....	....
Provide funding for a National Park Service Centennial Initiative	....	95	360	500	405	140	....	....	....	....	....	1,500	1,500
Total, conserve natural resources for future generations and provide recreation access to the public	....	246	876	1,490	1,362	1,051	900	900	900	900	900	5,025	9,525
Maintain commitments to communities and insular territories:													
Provide mandatory funding for tribal contract support costs:													
PAYGO effects	....	....	19	32	43	11	....	....	....	....	....	105	105
Nonscoreable reclassification	....	....	212	285	292	297	304	309	316	322	329	1,086	2,666
Total, provide mandatory funding for tribal contract support costs	....	....	231	317	335	308	304	309	316	322	329	1,191	2,771
Annual reduction to discretionary spending limits (non-add)	....	....	–212	–285	–292	–297	–304	–309	–316	–322	–329	–1,086	–2,666
Extend the Palau Compact of Free Association	....	41	29	20	18	17	16	10	7	5	....	125	163
Extend funding for Payments in Lieu of Taxes (PILT)	....	452	....	....	....	....	....	....	....	....	....	452	452
Improve coal miner retiree health and pension benefits	....	363	375	380	385	389	389	404	408	411	411	1,892	3,915
Total, maintain commitments to communities and insular territories	....	856	635	717	738	714	709	723	731	738	740	3,660	7,301
Total, Interior	....	1,020	1,218	1,635	1,582	1,320	1,152	1,163	1,102	1,054	972	6,775	12,218
Labor:													
Unemployment Insurance reform:[5]													
Strengthen Unemployment Insurance (UI) system solvency[3,6]	....	....	–3,634	–3,618	–3,457	–3,601	–3,901	–6,485	–6,313	–6,648	–7,100	–14,310	–44,757

Table S–9. Mandatory and Receipt Proposals—Continued

(Deficit increases (+) or decreases (–) in millions of dollars)

	2015	2016	2017	2018	2019	2020	2021	2022	2023	2024	2025	Totals 2016-2020	Totals 2016-2025
Improve UI Extended Benefits [3,6]	....	2,776	2,519	3,197	4,490	5,612	6,465	5,808	5,906	6,387	6,049	18,594	49,209
Modernize UI [3,6]	....	2,520	1,740	520	450	110	–40	....	....	....	....	5,340	5,300
Reform the Federal Employees' Compensation Act	....	–19	–9	–14	–21	–29	–34	–41	–49	–56	–64	–92	–336
Improve Pension Benefit Guaranty Corporation (PBGC) solvency	....	179	179	–1,194	–1,460	–1,823	–2,139	–2,589	–3,025	–3,402	–3,731	–4,119	–19,005
Extend the Trade Adjustment Assistance program	....	105	209	274	345	397	459	533	569	592	600	1,330	4,083
Implement cap adjustments for UI program integrity [3,6]	....	–34	–96	–110	–121	–131	–138	–147	–160	–173	–181	–492	–1,291
Outlays from discretionary cap adjustment (non-add)	....	30	35	40	45	50	55	60	65	70	75	200	525
Improve UI program integrity (mandatory SIDES) [3,6]	....	–5	–10	–15	–15	–16	–16	–13	–14	–14	–13	–61	–131
Create Connecting for Opportunity program	....	1,125	1,125	375	375	....	....	....	....	....	....	3,000	3,000
Allow use of prisoner database for UI program integrity [3,6]	....	–3	–7	–8	–7	–7	–8	–7	–7	–7	–7	–32	–68
Expand Foreign Labor Certification fees	....	....	....	....	....	....	....	....	....	....	....	....	....
Create an Apprenticeship Training Fund	....	500	500	500	500	....	....	....	....	....	....	2,000	2,000
Provide High-Growth Sector Training and Credentialing Grants	....	1,920	2,160	1,568	1,520	1,472	1,472	1,472	1,472	1,472	1,472	8,640	16,000
Establish Paid Leave Partnership Initiative	....	221	664	664	664	....	....	....	....	....	....	2,213	2,213
Total, Labor	....	9,285	5,340	2,139	3,263	1,984	2,120	–1,469	–1,621	–1,849	–2,975	22,011	16,217
Transportation:													
Invest in surface transportation reauthorization	....	3,056	9,622	14,565	16,516	17,707	18,837	15,640	9,528	6,003	4,115	61,466	115,589
Transfer to achieve trust fund solvency (non-add)	....	18,490	18,394	18,584	18,692	18,831	18,910	....	....	....	....	92,991	111,901
Treasury:													
Establish a Pay for Success Incentive Fund	....	29	21	10	24	40	56	46	42	24	8	124	300
Authorize Treasury to locate and recover assets of the United States and to retain a portion of amounts collected to pay for the costs of recovery	....	–3	–3	–3	–3	–3	–3	–3	–3	–3	–3	–15	–30
Increase delinquent Federal non-tax debt collections by authorizing administrative bank garnishment for non-tax debts	....	–32	–32	–32	–32	–32	–32	–32	–32	–32	–32	–160	–320
Increase levy authority for payments to Medicare providers with delinquent tax debt [3]	....	–34	–50	–50	–51	–52	–54	–54	–56	–56	–57	–237	–514
Allow offset of Federal income tax refunds to collect delinquent State income taxes for out-of-state residents	....	....	....	....	....	....	....	....	....	....	....	....	....
Reduce costs for States collecting delinquent income tax obligations	....	....	....	....	....	....	....	....	....	....	....	....	....

Table S–9. Mandatory and Receipt Proposals—Continued

(Deficit increases (+) or decreases (−) in millions of dollars)

	2015	2016	2017	2018	2019	2020	2021	2022	2023	2024	2025	Totals 2016-2020	Totals 2016-2025
Provide authority to contact delinquent debtors via their cell phones	......	−12	−12	−12	−12	−12	−12	−12	−12	−12	−12	−60	−120
Reauthorize the State Small Business Credit Initiative	......	216	735	525	6	6	6	6	......	......	......	1,488	1,500
Implement tax enforcement program integrity cap adjustment [3]		−432	−1,451	−2,926	−4,476	−6,095	−7,481	−8,475	−9,077	−9,503	−9,819	−15,380	−59,735
Outlays from discretionary cap adjustment (non-add)	......	667	1,039	1,403	1,781	2,170	2,232	2,276	2,329	2,382	2,437	7,060	18,716
Total, Treasury	......	−268	−792	−2,488	−4,544	−6,148	−7,520	−8,524	−9,138	−9,582	−9,915	−14,240	−58,919
Veterans Affairs:													
Extend round-down of cost of living adjustments (compensation)	......	−36	−74	−121	−159	−192	−204	−214	−225	−234	−244	−582	−1,703
Extend round-down of cost of living adjustments (education)	......	......	−1	−1	−1	−1	−1	−1	−1	−1	−2	−4	−10
Provide burial receptacles for certain new casketed gravesites	......	4	1	7	2	1	4	4	5	......	2	15	30
Improve housing grant program	......	3	3	3	3	3	1	1	1	1	1	15	20
Increase cap on vocational rehabilitation contract counseling		1	1	1	1	1	1	1	1	1	1	5	10
Extend supplemental service disabled veterans insurance coverage		......	......	......	......	1	......	......	1	1	1	1	4
Clarify evidentiary threshold at which VA is required to provide medical examination		−38	−39	−41	−42	−43	−44	−46	−47	−48	−50	−203	−438
Cap Post–9/11 GI Bill benefits for flight training		−26	−27	−28	−30	−31	−33	−35	−36	−39	−41	−142	−326
Expand eligibility for Montgomery GI Bill refund		4	4	4	5	5	4	4	4	4	5	22	43
Extend authorization of work-study activities		1	1	1	1	1	1	1	1	2	2	5	12
Pro-rate GI Bill benefit usage for certification tests		......	......	......	......	......	1	1	1	1	1	......	5
Modernize the definition of Automobile Adaptive Equipment (AAE)		−2	−2	−2	−2	−2	−2	−1	−1	−1	−1	−10	−16
Eliminate reductions of special monthly compensation for hospitalized veterans		......	......	1	1	1	1	1	1	1	1	3	7
Restore the eligibility of certain veterans for special aid and attendance allowance		2	2	2	2	2	3	3	3	3	3	10	25
Reissue VA benefit payments to all victims of fiduciary misuse		2	2	2	2	2	2	2	2	2	2	10	20
Total, Veterans Affairs	......	−85	−129	−172	−217	−252	−267	−279	−290	−307	−319	−855	−2,317
Corps of Engineers:													
Reform inland waterways funding [3]	......	−113	−113	−113	−113	−113	−113	−113	−113	−113	−113	−565	−1,130

Table S-9. Mandatory and Receipt Proposals—Continued

(Deficit increases (+) or decreases (−) in millions of dollars)

	2015	2016	2017	2018	2019	2020	2021	2022	2023	2024	2025	Totals 2016-2020	Totals 2016-2025
Environmental Protection Agency:													
Eliminate statutory cap on pre-manufacture notice fee	....	−4	−8	−8	−8	−8	−8	−8	−8	−8	−8	−36	−76
Enact confidential business information management fee	....	....	−2	−2	....	....	....	....	....	....	....	−4	−4
Create Clean Power State Incentive Fund	....	....	1,670	1,000	190	190	190	190	190	190	190	3,050	4,000
Total, Environmental Protection Agency	....	−4	1,660	990	182	182	182	182	182	182	182	3,010	3,920
Executive Office of the President:													
Promote Spectrum Relocation Fund flexibility[7]	....	50	−45	−75	−100	−160	−190	−230	−200	−50	....	−330	−1,000
International Assistance Programs:													
Mandatory effects of discretionary proposal to implement 2010 International Monetary Fund (IMF) agreement (non-scoreable)	....	−224	....	....	....	....	....	....	....	....	....	−224	−224
Other Defense–Civil Programs:													
Increase TRICARE pharmacy copayments	....	....	−71	−115	−344	−424	−483	−576	−676	−786	−832	−1,043	−4,396
Increase annual premiums for TRICARE-For-Life (TFL) enrollment	....	....	−3	−43	−83	−111	−141	−173	−206	−240	−276	−255	−1,291
Increase TRICARE pharmacy copayments (accrual effects)	....	315	328	343	361	382	403	426	451	476	505	1,729	3,990
Increase annual premiums for TFL enrollment (accrual effects)	....	83	85	87	89	92	97	103	109	115	123	436	983
Total, Other Defense–Civil Programs	....	324	309	272	23	−61	−124	−220	−322	−435	−480	867	−714
Office of Personnel Management (OPM):													
Streamline Federal Employee Health Benefit Plan (FEHBP) pharmacy benefit contracting	....	....	−59	−124	−143	−153	−164	−176	−187	−200	−213	−479	−1,419
Provide FEHBP benefits to domestic partners	....	....	−7	6	18	29	40	54	69	85	103	46	397
Expand FEHBP plan types	....	....	−1	−3	−4	−7	−9	−10	−14	−19	−21	−15	−88
Adjust FEHBP premiums for wellness	....	....	3	−12	−40	−78	−124	−177	−252	−344	−456	−127	−1,480
Total, Office of Personnel Management	....	....	−64	−133	−169	−209	−257	−309	−384	−478	−587	−575	−2,590
Social Security Administration (SSA):													
Provide dedicated, mandatory funding for program integrity:													
Administrative costs	....	....	1,805	1,728	1,676	1,582	1,575	1,631	1,688	1,747	1,808	6,791	15,240
Benefit savings	....	....	−238	−2,003	−3,163	−3,902	−4,532	−5,394	−5,714	−5,950	−6,796	−9,306	−37,692
Total, provide dedicated, mandatory funding for program integrity	....	....	1,567	−275	−1,487	−2,320	−2,957	−3,763	−4,026	−4,203	−4,988	−2,515	−22,452
Annual reduction to discretionary spending limits (non-add)	....	....	−273	−273	−273	−273	−273	−273	−273	−273	−273	−1,092	−2,457
Allow SSA to use commercial databases to verify wages in SSI	....	....	....	....	−71	−36	−24	−21	−19	−17	−18	−107	−206

Table S-9. Mandatory and Receipt Proposals—Continued

(Deficit increases (+) or decreases (−) in millions of dollars)

	2015	2016	2017	2018	2019	2020	2021	2022	2023	2024	2025	Totals 2016-2020	Totals 2016-2025
Expand authority to require authorization to verify financial information for overpayment waiver requests [8]	......	−5	−16	−17	−18	−19	−20	−20	−21	−22	−22	−75	−180
Hold fraud facilitators liable for overpayments [8]	......	......	......	−1	−1	−1	−1	−1	−1	−1	−1	−3	−8
Allow Government-wide use of CBP entry/exit data to prevent improper payments	......	......	......	−2	−7	−14	−22	−33	−40	−43	−52	−23	−213
Clarify penalties and prohibitions for misleading Internet advertising	......	......	......	......	......	......	......	......	......	......	......	......	......
Allow Social Security benefits for same sex married couples	1	5	8	9	11	13	13	14	14	14	14	46	115
Lower electronic wage reporting threshold to five employees	......	......	......	......	......	......	......	......	......	......	......	......	......
Move from annual to quarterly wage reporting	......	20	30	90	−131	−138	−168	−224	−257	−260	−301	−129	−1,339
Improve collection of pension information from States and localities	......	18	28	24	−351	−776	−1,047	−1,142	−1,085	−1,075	−1,054	−1,057	−6,460
Establish workers compensation information reporting	......	5	5	......	......	......	......	......	......	......	......	10	10
Extend SSI time limits for qualified refugees	......	45	50	......	......	......	......	......	......	......	......	95	95
Conform treatment of State and local government earned income tax credit (EITC) and child tax credit (CTC) for SSI [9]	......	......	......	......	......	......	......	......	......	......	......	......	......
Terminate step-child benefits in the same month as step-parent [10]	......	......	......	......	......	......	......	......	......	......	......	......	......
Allow SSA to electronically certify certain RRB payments	......	......	......	......	......	......	......	......	......	......	......	......	......
Use the Death Master File to prevent Federal improper payments	......	......	......	......	......	......	......	......	......	......	......	......	......
Offset DI benefits for period of concurrent UI receipt [3,6]	......	......	−35	−172	−253	−252	−253	−260	−264	−261	−269	−712	−2,019
Eliminate aggressive SSA claiming strategies	......	......	......	......	......	......	......	......	......	......	......	......	......
Reauthorize and expand demonstration authority for DI and SSI	......	......	70	105	115	60	......	......	......	......	......	350	350
Reallocate payroll taxes to address DI trust fund reserve depletion	......	......	......	......	......	......	......	......	......	......	......	......	......
Total, Social Security Administration	1	88	1,707	−239	−2,193	−3,483	−4,479	−5,450	−5,699	−5,868	−6,691	−4,120	−32,307
Other Independent Agencies:													
Federal Communications Commission:													
Enact Spectrum License User Fee and allow the FCC to auction predominantly domestic satellite services	......	−225	−325	−425	−550	−550	−550	−550	−550	−550	−550	−2,075	−4,825
Postal Service:													
Enact Postal Service financial relief and reform:													
PAYGO effect	769	−1,234	−2,182	−2,353	−4,226	−4,399	−4,472	−4,495	−4,419	−4,344	−4,318	−14,394	−36,442

Table S-9. Mandatory and Receipt Proposals—Continued

(Deficit increases (+) or decreases (−) in millions of dollars)

	2015	2016	2017	2018	2019	2020	2021	2022	2023	2024	2025	Totals 2016-2020	Totals 2016-2025
Non-scoreable effect	......	964	3,823	3,403	4,226	4,399	4,472	4,495	4,419	4,344	4,318	16,815	38,863
Total, enact Postal Service financial relief and reform	769	−270	1,641	1,050	......	......	......	......	......	......	......	2,421	2,421
Railroad Retirement Board (RRB):													
Amend Railroad Retirement Act and the Railroad Unemployment Insurance Act to include a felony charge for fraud	......	......	......	......	......	......	......	......	......	......	......		
Promote RRB program integrity	......	3	2	2	2	2	2	2	2	2	2	11	21
Total, Railroad Retirement Board	......	3	2	2	2	2	2	2	2	2	2	11	21
National Infrastructure Bank:													
Create infrastructure bank	......	33	153	373	595	831	1,058	1,158	1,233	1,207	1,062	1,985	7,703
Civilian Property Realignment Board:													
Dispose of unneeded real property	......	−87	−63	−136	−495	−65	−50	−60	−60	−40	−40	−846	−1,096
Total, Other Independent Agencies	769	−546	1,408	864	−448	218	460	550	625	619	474	1,496	4,224
Multi-Agency:													
Enact immigration reform [3]	......	6,000	−1,000	−10,000	−15,000	−17,000	−18,000	−20,000	−23,000	−29,000	−31,000	−37,000	−158,000
Establish a consolidated TRICARE program (mandatory effects in Coast Guard, Public Health Service, and National Oceanic and Atmospheric Administration)	......	1	−7	−14	−14	−15	−17	−17	−19	−20	−21	−49	−143
Auction or assign via fee 1675–1680 megahertz	......	......	−80	−150	......	......	......	......	......	......	......	−230	−230
Reconcile OPM/SSA retroactive disability payments	6	......	......	......	−48	−48	−48	−48	−48	−48	−48	−144	−384
Index the $750 benefit protection threshold for inflation	......	1,890	9	14	21	27	33	40	46	53	60	1,961	2,193
Establish hold harmless for Federal poverty guidelines	......	......	......	......	......	......	......	......	......	......	......		
Adjust payment timing	......	−37,600	......	37,600	......	......	......	−48,900	......	48,900	......		
Mandatory effects of proposal to authorize additional Afghan SIVs	......	......	21	20	18	19	18	17	15	16	16	78	160
Total, Multi-Agency	6	−29,709	−1,057	27,422	−15,023	−17,017	−18,014	−68,908	−23,006	19,901	−30,993	−35,384	−156,404
Total, mandatory initiatives and savings	6,069	−9,342	23,132	42,777	−6,326	−19,678	−26,070	−90,053	−55,765	−26,168	−86,980	30,563	−254,473
Tax proposals:													
Middle-class and pro-work tax reforms:													
Reform child care tax incentives [11]	......	4,024	4,191	4,429	4,639	4,841	5,052	5,292	5,532	5,615	6,257	22,124	49,872
Simplify and better target tax benefits for education [11]	......	5	1,861	4,753	4,660	5,027	5,242	5,730	5,878	6,337	6,205	16,306	45,698

Table S–9. Mandatory and Receipt Proposals—Continued

(Deficit increases (+) or decreases (−) in millions of dollars)

	2015	2016	2017	2018	2019	2020	2021	2022	2023	2024	2025	Totals 2016-2020	Totals 2016-2025
Provide for automatic enrollment in IRAs, including a small employer tax credit, increase the tax credit for small employer plan start-up costs, and provide an additional tax credit for small employer plans newly offering auto-enrollment [11]	......	......	993	1,589	1,700	1,754	1,831	2,005	2,176	2,410	2,661	6,036	17,119
Expand penalty-free withdrawals for long-term unemployed	......	162	235	240	245	250	255	260	265	270	276	1,132	2,458
Require retirement plans to allow long-term part-time workers to participate	......	39	55	54	53	52	50	47	44	40	34	253	468
Facilitate annuity portability	......	5	5	3	−4	−14	−30	−51	−74	−105	−142	−5	−407
Simplify minimum required distribution rules	......	......	......	......	......	......	......	......	......	......	......	......	......
Allow all inherited plan and IRA balances to be rolled over within 60 days	......	......	......	......	......	......	......	......	......	......	......	......	......
Expand EITC for workers without qualifying children [11]	......	460	6,256	6,297	6,350	6,481	6,612	6,716	6,804	6,921	7,047	25,844	59,944
Simplify the rules for claiming the EITC for workers without qualifying children [11]	......	44	593	599	588	605	620	631	642	653	678	2,429	5,653
Provide a second-earner tax credit [11]	......	2,067	9,007	9,104	9,383	9,502	9,727	9,872	9,936	10,127	10,306	39,063	89,031
Extend exclusion from income for cancellation of certain home mortgage debt	2,542	3,265	2,978	724	......	......	......	......	......	......	......	6,967	6,967
Total, middle-class and pro-work tax reforms	2,542	10,071	26,174	27,792	27,614	28,498	29,359	30,502	31,203	32,268	33,322	120,149	276,803
Reforms to capital gains taxation, upper-income tax benefits, and the taxation of financial institutions:													
Reduce the value of certain tax expenditures	......	−28,028	−46,032	−50,592	−54,995	−59,478	−63,843	−68,379	−72,914	−77,231	−81,734	−239,125	−603,226
Reform the taxation of capital income	−3,634	−9,048	−20,705	−18,041	−21,448	−21,892	−21,538	−22,276	−23,178	−24,292	−25,466	−91,134	−207,884
Implement the Buffett Rule by imposing a new "Fair Share Tax"	......	−6,671	93	−1,178	−2,810	−3,695	−3,872	−4,008	−4,177	−4,351	−4,507	−14,261	−35,176
Impose a financial fee	......	−5,644	−11,084	−10,978	−11,208	−11,470	−11,734	−12,003	−12,280	−12,562	−12,851	−50,384	−111,814
Total, reforms to capital gains taxation, upper-income tax benefits, and the taxation of financial institutions	−3,634	−49,391	−77,728	−80,789	−90,461	−96,535	−100,987	−106,666	−112,549	−118,436	−124,558	−394,904	−958,100
Loophole closers:													
Require current inclusion in income of accrued market discount and limit the accrual amount for distressed debt	......	−4	−12	−20	−27	−34	−41	−49	−58	−68	−78	−97	−391
Require that the cost basis of stock that is a covered security must be determined using an average cost basis method	......	......	−69	−209	−353	−507	−597	−620	−645	−673	−702	−1,138	−4,375
Tax carried (profits) interests as ordinary income	......	−1,294	−2,417	−2,421	−2,316	−2,204	−2,094	−1,692	−1,271	−1,036	−953	−10,652	−17,698

Table S-9. Mandatory and Receipt Proposals—Continued

(Deficit increases (+) or decreases (−) in millions of dollars)

	2015	2016	2017	2018	2019	2020	2021	2022	2023	2024	2025	Totals 2016-2020	Totals 2016-2025
Require non-spouse beneficiaries of deceased IRA owners and retirement plan participants to take inherited distributions over no more than five years	....	−87	−237	−400	−567	−737	−786	−748	−694	−640	−583	−2,028	−5,479
Limit the total accrual of tax-favored retirement benefits	....	−1,418	−1,987	−2,213	−2,287	−2,438	−2,634	−2,785	−3,183	−3,396	−3,702	−10,343	−26,043
Conform SECA taxes for professional service businesses	....	−4,465	−6,268	−6,622	−6,977	−7,372	−7,837	−8,371	−8,837	−9,248	−8,554	−31,704	−74,551
Limit Roth conversions to pre-tax dollars	....	....	−14	−23	−24	−38	−49	−50	−51	−67	−79	−99	−395
Eliminate deduction for dividends on stock of publicly-traded corporations held in ESOPs	....	−589	−830	−851	−865	−879	−892	−907	−922	−936	−951	−4,014	−8,622
Repeal exclusion of net unrealized appreciation in employer securities	....	−145	−245	−249	−254	−260	−265	−270	−275	−281	−287	−1,153	−2,531
Disallow the deduction for charitable contributions that are a prerequisite for purchasing tickets to college sporting events	....	−126	−201	−218	−233	−249	−266	−283	−302	−323	−345	−1,027	−2,546
Total, loophole closers	....	−8,128	−12,280	−13,226	−13,903	−14,718	−15,461	−15,775	−16,238	−16,668	−16,234	−62,255	−142,631
Incentives for job creation, clean energy, and manufacturing:													
Designate Promise Zones [11]	....	604	1,130	1,010	938	890	852	813	791	792	807	4,572	8,627
Provide a tax credit for the production of advanced technology vehicles	....	581	475	512	567	507	418	299	−6	−197	−209	2,642	2,947
Provide a tax credit for medium- and heavy-duty alternative-fuel commercial vehicles	....	46	76	77	80	61	26	5	....	....	....	340	371
Modify and extend the tax credit for the construction of energy-efficient new homes	60	132	164	195	227	252	270	286	302	329	341	970	2,498
Reduce excise taxes on LNG to bring into parity with diesel [12]		4	5	6	6	6	7	7	9	9	10	27	69
Enhance and modify the conservation easement deduction	57	144	76	−22	−54	−59	−61	−67	−71	−76	−82	85	−272
Total, incentives for job creation, clean energy, and manufacturing	117	1,511	1,926	1,778	1,764	1,657	1,512	1,343	1,025	857	867	8,636	14,240
Modify estate and gift tax provisions:													
Restore the estate, gift, and generation-skipping transfer (GST) tax parameters in effect in 2009	....	....	−14,611	−15,938	−17,310	−18,723	−20,444	−22,230	−24,261	−26,612	−29,182	−66,582	−189,311
Require consistency in value for transfer and income tax purposes	....	....	−267	−279	−303	−337	−356	−383	−407	−438	−467	−1,186	−3,237
Modify transfer tax rules for grantor retained annuity trusts (GRATs) and other grantor trusts	....	....	−1,054	−1,198	−1,359	−1,574	−1,892	−2,294	−2,637	−3,073	−3,273	−5,185	−18,354
Limit duration of GST tax exemption	....	....	....	....	....	....	....	....	....	....	....	....	....
Extend the lien on estate tax deferrals where estate consists largely of interest in closely held business	....	....	−23	−23	−24	−25	−27	−29	−31	−32	−34	−95	−248

Table S-9. Mandatory and Receipt Proposals—Continued

(Deficit increases (+) or decreases (–) in millions of dollars)

	2015	2016	2017	2018	2019	2020	2021	2022	2023	2024	2025	Totals 2016-2020	Totals 2016-2025
Modify GST tax treatment of Health and Education Exclusion Trusts	....	....	32	31	29	28	25	24	22	21	19	120	231
Simplify gift tax exclusion for annual gifts	....	....	–78	–155	–217	–320	–389	–428	–517	–618	–724	–770	–3,446
Expand applicability of definition of executor	....	....	....	....	....	....	....	....	....	....	....	....	....
Total, modify estate and gift tax provisions	....	....	–16,001	–17,562	–19,184	–20,951	–23,083	–25,340	–27,831	–30,752	–33,661	–73,698	–214,365
Other revenue raisers:													
Increase and modify Oil Spill Liability Trust Fund financing [12]	....	–105	–150	–155	–160	–165	–168	–176	–177	–181	–191	–735	–1,628
Reinstate Superfund taxes [12]	....	–1,585	–2,048	–2,080	–2,110	–2,126	–2,160	–2,205	–2,259	–2,307	–2,363	–9,949	–21,243
Increase tobacco taxes and index for inflation [12]	....	–8,434	–10,826	–10,663	–10,633	–10,301	–9,860	–9,403	–8,850	–8,342	–7,830	–50,857	–95,142
Make unemployment insurance surtax permanent [6]	....	–1,108	–1,527	–1,552	–1,575	–1,596	–1,620	–1,643	–1,669	–1,695	–1,701	–7,358	–15,686
Total, other revenue raisers	....	–11,232	–14,551	–14,450	–14,478	–14,188	–13,808	–13,427	–12,955	–12,525	–12,085	–68,899	–133,699
Reduce the tax gap and make reforms:													
Expand information reporting:													
Improve information reporting for certain businesses and contractors	....	–16	–39	–65	–89	–93	–97	–101	–106	–110	–115	–302	–831
Provide an exception to the limitation on disclosing tax return information to expand TIN matching beyond forms where payments are subject to backup withholding	....	....	....	....	....	....	....	....	....	....	....	....	....
Provide for reciprocal reporting of information in connection with the implementation of FATCA	....	....	....	....	....	....	....	....	....	....	....	....	....
Improve mortgage interest deduction reporting	....	–104	–160	–171	–182	–192	–203	–213	–222	–231	–240	–809	–1,918
Require Form W–2 reporting for employer contributions to defined contribution plans	....	....	....	....	....	....	....	....	....	....	....	....	....
Improve compliance by businesses:													
Increase certainty with respect to worker classification	....	–85	–420	–818	–978	–1,063	–1,155	–1,250	–1,356	–1,465	–1,580	–3,364	–10,170
Increase information sharing to administer excise taxes [12]	....	–4	–9	–13	–14	–16	–17	–18	–18	–19	–19	–56	–147
Provide authority to readily share information about beneficial ownership information of U.S. companies with law enforcement	....	....	–1	–2	–9	–6	–4	–3	–3	–3	–3	–18	–34
Strengthen tax administration:													

Table S–9. Mandatory and Receipt Proposals—Continued

(Deficit increases (+) or decreases (−) in millions of dollars)

	2015	2016	2017	2018	2019	2020	2021	2022	2023	2024	2025	Totals 2016-2020	Totals 2016-2025
Impose liability on shareholders to collect unpaid income taxes of applicable corporations		−442	−463	−484	−505	−528	−550	−574	−600	−626	−652	−2,422	−5,424
Streamline audit and adjustment procedures for large partnerships		−190	−252	−249	−242	−236	−238	−243	−248	−253	−256	−1,169	−2,407
Revise offer-in-compromise application rules		−1	−1	−2	−2	−2	−2	−2	−2	−2	−2	−8	−18
Expand IRS access to information in the National Directory of New Hires for tax administration purposes													
Make repeated willful failure to file a tax return a felony					−1	−1	−1	−1	−2	−2	−2	−2	−10
Facilitate tax compliance with local jurisdictions		−1	−1	−1	−2	−2	−2	−2	−2	−2	−2	−7	−17
Extend statute of limitations for assessment for overstated basis and State adjustments					−77	−90	−103	−118	−135	−155	−178	−167	−856
Improve investigative disclosure statute					−1	−1	−1	−1	−2	−2	−2	−2	−10
Allow the IRS to absorb credit and debit card processing fees for certain tax payments		−2	−2	−2	−2	−2	−2	−2	−2	−2	−2	−10	−20
Provide the IRS with greater flexibility to address correctable errors [11]		−30	−62	−64	−65	−65	−67	−68	−71	−72	−75	−286	−639
Enhance electronic filing of returns					−1	−1	−1	−1	−2	−2	−2	−2	−10
Improve the whistleblower program													
Index all civil tax penalties for inflation													
Extend IRS authority to require truncated Social Security Numbers on Form W–2													
Combat tax-related identity theft													
Allow States to send notices of intent to offset Federal tax refunds to collect State tax obligations by regular first-class mail instead of certified mail													
Rationalize tax return filing due dates so they are staggered [11]		180	−173	−181	−190	−196	−199	−207	−215	−221	−228	−560	−1,630
Increase oversight and due diligence of tax return preparers:													
Extend paid preparer EITC due diligence requirements to the child tax credit													
Explicitly provide that the Department of the Treasury and IRS have authority to regulate all paid return preparers [11]		−14	−32	−34	−38	−41	−45	−49	−53	−58	−63	−159	−427

Table S–9. Mandatory and Receipt Proposals—Continued

(Deficit increases (+) or decreases (–) in millions of dollars)

	2015	2016	2017	2018	2019	2020	2021	2022	2023	2024	2025	Totals 2016-2020	Totals 2016-2025
Increase the penalty applicable to paid tax preparers who engage in willful or reckless conduct		....	....	–1	–1	–1	–1	–1	–1	–1	–1	–3	–8
Enhance administrability of the appraiser penalty		....	....	....	....	....	....	....	....	....	....	....	....
Total, reduce the tax gap and make reforms		–709	–1,615	–2,087	–2,399	–2,536	–2,688	–2,854	–3,040	–3,226	–3,422	–9,346	–24,576
Simplify the tax system:													
Modify adoption credit to allow tribal determination of special needs		....	....	....	....	....	1	1	1	1	1	....	5
Repeal non-qualified preferred stock designation		–26	–44	–43	–41	–38	–35	–30	–26	–23	–20	–192	–326
Repeal preferential dividend rule for publicly traded and publicly offered REITs		....	....	....	....	....	....	....	....	....	....	....	....
Reform excise tax based on investment income of private foundations		....	6	5	5	6	6	6	6	6	7	22	53
Remove bonding requirements for certain taxpayers subject to Federal excise taxes on distilled spirits, wine, and beer		....	....	....	....	....	....	....	....	....	....	....	....
Simplify arbitrage investment restrictions		....	2	10	18	28	38	46	58	68	76	58	344
Simplify single-family housing mortgage bond targeting requirements		....	1	3	5	7	10	12	17	20	22	16	97
Streamline private business limits on governmental bonds		....	1	3	5	7	9	11	13	15	17	16	81
Repeal technical terminations of partnerships		–10	–16	–18	–20	–22	–24	–26	–28	–29	–31	–86	–224
Repeal anti-churning rules of section 197		24	99	198	281	338	370	378	378	378	378	940	2,822
Repeal special estimated tax payment provision for certain insurance companies		....	....	....	....	....	....	....	....	....	....	....	....
Repeal the telephone excise tax [12]		296	349	308	266	225	208	161	128	80	31	1,444	2,052
Increase the standard mileage rate for automobile use by volunteers		15	47	48	49	50	51	52	53	55	56	209	476
Consolidate contribution limitations for charitable deductions and extend the carryforward period for excess charitable contribution deduction amounts		88	49	5	6	6	6	482	1,168	1,801	2,379	154	5,990
Exclude from gross income subsidies from public utilities for purchase of water runoff management		....	....	....	....	....	....	....	....	....	....	....	....
Provide relief for certain accidental dual citizens		60	103	55	23	24	25	26	28	29	30	265	403
Total, simplify the tax system		447	597	574	597	631	665	1,119	1,796	2,401	2,946	2,846	11,773
Trade initiatives:													
Extend Generalized System of Preferences (GSP) [12]		381	164	....	....	....	....	....	....	....	....	545	545
Extend African Growth and Opportunity Act (AGOA) [12]		88	120	133	147	162	178	195	215	235	256	650	1,729

Table S–9. Mandatory and Receipt Proposals—Continued

(Deficit increases (+) or decreases (−) in millions of dollars)

	2015	2016	2017	2018	2019	2020	2021	2022	2023	2024	2025	Totals 2016-2020	Totals 2016-2025
Total, trade initiatives	......	469	284	133	147	162	178	195	215	235	256	1,195	2,274
Other initiatives:													
Allow offset of Federal income tax refunds to collect delinquent State income taxes for out-of-state residents	......	......	......	......	......	......	......	......	......	......	......	......	......
Authorize the limited sharing of business tax return information to improve the accuracy of important measures of the economy	......	......	......	......	......	......	......	......	......	......	......	......	......
Eliminate certain reviews conducted by the U.S. Treasury Inspector General for Tax Administration	......	......	......	......	......	......	......	......	......	......	......	......	......
Modify indexing to prevent deflationary adjustments	......	......	......	......	......	......	......	......	......	......	......	......	......
Extend reserve depletion date for Social Security's Disability Insurance program	......	......	......	......	......	......	......	......	......	......	......	......	......
Impose a 14-percent one-time tax on previously untaxed foreign income	......	−34,559	−56,407	−54,420	−52,434	−50,448	−19,861					−248,268	−268,129
Total, other initiatives	......	−34,559	−56,407	−54,420	−52,434	−50,448	−19,861					−248,268	−268,129
Total, tax proposals	−975	−91,521	−149,601	−152,257	−162,737	−168,428	−144,174	−130,903	−138,374	−145,846	−152,569	−724,544	−1,456,410
Grand total	5,094	−100,863	−126,469	−109,480	−169,063	−188,106	−170,244	−220,956	−194,139	−172,014	−239,549	−693,981	−1,690,883
Addendum, Reserve for long-run revenue-neutral business tax reform:													
Reform the U.S. international tax system:													
Restrict deductions for excessive interest of members of financial reporting groups	......	−2,566	−4,533	−4,987	−5,485	−6,034	−6,637	−7,301	−8,031	−8,834	−9,718	−23,605	−64,126
Provide tax incentives for locating jobs and business activity in the United States and remove tax deductions for shipping jobs overseas		13	22	23	24	25	25	27	28	29	31	107	247
Repeal delay in the implementation of worldwide interest allocation		1,352	2,308	2,400	2,496	2,596	1,055					11,152	12,207
Extend the exception under subpart F for active financing income		4,081	7,006	7,356	7,724	8,110	8,516	8,942	9,389	9,858	10,351	34,277	81,333
Extend the look-through treatment of payments between related CFCs		488	838	880	924	971	1,019	1,070	1,124	1,180	1,239	4,101	9,733
Impose a 19-percent minimum tax on foreign income		−11,881	−19,710	−19,873	−20,246	−20,633	−21,200	−21,799	−22,675	−23,478	−24,481	−92,343	−205,976
Impose a 14-percent one-time tax on previously untaxed foreign income [13]		......	......	......	......	......	......	......	......	......	......	......	......
Limit shifting of income through intangible property transfers		−88	−167	−201	−237	−275	−315	−361	−413	−473	−542	−968	−3,072
Disallow the deduction for excess non-taxed reinsurance premiums paid to affiliates		−346	−616	−667	−708	−744	−784	−829	−863	−897	−934	−3,081	−7,388

Table S–9. Mandatory and Receipt Proposals—Continued

(Deficit increases (+) or decreases (−) in millions of dollars)

	2015	2016	2017	2018	2019	2020	2021	2022	2023	2024	2025	Totals 2016-2020	Totals 2016-2025
Modify tax rules for dual capacity taxpayers	....	−533	−914	−956	−999	−1,043	−1,089	−1,119	−1,168	−1,220	−1,274	−4,445	−10,315
Tax gain from the sale of a partnership interest on look-through basis	....	−183	−253	−266	−279	−293	−308	−323	−339	−356	−374	−1,274	−2,974
Modify sections 338(h)(16) and 902 to limit credits when non-double taxation exists	....	−55	−95	−102	−105	−105	−105	−105	−105	−106	−106	−462	−989
Close loopholes under subpart F	....	−1,449	−2,519	−2,699	−2,890	−3,094	−3,312	−3,543	−3,789	−4,051	−4,330	−12,651	−31,676
Restrict the use of hybrid arrangements that create stateless income	....	−116	−201	−215	−230	−246	−264	−283	−304	−326	−350	−1,008	−2,535
Limit the ability of domestic entities to expatriate	....	−113	−311	−530	−769	−1,031	−1,317	−1,630	−1,970	−2,340	−2,743	−2,754	−12,754
Total, reform the U.S. international tax system	....	−11,396	−19,145	−19,837	−20,780	−21,796	−24,716	−27,254	−29,116	−31,014	−33,231	−92,954	−238,285
Simplification and tax relief for small business:													
Expand and permanently extend increased expensing for small business	7,200	10,941	8,935	7,300	6,254	5,502	5,108	4,968	4,896	4,929	5,012	38,932	63,845
Expand simplified accounting for small business and establish a uniform definition of small business for accounting methods	....	5,812	3,809	1,443	762	507	492	493	488	479	472	12,333	14,757
Eliminate capital gains taxation on investments in small business stock	....	....	....	....	....	206	710	1,277	1,811	2,342	2,869	206	9,215
Increase the limitations for deductible new business expenditures and consolidate provisions for start-up and organizational expenditures	....	359	446	440	434	431	428	426	423	419	415	2,110	4,221
Expand and simplify the tax credit provided to qualified small employers for non-elective contributions to employee health insurance [11]	24	305	328	218	174	148	102	113	76	60	26	1,173	1,550
Total, simplification and tax relief for small business	7,224	17,417	13,518	9,401	7,624	6,794	6,840	7,277	7,694	8,229	8,794	54,754	93,588
Incentives for manufacturing, research, and clean energy:													
Enhance and make permanent research incentives	3,552	7,529	9,290	10,356	11,389	12,396	13,387	14,370	15,352	16,336	17,327	50,960	127,732
Extend and modify certain employment tax credits, including incentives for hiring veterans	403	796	885	950	997	1,033	1,074	1,121	1,167	1,210	1,255	4,661	10,488
Modify and permanently extend renewable electricity production tax credit and investment tax credit [11]	....	−596	869	2,323	2,775	3,283	3,695	4,075	4,524	4,991	5,513	8,654	31,452
Modify and permanently extend the deduction for energy-efficient commercial building property	....	170	256	294	302	298	290	280	270	260	252	1,320	2,672
Provide a carbon dioxide investment and sequestration tax credit [11]	....	....	....	174	1,094	1,149	600	466	495	521	541	2,417	5,040

Table S-9. Mandatory and Receipt Proposals—Continued

(Deficit increases (+) or decreases (−) in millions of dollars)

	2015	2016	2017	2018	2019	2020	2021	2022	2023	2024	2025	Totals 2016-2020	Totals 2016-2025
Provide additional tax credits for investment in qualified property used in a qualifying advanced energy manufacturing project	......	......	73	192	1,111	772	94	−14	−48	−40	−37	2,148	2,103
Provide new Manufacturing Communities tax credit	......	87	256	457	600	683	745	784	689	447	145	2,083	4,893
Extend the tax credit for second generation biofuel production	35	80	119	149	163	175	183	158	113	65	18	686	1,223
Total, incentives for manufacturing, research, and clean energy	3,990	8,066	11,748	14,895	18,431	19,789	20,068	21,240	22,562	23,790	25,014	72,929	185,603
Incentives to promote regional growth:													
Modify and permanently extend the New Markets tax credit	18	119	289	491	720	968	1,226	1,470	1,605	1,620	1,586	2,587	10,094
Reform and expand the Low-Income Housing tax credit	......	9	42	130	233	345	441	541	641	751	860	759	3,993
Total, incentives to promote regional growth	18	128	331	621	953	1,313	1,667	2,011	2,246	2,371	2,446	3,346	14,087
Incentives for investment in infrastructure:													
Provide America Fast Forward Bonds and expand eligible uses [11]	......	1	5	11	14	22	28	35	41	48	53	53	258
Allow current refundings of State and local governmental bonds	......	1	5	5	5	5	5	5	5	5	5	21	46
Repeal the $150 million non-hospital bond limitation on all qualified 501(c)(3) bonds	......	......	1	3	5	7	9	11	13	16	17	16	82
Increase national limitation amount for qualified highway or surface freight transfer facility bonds	6	28	60	93	125	153	167	163	136	96	55	459	1,076
Provide a new category of qualified private activity bonds for infrastructure projects referred to as qualified public infrastructure bonds	......	25	117	251	386	524	638	695	714	733	751	1,303	4,834
Modify qualified private activity bonds for public education facilities	......	......	......	......	......	......	......	......	......	......	......	......	......
Modify treatment of banks investing in tax-exempt bonds	......	5	38	131	225	317	405	493	574	630	616	716	3,434
Repeal tax-exempt bond financing of professional sports facilities	......	−3	−11	−23	−35	−47	−60	−72	−85	−97	−109	−119	−542
Allow more flexible research arrangements for purposes of private business use limits	......	......	......	......	1	1	1	3	3	3	4	2	16
Modify tax-exempt bonds for Indian tribal governments	......	4	12	12	12	12	12	12	12	12	12	52	112
Exempt foreign pension funds from the application of FIRPTA	......	120	206	216	227	238	250	263	276	290	304	1,007	2,390
Total, incentives for investment in infrastructure	6	181	433	699	965	1,232	1,455	1,608	1,689	1,736	1,708	3,510	11,706

Eliminate fossil fuel tax preferences:

Table S–9. Mandatory and Receipt Proposals—Continued

(Deficit increases (+) or decreases (−) in millions of dollars)

	2015	2016	2017	2018	2019	2020	2021	2022	2023	2024	2025	Totals 2016-2020	Totals 2016-2025
Treat publicly-traded partnerships for fossil fuels as C corporations	......	......	......	......	......	......	-303	-322	-341	-358	-375	......	-1,699
Eliminate oil and natural gas preferences:													
Repeal enhanced oil recovery credit [14]	......	......	......	......	......	......	......	......	......	......	......	......	......
Repeal credit for oil and natural gas produced from marginal wells [14]	......	......	......	......	......	......	......	......	......	......	......	......	......
Repeal expensing of intangible drilling costs	......	-2,267	-3,182	-2,351	-1,867	-1,566	-1,243	-848	-695	-723	-753	-11,233	-15,495
Repeal deduction for tertiary injectants	......	-7	-10	-10	-10	-10	-10	-10	-10	-10	-10	-47	-97
Repeal exception to passive loss limitations for working interests in oil and natural gas properties	......	-9	-17	-19	-20	-20	-20	-20	-20	-20	-20	-85	-185
Repeal percentage depletion for oil and natural gas wells	......	-1,118	-1,790	-1,669	-1,585	-1,498	-1,375	-1,246	-1,122	-994	-856	-7,660	-13,253
Repeal domestic manufacturing deduction for oil and natural gas production	......	-647	-1,115	-1,139	-1,173	-1,208	-1,242	-1,280	-1,321	-1,366	-1,413	-5,282	-11,904
Increase geological and geophysical amortization period for independent producers to seven years	......	-91	-341	-537	-532	-440	-337	-226	-147	-125	-100	-1,941	-2,876
Subtotal, eliminate oil and natural gas preferences	......	-4,139	-6,455	-5,725	-5,187	-4,742	-4,530	-3,952	-3,656	-3,596	-3,527	-26,248	-45,509
Eliminate coal preferences:													
Repeal expensing of exploration and development costs	......	-40	-68	-70	-74	-77	-77	-75	-73	-71	-69	-329	-694
Repeal percentage depletion for hard mineral fuels	......	-183	-299	-288	-278	-266	-254	-241	-228	-214	-199	-1,314	-2,450
Repeal capital gains treatment for royalties	......	-27	-54	-53	-54	-55	-58	-61	-61	-62	-62	-243	-547
Repeal domestic manufacturing deduction for the production of coal and other hard mineral fuels	......	-45	-48	-50	-53	-54	-57	-59	-62	-65	-68	-250	-561
Subtotal, eliminate coal preferences	......	-295	-469	-461	-459	-452	-446	-436	-424	-412	-398	-2,136	-4,252
Total, eliminate fossil fuel tax preferences	......	-4,434	-6,924	-6,186	-5,646	-5,194	-4,976	-4,388	-4,080	-4,008	-3,925	-28,384	-49,761
Reform the treatment of financial and insurance industry products:													
Require that derivative contracts be marked to market with resulting gain or loss treated as ordinary	......	-2,926	-4,769	-4,138	-2,731	-1,733	-1,186	-731	-531	-535	-516	-16,297	-19,796

Table S-9. Mandatory and Receipt Proposals—Continued

(Deficit increases (+) or decreases (−) in millions of dollars)

	2015	2016	2017	2018	2019	2020	2021	2022	2023	2024	2025	Totals 2016-2020	Totals 2016-2025
Modify rules that apply to sales of life insurance contracts	....	−23	−43	−46	−48	−50	−54	−56	−58	−61	−63	−210	−502
Modify proration rules for life insurance company general and separate accounts	....	−385	−676	−722	−762	−792	−816	−836	−843	−849	−862	−3,337	−7,543
Expand pro rata interest expense disallowance for corporate-owned life insurance	....	−65	−159	−252	−364	−492	−641	−809	−980	−1,160	−1,357	−1,332	−6,279
Conform net operating loss (NOL) rules of life insurance companies to those of other corporations	....	−15	−27	−29	−30	−32	−34	−36	−37	−39	−40	−133	−319
Total, reform the treatment of financial and insurance industry products	....	−3,414	−5,674	−5,187	−3,935	−3,099	−2,731	−2,468	−2,449	−2,644	−2,838	−21,309	−34,439
Other revenue changes and loophole closers:													
Repeal LIFO method of accounting for inventories	....	−5,505	−7,866	−7,812	−8,012	−7,908	−8,070	−7,752	−7,644	−7,931	−7,592	−37,103	−76,092
Repeal lower-of-cost-or-market inventory accounting method	....	−743	−1,491	−1,501	−1,511	−889	−266	−278	−291	−304	−317	−6,135	−7,591
Repeal like-kind exchange rules for real property and collectibles	....	−659	−2,005	−2,026	−2,048	−2,070	−2,094	−2,119	−2,145	−2,174	−2,202	−8,808	−19,542
Modify depreciation rules for purchases of general aviation passenger aircraft	....	−108	−338	−499	−531	−596	−593	−395	−198	−139	−141	−2,072	−3,538
Expand the definition of substantial built-in loss for purposes of partnership loss transfers	....	−6	−7	−7	−7	−7	−8	−8	−10	−10	−10	−34	−80
Extend partnership basis limitation rules to nondeductible expenditures	....	−69	−97	−102	−105	−108	−110	−112	−114	−116	−118	−481	−1,051
Limit the importation of losses under related party loss limitation rules	....	−63	−87	−92	−95	−97	−99	−100	−102	−104	−106	−434	−945
Deny deduction for punitive damages	....	−30	−43	−44	−45	−46	−47	−48	−49	−51	−52	−208	−455
Conform corporate ownership standards	....	−1	−17	−32	−33	−34	−35	−36	−38	−40	−42	−117	−308
Tax corporate distributions as dividends	....	−48	−82	−86	−90	−94	−98	−103	−108	−113	−118	−400	−940
Repeal FICA tip credit	....	−480	−993	−1,062	−1,137	−1,216	−1,301	−1,389	−1,483	−1,581	−1,687	−4,888	−12,329
Repeal the excise tax credit for distilled spirits with flavor and wine additives[12]	....	−85	−112	−112	−112	−112	−112	−112	−112	−112	−112	−533	−1,093
Total, other revenue changes and loophole closers	....	−7,797	−13,138	−13,375	−13,726	−13,177	−12,833	−12,452	−12,294	−12,675	−12,497	−61,213	−123,964
Total, reserve for long-run revenue-neutral business tax reform	11,238	−1,249	−18,851	−18,969	−16,114	−14,138	−15,226	−14,426	−13,748	−14,215	−14,529	−69,321	−141,465

Note: For receipt effects, positive figures indicate lower receipts. For outlay effects, positive figures indicate higher outlays. For net costs, positive figures indicate higher deficits.

[1] For 2016, the additional funding is proposed as a discretionary change in mandatory programs (CHIMP).

[2] Last summer, the President took action within his existing authority to implement eligibility expansions to income-based repayment plans proposed in the 2015 Budget. However, the Administration continues to seek to work with the Congress to create a unified, simple, and better targeted PAYE program. The Budget would use the resulting savings presented in this table to help students and expand college access.

[3] The estimates for this proposal include effects on receipts. The receipt effects included in the totals above are as follows:

Table S–9. Mandatory and Receipt Proposals—Continued

(Deficit increases (+) or decreases (−) in millions of dollars)

	2015	2016	2017	2018	2019	2020	2021	2022	2023	2024	2025	Totals 2016-2020	Totals 2016-2025
Reauthorize special assessment from domestic nuclear utilities		−204	−208	−213	−218	−223	−228	−233	−238	−244	−249	−1,066	−2,258
Create State option to provide 12-month continuous Medicaid eligibility for adults			−51	−103	−224	−203	−204	−212	−222	−229	−241	−581	−1,689
Extend CHIP funding through 2019		−24	−351	−750	−835	−515						−2,475	−2,475
Establish an AML hardrock reclamation fund			−200	−200	−200	−200	−200	−200	−200	−200	−200	−800	−1,800
Increase coal AML fee to pre–2006 levels		−49	−50	−51	−52	−52	−52					−254	−306
Strengthen Unemployment Insurance (UI) system solvency			−3,634	−3,618	−3,457	−3,601	−3,901	−6,485	−6,313	−6,648	−7,100	−14,310	−44,757
Improve UI Extended Benefits		−52	−201	−208	−269	−363	−443	−483	−448	−462	−483	−1,093	−3,412
Modernize UI				−200	−120	−40	−40					−360	−400
Implement cap adjustments for UI program integrity				4	12	20	34	45	55	67	78	36	315
Improve UI program integrity (mandatory SIDES)				1	2	2	3	6	6	7	9	5	36
Allow use of prisoner database for UI program integrity					1	2	2	3	3	4	4	3	19
Increase levy authority for payments to Medicare providers with delinquent tax debt		−34	−50	−50	−51	−52	−54	−54	−56	−56	−57	−237	−514
Implement tax enforcement program integrity cap adjustment		−432	−1,451	−2,926	−4,476	−6,095	−7,481	−8,475	−9,077	−9,503	−9,819	−15,380	−59,735
Reform inland waterways funding		−113	−113	−113	−113	−113	−113	−113	−113	−113	−113	−565	−1,130
Offset DI benefits for period of concurrent UI receipt					2	6	11	16	23	38	42	8	138
Enact immigration reform		−2,000	−12,000	−28,000	−39,000	−45,000	−47,000	−55,000	−64,000	−77,000	−87,000	−126,000	−456,000
Total receipt effects of mandatory proposals		−2,908	−18,309	−36,427	−48,998	−56,427	−59,666	−71,185	−80,580	−94,339	−105,129	−163,069	−573,968

[4] Health savings in Table S-2 includes all HHS health savings and OPM FEHBP savings.

[5] Unemployment insurance reform also includes the proposal to make the unemployment insurance surtax permanent. On net, the package reduces the deficit by $5.9 billion over 10 years.

[6] Revenues are net of the 20% Treasury offset.

[7] Deficit savings achieved through the increased value of monetized spectrum achieved via targeted investments that will enhance Federal spectrum efficiency and create more opportunity for spectrum sharing.

[8] This proposal also saves less than $500,000 in SSI over 10 years.

[9] This proposal costs less than $500,000 in each year and over 5 and 10 years.

[10] Savings of $1 million over 5 years and $4 million over 10 years.

[11] The estimates for this proposal include effects on outlays. The outlay effects included in the totals above are as follows:

	2015	2016	2017	2018	2019	2020	2021	2022	2023	2024	2025	Totals 2016-2020	Totals 2016-2025

Table S–9.　Mandatory and Receipt Proposals—Continued

(Deficit increases (+) or decreases (−) in millions of dollars)

	2015	2016	2017	2018	2019	2020	2021	2022	2023	2024	2025	Totals 2016-2020	Totals 2016-2025
Reform child care tax incentives	......	932	969	1,014	1,066	1,107	1,139	1,190	1,231	1,227	1,265	5,088	11,140
Simplify and better target tax benefits for education	......	......	1,862	4,822	4,774	4,829	5,177	5,471	5,785	6,075	6,135	16,287	44,930
Provide for automatic enrollment in IRAs, including a small employer tax credit, increase the tax credit for small employer plan start-up costs, and provide an additional tax credit for small employer plans newly offering auto-enrollment		......	127	195	200	209	212	215	220	225	229	731	1,832
Expand EITC for workers without qualifying children		276	5,519	5,553	5,600	5,709	5,825	5,914	5,997	6,090	6,198	22,657	52,681
Simplify the rules for claiming the EITC for workers without qualifying children		26	522	527	517	532	545	555	565	574	596	2,124	4,959
Provide a second-earner tax credit		......	732	729	750	740	761	768	770	762	767	2,951	6,779
Designate Promise Zones		12	28	29	31	32	34	35	37	38	41	132	317
Provide the IRS with greater flexibility to address correctable errors		−26	−53	−54	−55	−55	−56	−57	−59	−60	−62	−243	−537
Rationalize tax return filing due dates so they are staggered		−22	−22	−22	−23	−23	−23	−24	−24	−25	−25	−112	−233
Explicitly provide that the Department of the Treasury and IRS have authority to regulate all paid return preparers	......	−2	−14	−15	−17	−18	−20	−21	−23	−25	−27	−66	−182
Total, outlay effects of receipt proposals		1,196	9,670	12,778	12,843	13,062	13,594	14,046	14,499	14,881	15,117	49,549	121,686
Addendum, reserve for long-run revenue-neutral business tax reform:													
Expand and simplify the tax credit provided to qualified small employers for non-elective contributions to employee health insurance	6	76	68	32	23	21	11	10	8	8	4	220	261
Modify and permanently extend renewable electricity production tax credit and investment tax credit		......	20	47	63	71	78	83	90	95	101	201	648
Provide a carbon dioxide investment and sequestration tax credit		......	......	......	729	728	170	28	48	65	76	1,457	1,844
Provide America Fast Forward Bonds and expand eligible uses		306	1,397	3,006	4,689	6,438	8,244	10,101	11,994	13,911	15,845	15,836	75,931

[12] Revenues are net of the 25% Treasury offset.
[13] The effect of this proposal on receipts is shown above under tax proposals.
[14] This provision is estimated to have zero receipt effect under the Administration's current economic projections.

Table S–10. Funding Levels for Appropriated ("Discretionary") Programs by Category

(Budget authority in billions of dollars)

	Actual 2014	Enacted 2015	Request 2016	Outyears 2017	2018	2019	2020	2021	2022	2023	2024	2025	Totals 2016–2020	2016–2025
Discretionary Adjusted Baseline by Category:[1]														
Defense Category	521	522	523	536	549	562	576	590	660	676	693	710	2,746	6,075
Non-Defense Category	514	512	493	504	516	530	543	556	604	619	635	650	2,587	5,651
Total, Base Discretionary Funding	1,035	1,033	1,017	1,040	1,065	1,092	1,119	1,146	1,264	1,295	1,327	1,360	5,333	11,726
Discretionary Policy Changes to Baseline Caps:														
Proposed Cap Changes:[2]														
Defense Category	....	*	+38	+37	+35	+30	+22	+20	–38	–41	–45	–49	+162	+9
Non-Defense Category	....	–2	+37	+37	+35	+30	+22	+20	–16	–18	–21	–23	+160	+102
Non-Defense Category Reclassifications:														
Surface Transportation Programs	–4	–4	–4	–4	–4	–4	–5	–5	–5	–5	–5	–5	–22	–46
Program Integrity	....	....	*	*	*	*	*	*	*	*	*	*	–1	–2
Contract Support Costs	....	....	....	–1	–1	–1	–1	–1	–1	–1	–1	–1	–4	–10
Proposed Discretionary Policy by Category:														
Defense Category	521	522	561	573	584	592	598	610	622	635	648	661	2,908	6,084
Non-Defense Category	510	506	526	535	545	554	559	570	582	595	608	620	2,720	5,694
Total, Base Discretionary Funding	1,031	1,027	1,087	1,108	1,129	1,146	1,157	1,180	1,204	1,230	1,256	1,281	5,628	11,778
Discretionary Cap Adjustments and Other Funding (not included above):[3]														
Overseas Contingency Operations[4]	92	73	58	27	27	27	27	27	....	....	....	....	165	191
Disaster Relief	6	7	7	7	7	7	7	7	....	....	....	....	7	7
Program Integrity	1	1	2	1	2	2	3	3	3	3	3	3	11	25
Wildfire Suppression	....	....	1	1	1	1	1	1	1	1	1	1	5	11
Other Emergency/Supplemental Funding	*	5	....	....	....	....	....	....	....	....	....	....	....	....
Total, Cap Adjustments and Other	99	87	68	29	30	30	30	31	4	4	4	4	188	235
Grand Total, Discretionary Budget Authority	1,129	1,114	1,155	1,138	1,159	1,176	1,188	1,211	1,208	1,234	1,260	1,286	5,815	12,013

Memorandum: Current Law and Proposed Changes to Existing BBEDCA Caps:[5]	2016	2017	2018	2019	2020	2021	2016–2021
Joint Committee Reductions	–90	–90	–91	–90	–89	–88	–539
2016 Budget Proposed Addback to caps	+74	+74	+70	+60	+44	+40	+362

Table S–10. Funding Levels for Appropriated ("Discretionary") Programs by Category—Continued

(Budget authority in billions of dollars)

* $500 million or less.

[1] The discretionary funding levels from OMB's adjusted baseline are consistent with the caps in the Balanced Budget and Emergency Deficit Control Act of 1985 (BBEDCA), as amended, with separate categories of funding for "defense" (or Function 050) and "non-defense" for 2015–2021. These baseline levels assume Joint Committee enforcement cap reductions are in effect through 2021. For 2022 through 2025, programs are assumed to grow at current services growth rates with Joint Committee enforcement no longer in effect, consistent with current law. The levels shown here for the non-defense category do not include the reclassification of surface transportation programs shown later in the table.

[2] The 2016 Budget provides a detailed request for 2016 at the cap levels requested in the 2015 Budget and, after 2016, continues the 2015 Budget framework of providing additional investments in both defense and non-defense programs above the baseline levels that include Joint Committee enforcement. In addition, the 2015 Enacted levels are illustratively adjusted to reflect the 2015 Request for the Department of Homeland Security since the programs and activities in the Department were under a short-term continuing resolution at the time the 2016 Budget was developed.

[3] Where applicable, amounts in 2014 through 2025 are existing or proposed cap adjustments designated pursuant to Section 251(b)(2) of BBEDCA, as amended. The 2016 Budget proposes new cap adjustments for program integrity and wildfire suppression activities. For 2017 through 2025, the cap adjustment levels for wildfire suppression are a placeholder that increase at the policy growth rates in the President's Budget. The existing disaster relief cap adjustment ceiling (which is determined one year at a time) would be reduced by the amount provided for wildfire suppression activities under the cap adjustment for the preceding fiscal year. The amounts will be refined in subsequent Budgets as data on the average costs for wildfire suppression are updated annually.

[4] The 2016 Budget includes placeholder amounts of nearly $27 billion per year for Government-wide OCO funding from 2017 to 2021. The placeholder amounts continue to reflect a total OCO budget authority cap from 2013 to 2021 of $450 billion, in line with previous years' policy, but do not reflect any specific decisions or assumptions about OCO funding in any particular year. These amounts do not reflect the Administration's intent to transition all enduring costs currently funded in the OCO budget to the base budget beginning in 2017 and ending by 2020. Those amounts will be refined in subsequent Budgets as the Administration develops its OCO transition plan.

[5] Under Joint Committee enforcement, the current law defense and non-defense discretionary caps specified in BBEDCA are estimated to be reduced by a combined $539 billion over the 2016 through 2021 period. The 2016 Budget proposes to restore approximately two-thirds of those reductions.

Table S–11. Funding Levels for Appropriated ("Discretionary") Programs by Agency

(Budget authority in billions of dollars)

	Actual	Enacted	Request	Outyears									Totals	
	2014	2015	2016	2017	2018	2019	2020	2021	2022	2023	2024	2025	2016-2020	2016-2025
Base Discretionary Funding by Agency:[1]														
Agriculture	24.3	23.8	23.5	25.2	25.5	25.7	26.0	26.5	27.1	27.6	28.2	28.7	125.9	264.0
Commerce	8.3	8.8	9.8	10.3	10.7	11.9	15.5	10.6	10.4	10.7	10.8	11.3	58.3	112.0
Census Bureau	*0.9*	*1.1*	*1.5*	*1.8*	*2.1*	*3.2*	*6.7*	*1.6*	*1.2*	*1.3*	*1.3*	*1.5*	*15.2*	*22.1*
Defense[2]	496.0	496.1	534.3	547.3	556.4	564.4	570.0	581.4	593.0	604.9	617.0	629.3	2,772.4	5,798.1
Education[2]	67.3	67.1	70.7	71.7	72.7	73.2	73.7	74.7	75.8	76.8	77.9	79.0	362.0	746.3
Energy	27.2	27.3	29.9	29.3	29.9	30.6	31.0	31.6	32.2	32.8	33.5	34.2	150.7	315.1
National Nuclear Security Administration[2]	*11.2*	*11.4*	*12.6*	*11.5*	*11.7*	*12.2*	*12.3*	*12.6*	*12.8*	*13.1*	*13.3*	*13.6*	*60.3*	*125.7*
Health & Human Services[3]	79.8	80.2	79.9	86.3	88.0	88.8	89.7	91.5	93.3	95.2	97.1	99.0	432.6	908.9
Homeland Security[4]	39.8	38.2	41.2	41.6	42.2	42.5	43.0	43.8	44.8	45.7	46.6	47.5	210.4	438.8
Housing and Urban Development	34.2	34.8	41.0	41.8	42.6	43.0	43.4	44.2	45.0	45.8	46.7	47.5	211.8	441.1
Interior	11.7	12.1	12.9	12.9	13.1	13.3	13.4	13.7	14.0	14.2	14.5	14.8	65.6	136.7
Justice	27.3	27.3	14.9	29.4	30.0	30.3	30.6	31.2	31.9	32.5	33.1	33.8	135.2	297.8
Labor	12.0	11.9	13.2	13.4	13.6	13.7	13.8	14.1	14.3	14.6	14.8	15.1	67.7	140.6
State and Other International Programs	42.9	40.1	46.3	47.2	48.1	48.6	48.9	49.9	50.8	51.9	52.9	53.9	239.0	498.4
Transportation	13.6	13.8	14.3	14.6	14.9	15.1	15.2	15.5	15.8	16.2	16.5	16.8	74.2	155.0
Treasury	12.7	12.2	12.8	14.0	14.3	14.5	14.8	15.1	15.5	15.8	16.2	16.5	70.4	149.5
Veterans Affairs	63.3	65.1	70.2	74.8	76.4	78.0	79.6	81.2	83.2	85.2	87.3	89.4	379.0	805.3
Corps of Engineers	5.7	5.5	4.7	4.8	4.9	5.0	5.0	5.1	5.2	5.3	5.4	5.5	24.5	51.1
Environmental Protection Agency	8.2	8.1	8.6	8.8	8.9	9.0	9.1	9.3	9.5	9.7	9.9	10.1	44.4	92.8
General Services Administration	2.0	-0.4	0.8	0.3	0.3	0.3	0.3	0.3	0.3	0.3	0.3	0.3	1.9	3.4
National Aeronautics & Space Administration	17.6	18.0	18.5	18.9	19.3	19.5	19.7	20.1	20.5	20.9	21.3	21.7	95.8	200.2
National Science Foundation	7.2	7.3	7.7	7.9	8.0	8.1	8.2	8.4	8.5	8.7	8.9	9.1	39.9	83.5
Small Business Administration	0.9	0.9	0.7	0.7	0.7	0.7	0.7	0.8	0.8	0.8	0.8	0.8	3.6	7.6
Social Security Administration[3]	8.9	9.0	9.6	9.4	9.6	9.7	9.8	10.0	10.2	10.4	10.6	10.8	48.1	100.1
Corporation for National & Community Service	1.0	1.1	1.2	1.2	1.2	1.2	1.3	1.3	1.3	1.3	1.4	1.4	6.1	12.8
Other Agencies	18.8	19.0	20.0	20.0	20.4	20.6	20.8	21.1	21.6	22.0	22.4	22.9	101.8	211.8
Allowances[5]				-23.1	-22.7	-21.7	-26.5	-21.5	-21.1	-19.5	-18.3	-18.1	-93.9	-192.4
Subtotal, Base Discretionary Funding	**1,030.8**	**1,027.4**	**1,086.8**	**1,108.4**	**1,129.3**	**1,146.2**	**1,157.1**	**1,180.0**	**1,203.8**	**1,229.7**	**1,255.6**	**1,281.5**	**5,627.7**	**11,778.3**

Table S–11. Funding Levels for Appropriated ("Discretionary") Programs by Agency—Continued

(Budget authority in billions of dollars)

	Actual 2014	Enacted 2015	Request 2016	Outyears 2017	2018	2019	2020	2021	2022	2023	2024	2025	Totals 2016-2020	2016-2025
Discretionary Cap Adjustments and Other Funding (not included above):[6]														
Overseas Contingency Operations	91.9	73.5	58.0	26.7	26.7	26.7	26.7	26.7	......	......	......	......	164.7	191.3
Defense[4]	85.2	64.2	50.9	......	......	......	......	......	......	......	......	......	50.9	50.9
Homeland Security[4]	0.2	......	......	......	......	......	......	......	......	......	......	......	......	......
State and Other International Programs	6.5	9.3	7.0	......	......	......	......	......	......	......	......	......	7.0	7.0
Overseas Contingency Operations Outyears[7]	......	......	......	26.7	26.7	26.7	26.7	26.7	26.7	26.7	26.7	26.7	106.7	133.3
Program Integrity	0.9	1.5	2.3	1.5	1.9	2.3	2.7	2.8	2.8	2.9	3.0	3.1	10.6	25.1
Health & Human Services	......	0.4	0.4	0.4	0.4	0.5	0.5	0.5	0.5	0.5	0.6	0.6	2.2	4.9
Labor	......	......	*	*	*	*	*	0.1	0.1	0.1	0.1	0.1	0.2	0.5
Treasury	......	......	0.7	1.0	1.4	1.8	2.2	2.2	2.3	2.3	2.4	2.4	7.0	18.6
SSA	0.9	1.1	1.2	......	......	......	......	......	......	......	......	......	1.2	1.2
Disaster Relief	5.6	6.5	6.9	......	......	......	......	......	......	......	......	......	6.9	6.9
Agriculture	......	0.1	......	......	......	......	......	......	......	......	......	......	......	......
Homeland Security[4]	5.6	6.4	6.7	......	......	......	......	......	......	......	......	......	6.7	6.7
Small Business Administration	......	......	0.2	......	......	......	......	......	......	......	......	......	0.2	0.2
Wildfire Suppression[8]	......	......	1.1	1.1	1.1	1.1	1.1	1.1	1.2	1.2	1.2	1.2	5.5	11.4
Agriculture	......	......	0.9	0.9	0.9	0.9	0.9	0.9	0.9	1.0	1.0	1.0	4.4	9.2
Interior	......	......	0.2	0.2	0.2	0.2	0.2	0.2	0.2	0.2	0.2	0.2	1.0	2.2
Other Emergency Funding	0.2	5.4	......	......	......	......	......	......	......	......	......	......	......	......
Defense	0.2	0.1	......	......	......	......	......	......	......	......	......	......	......	......
Health & Human Services	......	2.8	......	......	......	......	......	......	......	......	......	......	......	......
State and Other International Programs	......	2.5	......	......	......	......	......	......	......	......	......	......	......	......
Grand Total, Discretionary Funding	1,129.5	1,114.3	1,154.9	1,137.6	1,158.9	1,176.2	1,187.5	1,210.5	1,207.8	1,233.8	1,259.8	1,285.8	5,815.3	12,013.0

* $50 million or less.

[1] Amounts in the actual and enacted years of 2014 and 2015 exclude changes in mandatory programs enacted in appropriations bills since those amounts have been rebased as mandatory, whereas amounts in 2016 are net of these proposals.

[2] The Department of Defense (DOD) levels in 2017–2025 include funding that will be allocated, in annual increments, to the National Nuclear Security Administration (NNSA). Current estimates by which DOD's budget authority will decrease and NNSA's will increase are, in millions of dollars: 2017: $1,602; 2018: $1,665; 2019: $1,698; 2020: $1,735; 2017–2025: $15,910. DOD and NNSA are reviewing NNSA's outyear requirements and these will be included in future reports to the Congress.

[3] Funding from the Hospital Insurance and Supplementary Medical Insurance trust funds for administrative expenses incurred by the Social Security Administration that support the Medicare program are included in the Health and Human Services total and not in the Social Security Administration total.

[4] The 2015 Enacted levels are illustratively adjusted to reflect the 2015 Request for the Department of Homeland Security since the programs and activities in the Department were under a short-term continuing resolution at the time the 2016 Budget was developed.

Table S–11. Funding Levels for Appropriated ("Discretionary") Programs by Agency—Continued

(Budget authority in billions of dollars)

[5] The 2016 Budget includes allowances, similar to the Function 920 allowances used in Budget Resolutions, to represent amounts to be allocated among the respective agencies to reach the proposed defense and non-defense caps for 2017 and beyond. These levels are determined for illustrative purposes but do not reflect specific policy decisions.

[6] Where applicable, amounts in 2014 through 2025 are existing or proposed cap adjustments designated pursuant to Section 251(b)(2) of the BBEDCA, as amended.

[7] The 2016 Budget includes placeholder amounts of nearly $27 billion per year for Government-wide OCO funding from 2017 to 2021. The placeholder amounts continue to reflect a total OCO budget authority cap from 2013 to 2021 of $450 billion, in line with previous years' policy, but do not reflect any specific decisions or assumptions about OCO funding in any particular year. These amounts do not reflect the Administration's intent to transition all enduring costs currently funded in the OCO budget to the base budget beginning in 2017 and ending by 2020. Those amounts will be refined in subsequent Budgets as the Administration develops its OCO transition plan.

[8] For 2017 through 2025, the cap adjustment levels are a placeholder that increase at the policy growth rates in the President's Budget. The existing disaster relief cap adjustment ceiling (which is determined one year at a time) would be reduced by the amount provided for wildfire suppression activities under the cap adjustment for the preceding fiscal year. Those amounts will be refined in subsequent Budgets as data on the average costs for wildfire suppression are updated annually.

Table S–12. Economic Assumptions[1]

(Calendar years)

	Actual 2013	2014	2015	2016	2017	2018	Projections						
							2019	2020	2021	2022	2023	2024	2025
Gross Domestic Product (GDP):													
Nominal level, billions of dollars	16,768	17,394	18,188	19,039	19,933	20,847	21,770	22,717	23,705	24,736	25,812	26,934	28,106
Percent change, nominal GDP, year/year	3.7	3.7	4.6	4.7	4.7	4.6	4.4	4.3	4.3	4.3	4.3	4.3	4.3
Real GDP, percent change, year/year	2.2	2.2	3.1	3.0	2.8	2.6	2.4	2.3	2.3	2.3	2.3	2.3	2.3
Real GDP, percent change, Q4/Q4	3.1	2.1	3.0	3.0	2.7	2.5	2.3	2.3	2.3	2.3	2.3	2.3	2.3
GDP chained price index, percent change, year/year	1.5	1.5	1.4	1.6	1.8	2.0	2.0	2.0	2.0	2.0	2.0	2.0	2.0
Consumer Price Index,[2] percent change, year/year	1.5	1.7	1.4	1.9	2.1	2.2	2.3	2.3	2.3	2.3	2.3	2.3	2.3
Interest rates, percent:[3]													
91-day Treasury bills[4]	0.1	*	0.4	1.5	2.4	2.9	3.2	3.3	3.4	3.4	3.5	3.5	3.5
10-year Treasury notes	2.4	2.6	2.8	3.3	3.7	4.0	4.3	4.5	4.5	4.5	4.5	4.5	4.5
Unemployment rate, civilian, percent[3]	7.4	6.2	5.4	5.1	4.9	4.9	5.0	5.1	5.2	5.2	5.2	5.2	5.2

* 0.05 percent or less.

Note: A more detailed table of economic assumptions appears in Chapter 2, "Economic Assumptions and Interactions with the Budget," in the *Analytical Perspectives* volume of the Budget.

[1] Based on information available as of mid-November 2014.

[2] Seasonally adjusted CPI for all urban consumers.

[3] Annual average.

[4] Average rate, secondary market (bank discount basis).

Table S–13. Federal Government Financing and Debt

(Dollar amounts in billions)

	Actual 2014	Estimate										
		2015	2016	2017	2018	2019	2020	2021	2022	2023	2024	2025
Financing:												
Unified budget deficit:												
Primary deficit (+)/surplus (−)	256	353	191	102	55	34	10	4	−23	−65	−106	−99
Net interest	229	229	283	361	424	483	544	597	649	700	744	785
Unified budget deficit	485	583	474	463	479	518	554	600	626	635	639	687
As a percent of GDP	2.8%	3.2%	2.5%	2.3%	2.3%	2.4%	2.5%	2.6%	2.6%	2.5%	2.4%	2.5%
Other transactions affecting borrowing from the public:												
Changes in financial assets and liabilities:[1]												
Change in Treasury operating cash balance	70	42	......									
Net disbursements of credit financing accounts:												
Direct loan accounts	121	96	132	137	133	129	125	119	117	119	117	116
Guaranteed loan accounts	12	8	−3	−3	−1	−2	−2	−4	−5	−8	−8	−8
Troubled Asset Relief Program (TARP) equity purchase accounts	−6	−1	−*	−*	−*	−*	−*	−*	−*	−*	−*	−*
Net purchases of non-Federal securities by the National Railroad Retirement Investment Trust (NRRIT)	1	−*	−1	−1	−1	−1	−1	−1	−1	−1	−1	−*
Net change in other financial assets and liabilities:[2]	114	......										
Subtotal, changes in financial assets and liabilities	313	144	128	134	131	127	122	114	111	111	108	108
Seigniorage on coins	−*	−*	−*	−*	−*	−*	−*	−*	−*	−*	−*	−*
Total, other transactions affecting borrowing from the public	313	144	128	134	131	127	121	114	110	111	108	107
Total, requirement to borrow from the public (equals change in debt held by the public)	797	726	602	596	610	644	676	714	736	746	747	794
Changes in Debt Subject to Statutory Limitation:												
Change in debt held by the public	797	726	602	596	610	644	676	714	736	746	747	794
Change in debt held by Government accounts	278	107	104	165	165	126	97	86	4	16	33	−26
Change in other factors	7	1	2	2	2	3	2	2	2	2	1	−*
Total, change in debt subject to statutory limitation	1,082	834	708	763	778	773	775	803	742	763	781	768
Debt Subject to Statutory Limitation, End of Year:												
Debt issued by Treasury	17,768	18,600	19,307	20,068	20,845	21,616	22,389	23,191	23,931	24,693	25,474	26,242
Adjustment for discount, premium, and coverage[3]	13	15	17	18	19	21	22	24	25	26	27	27
Total, debt subject to statutory limitation[4]	17,781	18,615	19,323	20,087	20,864	21,637	22,412	23,214	23,956	24,720	25,501	26,269

Table S–13. Federal Government Financing and Debt—Continued

(Dollar amounts in billions)

	Actual 2014	Estimate 2015	2016	2017	2018	2019	2020	2021	2022	2023	2024	2025
Debt Outstanding, End of Year:												
Gross Federal debt:[5]												
Debt issued by Treasury	17,768	18,600	19,307	20,068	20,845	21,616	22,389	23,191	23,931	24,693	25,474	26,242
Debt issued by other agencies	26	27	27	27	25	24	24	23	22	22	21	21
Total, gross Federal debt	17,794	18,628	19,334	20,095	20,870	21,640	22,413	23,213	23,953	24,715	25,494	26,262
Held by:												
Debt held by Government accounts	5,015	5,121	5,225	5,390	5,555	5,681	5,778	5,864	5,868	5,885	5,917	5,891
Debt held by the public[6]	12,780	13,506	14,108	14,705	15,315	15,959	16,635	17,349	18,085	18,830	19,577	20,371
As a percent of GDP	74.1%	75.1%	75.0%	74.6%	74.3%	74.1%	74.0%	74.0%	73.9%	73.7%	73.5%	73.3%
Debt Held by the Public Net of Financial Assets:												
Debt held by the public	12,780	13,506	14,108	14,705	15,315	15,959	16,635	17,349	18,085	18,830	19,577	20,371
Less financial assets net of liabilities:												
Treasury operating cash balance	158	200	200	200	200	200	200	200	200	200	200	200
Credit financing account balances:												
Direct loan accounts	1,065	1,161	1,293	1,430	1,564	1,693	1,818	1,936	2,053	2,173	2,290	2,406
Guaranteed loan accounts	2	10	7	4	3	2	–*	–4	–10	–17	–26	–34
TARP equity purchase accounts	1	*	*	*	–*	–*	–*	–*	–*	–1	–1	–1
Government-sponsored enterprise preferred stock	96	96	96	96	96	96	96	96	96	96	96	96
Non-Federal securities held by NRRIT	25	25	24	23	22	22	21	20	19	19	18	18
Other assets net of liabilities	–23	–23	–23	–23	–23	–23	–23	–23	–23	–23	–23	–23
Total, financial assets net of liabilities	1,324	1,469	1,597	1,731	1,862	1,989	2,111	2,225	2,335	2,447	2,555	2,663
Debt held by the public net of financial assets	11,455	12,038	12,512	12,974	13,453	13,970	14,524	15,124	15,749	16,384	17,022	17,709
As a percent of GDP	66.4%	66.9%	66.5%	65.8%	65.3%	64.9%	64.6%	64.5%	64.4%	64.2%	63.9%	63.7%

* $500 million or less.

[1] A decrease in the Treasury operating cash balance (which is an asset) is a means of financing a deficit and therefore has a negative sign. An increase in checks outstanding (which is a liability) is also a means of financing a deficit and therefore also has a negative sign.

[2] Includes checks outstanding, accrued interest payable on Treasury debt, uninvested deposit fund balances, allocations of special drawing rights, and other liability accounts; and, as an offset, cash and monetary assets (other than the Treasury operating cash balance), other asset accounts, and profit on sale of gold.

[3] Consists mainly of debt issued by the Federal Financing Bank (which is not subject to limit), Treasury securities held by the Federal Financing Bank, the unamortized discount (less premium) on public issues of Treasury notes and bonds (other than zero-coupon bonds), and the unrealized discount on Government account series securities.

[4] Legislation enacted February 15, 2014, (P.L. 113-83) temporarily suspends the debt limit through March 15, 2015.

[5] Treasury securities held by the public and zero-coupon bonds held by Government accounts are almost all measured at sales price plus amortized discount or less amortized premium. Agency debt securities are almost all measured at face value. Treasury securities in the Government account series are otherwise measured at face value less unrealized discount (if any).

[6] At the end of 2014, the Federal Reserve Banks held $2,451.7 billion of Federal securities and the rest of the public held $10,328.1 billion. Debt held by the public held by the Federal Reserve Banks is not estimated for future years.

OMB CONTRIBUTORS TO THE 2016 BUDGET

The following personnel contributed to the preparation of this publication. Hundreds, perhaps thousands, of others throughout the Government also deserve credit for their valuable contributions.

A

Andrew Abrams
Chandana L. Achanta
Brenda Aguilar
Shagufta Ahmed
Steven Aitken
David W. Alekson
Emily R. Alinikoff
Victoria L. Allred
Lois E. Altoft
Jessica A. Andreasen
Benton T. Arnett
Aviva R. Aron-Dine
Anna R. Arroyo
Jeramie T. Ashton
Emily E. Askew
Scott B. Astrada
Lisa L. August
Renee Austin
Kristin B. Aveille

B

Peter Babb
Michelle B. Bacon
Jessie W. Bailey
Paul W. Baker
Carol A. Bales
Pratik S. Banjade
Avital Bar-Shalom
Taylor J. Barnard
Bethanne Barnes
Patti A. Barnett
Jody M. Barringer
Mary Barth
Sarah O. Bashadi
Kheira Z. Benkreira
Joseph J. Berger

Sam K. Berger
Elizabeth A. Bernhard
Jamie L. Berryhill
Mathew C. Blum
James Boden
Erin Boeke Burke
Cassie L. Boles
Melissa B. Bomberger
Cole A. Borders
Ariel V. Boyarsky
William J. Boyd
Mollie Bradlee
Bing Bradshaw
Joshua Brammer
Michael Branson
Alex M. Brant
Joseph F. Breighner
Eric J. Bremen
Andrea M. Brian
Candice M. Bronack
Jonathan M. Brooks
Andrew R. Brown
Dustin S. Brown
Jamal T. Brown
James A. Brown
Michael T. Brunetto
Robert W. Buccigrosso
Paul Bugg
Tom D. Bullers
Scott H. Burgess
Ben Burnett
Ryan M. Burnette
John D. Burnim
John C. Burton
Mark Bussow

C

Steven Cahill
Jeffrey B. Cahoon
Emily E. Cain
Gregory J. Callanan
Erin L. Campbell
Mark F. Cancian
Eric Cardoza
Matthew B. Carney
Todd S. Carolin
J. Kevin Carroll
William S. S. Carroll
Scott D. Carson
Alexandra M. Casiano
Mary I. Cassell
Daniel E. Chandler
Maureen M. Charan-
    Danzot
James Chase
Anita Chellaraj
Yungchih Chen
Robert G. Chun
Edward K. Chung
Deidre A. Ciliento
Michael Clark
Beth F. Cobert
Michael L. Cohen
William P. Cole
Victoria W. Collin
Debra M. Collins
Kelly T. Colyar
Jose A. Conde
Sarah Haile Coombs
Justin P. Cormier
Martha B. Coven
Catherine E. Crato
Joseph Crilley
Rose Crow

Albert T. Crowley
Juliana Crump
Craig Crutchfield
David M. Cruz-
    Glaudemans
Edna Falk Curtin
C. Tyler Curtis
William Curtis

D

D. Michael Daly
Neil B. Danberg
Lisa E. Danzig
Kristy L. Daphnis
Alexander J. Daumit
Joanne Chow
    Davenport
Kenneth L. Davis
Margaret B. Davis-
    Christian
Chad J. Day
Carolyn M. Dee
Brian C. Deese
John H. Dick
Julie Allen Dingley
Derek M. Donahoo
Angela M. Donatelli
Paul S. Donohue
Shaun L. S. Donovan
Bridget C. Dooling
Vladik Dorjets
Lisa Cash Driskill
Julia M. Druhan
Robin Duddy-
    Tenbrunsel
Francis J. DuFrayne
Laura E. Duke
Matthew S. Dunn

E

Jacqueline A. Easley
Russell J. Edmiston
Jeanette Edwards
Emily M. Eelman
Christopher J. Elliott
Tonya L. Ellison-Mays
Noah Engelberg
Michelle A. Enger
Leandra English
Mark T. Erwin
Edward V. Etzkorn
Yasmine S. Evans

F

Chris Fairhall
Robert Fairweather
Michael C. Falkenheim
Michael-Kourosh B.
  Fallahkhair
Shao W. Fang
Kara L. Farley-Cahill
Christine E.
  Farquharson
Kira R. Fatherree
Andrew R. Feldman
Patricia A. Ferrell
Lesley A. Field
Mary S. Fischietto
E Holly Fitter
John Joseph
  Fitzpatrick
Darlene B. Fleming
Ibrahima Fofana
Daniel E. Folliard
Tera L. Fong
Harvey D. Fort
Nicholas A. Fraser
Elizabeth A. Frederick
Marc P. Freiman
Farrah B. Freis
Nathan J. Frey
Patrick J. Fuchs
Tamara L. Fucile

G

Germaine G. Gabriel
Janice Gallant
Marc Garufi
Thomas O. Gates
Benjamin Patrick
  O'Hora Geare
Jeremy J. Gelb
Brian Gillis
Janelle R. Gingold
Joshua S. Glazer
Porter O. Glock
Ja'Cia D. Goins
Melanie R. Goldberg
Jeffrey D. Goldstein
Oscar Gonzalez
Thomas W.
  Grannemann
Kathleen A. Gravelle
Richard E. Green
Aron Greenberg
Hester C. Grippando
Andrea L. Grossman

H

Michael B. Hagan
Erika S. Hamalainen
William F. Hamele
Christina L. Hansen
Jennifer L. Hanson
Anetra L. Harbor
Linda W. Hardin
Derek M. Hardison
Dionne Hardy
Julian J. Harris
Letetia M. Harris
Patsy W. Harris
Brian A. Harris-
  Kojetin
Nicholas R. Hart
Paul Harvey
Ryan Bensussan
  Harvey
Tomer Hasson
Alyson M. Hatchett
Kyle W. Hathaway

David Haun
Laurel S. Havas
Nora K. Hawkins
Nichole M. Hayden
Mark Hazelgren
Margaret A. Heins
Jeffrey K. Hendrickson
John David Henson
Kevin W. Herms
Alexander G.
  Hettinger
Gretchen T. Hickey
Michael J. Hickey
Cortney J. Higgins
Mary Lou Hildreth
Amanda M. Hill
Andrew D. Hire
Thomas E. Hitter
Jennifer E. Hoef
Joanne Cianci Hoff
Adam Hoffberg
Stuart Hoffman
James S. Holm
Glenn L. Holmes
Brian R. Hooker
Shannon C. Horn
Daniel Hornung
Lynette Hornung-
  Kobes
Brian M. Hoxie
Grace Hu
Jamie W. Huang
Rhea A. Hubbard
Kathy M. Hudgins
Jeremy D. Hulick
Alexander T. Hunt
Lorraine D. Hunt
James C. Hurban
Jaki Mayer Hurwitz

I

Adrian B. Ilagan
Tae H. Im
Mason C. Ingram
Janet E. Irwin
Patrick N. Issa
Paul Iwugo

J

Antoine L. Jackson
Brian M. Jacob
Laurence R. Jacobson
Erica L. Jacquez
Varun M. Jain
Carol Jenkins
Carol S. Johnson
Katherine B. Johnson
Kim I. Johnson
Michael D. Johnson
Bryant A. Jones
Danielle Y. Jones
Denise Bray Jones
Joshua S. Jones
Lisa M. Jones
Othni A. Jones
Hee Jun

K

Paul A. Kagan
Richard E. Kane
Jacob H. Kaplan
Michele D. Kaplan
Jenifer Liechty
  Karwoski
Regina L. Kearney
Daniel J. Keenaghan
Matthew J. Keeneth
Ioanna Kefalas
Grace Kelemen
Hunter S. Kellett
Nancy B. Kenly
Amanda R. Kepko
Alper A. Kerman
Meshach E. Keye
Paul E. Kilbride
James H. Kim
Jennifer M. Kim
Barry King
Kelly Kinneen
Carole Kitti
Benjamin W. Klay
Sarah B. Klein
Kevin E. Kobee
John Kraemer

Lori A. Krauss
Joydip Kundu
Alexander K. Kwon

L

Christopher D. LaBaw
Jonathan S. Lachman
Michael R. Lachowicz
Leonard L. Lainhart
Chad A. Lallemand
Lawrence L. Lambert
Daniel LaPlaca
Derek B. Larson
Eric P. Lauer
Jessie L. LaVine
Mary A. Lazzeri
Donald H. Leathem
Allina Lee
Jessica K. Lee
Karen F. Lee
Sarah S. Lee
Susan E. Leetmaa
Bryan León
Jeremy L. León
Andrea Leung
Malissa C. Levesque
John C. Levock
Matthew Alan Lewis
Sheila Lewis
Wendy L. Liberante
Daniel L. Lichliter
Richard Alan
   Lichtenberger
Sara R. Lichtenstein
Kristina E. Lilac
Jennifer M. Lipiew
Patrick Locke
Aaron M. Lopata
Sara R. López
Alexander W. Louie
Adrienne Lucas
Gideon F. Lukens
Sarah Lyberg

M

Chi T. Mac
Deborah L. Macaulay
Ryan J. MacMaster
John S. MacNeil
David A. Mader
Natalia Mahmud
Claire A. Mahoney
Lesley R. Maloney
Dominic J. Mancini
Robert Mann
Sharon Mar
Celinda A. Marsh
Brendan A. Martin
Kathryn E. Martin
Rochelle W. Martinez
Richard K. Mattick
Andrew Mayock
Shelly McAllister
George H. McArdle
Scott J. McCaughey
Alexander J.
   McClelland
Connor G. McCrone
Timothy D. McCrosson
Anthony W. McDonald
Christine A. McDonald
Katrina A. McDonald
Renford A. McDonald
Luther C. McGinty
Kevin J. McKernin
Christopher McLaren
Robin J. McLaughry
Megan B. McPhaden
William J. McQuaid
William J. Mea
Aalok S. Mehta
Dinesh Mehta
Inna L. Melamed
Patrick J. Mellon
Barbara A. Menard
Flavio Menasce
Jose A. Mendez
Jessica Nielsen Menter
P. Thaddeus
   Messenger
Ashley E. Miller
Julie L. Miller

Kimberly Miller
Susan M. Minson
Asma Mirza
RaShawn L. Mitchell
Rehana I. Mohammed
Cindy H. Moon
Martha Moorehouse
Todd M. Muehlenbeck
James S. Mulligan
Christian G. Music
Hayley W. Myers
Kimberley L Myers

N

Jennifer M. Nading
Jeptha E. Nafziger
Larry J. Nagl
Anna M. Naimark
Teresa B. Nankivell
Barry Napear
Ashley M. Nathanson
Allie R. Neill
Kimberly P. Nelson
Melissa K. Neuman
Betsy A. Newcomer
Joanie F. Newhart
John D. Newman
Kimberly Armstrong
   Newman
Melanie R. Newman
Teresa O. Nguyen
Brian A. Nichols
John T. Nichols
Tim H. Nusraty
Joseph B. Nye

O

Erin O'Brien
Devin L. O'Connor
Matthew J. O'Kane
Brendan J. O'Meara
Justin M. Oliveira
Paul Oliver
Somer Omar
Farouk Ophaso
Allison B. Orris
Jared L. Ostermiller

Tyler J. Overstreet
D. Brooke Owens
Adeniran O. Oyebade

P

Benjamin J. Page
Heather C. Pajak
Jennifer E. Park
Sangkyun Park
Sharon Parrott
John C. Pasquantino
Arati N. Patel
Terri B. Payne
Jacqueline M. Peay
Falisa L. Peoples-Tittle
Michael A. Perz
Andrea M. Petro
Stacey Que-Chi Pham
Carolyn R. Phelps
Karen A. Pica
Joseph Pipan
Jeffrey M. Pitts
Alisa M. Ple-Plakon
Kimberly A. Pohland
Rachel C. Pollock
Aaron W. Pollon
Mark J. Pomponio
Ruxandra Pond
Sarah R. Porter
Celestine M. Pressley
Larrimer S. Prestosa
Jamie M. Price
Daniel M. Proctor
Robert Purdy

R

Lucas R. Radzinschi
Latonda Glass Raft
Moshiur Rahman
Maria S. Raphael
Jeff Reczek
Julia G. Reed
Mark A. Reger
Rudolph G. Regner
Paul B. Rehmus
Sean C. Reilly
Thomas M. Reilly

Scott D. Renda
Richard J. Renomeron
Julianna P. Rice
Keri A. Rice
Shannon A. Richter
Kyle Stayton Riggs
Emma K. Roach
Benjamin T. Roberts
Beth Higa Roberts
Donovan Robinson
Marshall J. Rodgers
Juan C. Rodriguez
Alexandra N. Rogers
Meredith B. Romley
Dan T. Rosenbaum
David J. Rowe
Mario Roy
Danielle R. Royal
Brian Rozental
Joshua Rubin
Trevor H. Rudolph
Anne E. Rung
Latisha M. Russell

S

Fouad P. Saad
Preeya Saikia
John Asa Saldivar
Dominic K. Sale
Mark S. Sandy
Subu Sangameswar
Katherin Monica
   Santoro
Matthew R. Sarge
Lisa Schlosser
Tricia Schmitt
Grant M. Schneider
Andrew M. Schoenbach
Daniel K. Schory
Margo Schwab
Nancy E. Schwartz
Mariarosaria
   Sciannameo
Jasmeet K. Seehra
Robert B. Seidner
Will Sellheim
Patricia Moore Shaffer
Shahid N. Shah

Dianne Shaughnessy
Paul Shawcross
Howard A. Shelanski
Melissa Shih
Gary F. Shortencarrier
Sara R. Sills
Samantha E.
   Silverberg
Brandon A. Simons
John L. S. Simpkins
Daniel Liam Singer
Whitney O. Singletary
Benjamin J. Skidmore
Jack Smalligan
Curtina O. Smith
Jennifer A. Smith
Stannis M. Smith
Silvana Solano
Roderic A. Solomon
David A. Spett
Kathryn B. Stack
Travis C. Stalcup
Scott R. Stambaugh
Melanie A. Stansbury
Nora Stein
Lamar R. Stewart
Gary R. Stofko
Carla B. Stone
Thomas J. Suarez
Claire D. Suh
Kevin J. Sullivan
Sarah Sullivan
Jessica L. Sun
Erin Sutton
Jennifer A. Swartz
Ben Sweezy
Aaron L. Szabo

T

Teresa A. Tancre
Naomi Taransky
Benjamin K. Taylor
Myra L. Taylor
Nathaniel Nana Kojo
   Taylor
Amanda L. Thomas
Judith F. Thomas
Latina D. Thomas

Payton A. Thomas
Will Thomas
Courtney B.
   Timberlake
John R. Tindel
Philip Tizzani
Thomas Tobasko
Richard W. Toner
Rosanna Torres
   Pizarro
Mariel E. Townsend
Gil M. Tran
Natalie Trochimiuk
Lily C. Tsao
Donald L. Tuck
Melissa H. Turner
Benjamin J. Turpen

U

Christian Unkenholz
Darrell J. Upshaw
Taylor J. Urbanski

V

Matthew J. Vaeth
Ofelia M. Valeriano
Amanda L. Valerio
Cynthia Vallina
Haley Van Dyck
Sarita Vanka
Steven L. VanRoekel
David W. Varvel
Areletha L. Venson
Alexandra Ventura
Patricia A. Vinkenes
Sara M. Vitolo
Dean R. Vonk
Ann M. Vrabel

W

James A. Wade
Katherine K. Wallman
Heather V. Walsh
Kan Wang
Tim Wang
Sharon A. Warner

Geovette E.
   Washington
Gini S. Waters
Gary Waxman
Mark A. Weatherly
Bess Weaver
Jeffrey A. Weinberg
Sharon K. Weiner
David Weisshaar
Philip R. Wenger
Max W. West
Michael S. Wetklow
Arnette C. White
Catherine E. White
Kamela White
Kim S. White
Sherron R. White
Chad S. Whiteman
Mary Ellen Wiggins
Shimika Wilder
Calvin L. Williams
Debra (Debbie) L.
   Williams
Monique C. Williams
Paul A. Winters
Julia B. Wise
Julie Wise
Elizabeth D. Wolkomir
Raymond J.M. Wong
Charles E.
   Worthington
Lauren E. Wright
Sophia M. Wright
William Wu
Steven N. Wynands

Y

Abra S. Yeh
Melany N. Yeung
Carl H. Young, III

Z

Ali A. Zaidi
Charles H. Zhou
Gail S Zimmerman
Rita R. Zota

www.ingramcontent.com/pod-product-compliance
Lightning Source LLC
Chambersburg PA
CBHW080253290526
45790CB00005B/1790